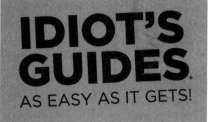

IDIOT'S
GUIDES.
AS EASY AS IT GETS!

Starting & Running a Restaurant

by Jody Pennette and Elizabeth Keyser

ALPHA
A member of Penguin Random House LLC

To my grandparents who taught me that sharing dinner with family is about so much more than good food.
—Jody Pennette

ALPHA BOOKS

Published by Penguin Random House LLC

Penguin Random House LLC, 375 Hudson Street, New York, New York 10014, USA • Penguin Random House LLC (Canada), 90 Eglinton Avenue East, Suite 700, Toronto, Ontario M4P 2Y3, Canada (a division of Pearson Penguin Canada Inc.) • Penguin Books Ltd., 80 Strand, London WC2R 0RL, England • Penguin Ireland, 25 St. Stephen's Green, Dublin 2, Ireland (a division of Penguin Books Ltd.) • Penguin Random House LLC (Australia), 250 Camberwell Road, Camberwell, Victoria 3124, Australia (a division of Pearson Australia Group Pty. Ltd.) • Penguin Books India Pvt. Ltd., 11 Community Centre, Panchsheel Park, New Delhi—110 017, India • Penguin Random House LLC (NZ), 67 Apollo Drive, Rosedale, North Shore, Auckland 1311, New Zealand (a division of Pearson New Zealand Ltd.) • Penguin Books (South Africa) (Pty.) Ltd., 24 Sturdee Avenue, Rosebank, Johannesburg 2196, South Africa • Penguin Books Ltd., Registered Offices: 80 Strand, London WC2R 0RL, England

001-283813-September2015

IDIOT'S GUIDES and Design are trademarks of Penguin Random House LLC

International Standard Book Number: 978-1-615-64852-8
Library of Congress Catalog Card Number: 2015933124

17 16 15   8 7 6 5 4 3 2 1

Interpretation of the printing code: The rightmost number of the first series of numbers is the year of the book's printing; the rightmost number of the second series of numbers is the number of the book's printing. For example, a printing code of 15-1 shows that the first printing occurred in 2015.

Printed in the United States of America

Note: This publication contains the opinions and ideas of its author. It is intended to provide helpful and informative material on the subject matter covered. It is sold with the understanding that the author and publisher are not engaged in rendering professional services in the book. If the reader requires personal assistance or advice, a competent professional should be consulted. The author and publisher specifically disclaim any responsibility for any liability, loss, or risk, personal or otherwise, which is incurred as a consequence, directly or indirectly, of the use and application of any of the contents of this book.

Most Alpha books are available at special quantity discounts for bulk purchases for sales promotions, premiums, fundraising, or educational use. Special books, or book excerpts, can also be created to fit specific needs. For details, write: Special Markets, Alpha Books, 375 Hudson Street, New York, NY 10014.

Publisher: *Mike Sanders*
Associate Publisher: *Billy Fields*
Acquisitions Editor: *Janette Lynn*
Development Editor: *John Etchison*

Cover Designer: *Laura Merriman*
Book Designer: *William Thomas*
Indexer: *Tonya Heard*
Layout: *Ayanna Lacey, Brian Massey*
Proofreader: *Claudia Bell*

Contents

Appendixes

Introduction

If there's one thing we want this book to do, it's to help readers realize the left-brain/right-brain qualities of owning and managing a restaurant. Yes, a restaurant needs to be a creative enterprise—but, it also must be managed as a business. This book will teach you how to balance these two aspects to build a successful—and fun!—restaurant.

Jody began his career managing restaurants, and then moved on to owning them. This grounded him in the hard work that's required, and the fragile nature of success in this industry. In the restaurant business, death comes from a thousand little cuts, not one massive blow. In this book, we'll show you how to stack up enough positives to be financially successful, and to get the most enjoyment from the work it takes to get there. You'll learn to distill creative thinking into an experience that is executed by an ensemble of fun peers. Restaurants are families, which helps balance the hard work and hours required to enjoy sustainable success. Building a strong, close team is essential.

The restaurant business is all about details. You'll learn how to script and blueprint all the minutiae to create the alchemy, the magic of the dining experience. It's all the little things that count—when you turn the lights down, when you turn the music up …. A successful restaurant goes far beyond good food and good service. The restaurant's concept and relevancy to the contemporary market are the keys to success in this industry.

Restaurants are all about the guests, indulging and entertaining them. When your restaurant is filled with the happy sound of guests eating, drinking, talking, laughing, and enjoying themselves, when it's filled with the energy of your restaurant team coming together to execute your restaurant concept, there's no greater feeling than being a restaurateur.

How This Book Is Organized

Part 1, An Introduction to the Restaurant Business, focuses on the reasons why you might want to start a restaurant. It helps you define your market relevancy so you don't start a restaurant in a location where customers just have no need for your fare. This part covers how to focus your concept so you hone in on exactly what you want to offer your customers. Finally, it covers how to deal with the daily business of ensuring your restaurant is up to all local government codes.

Part 2, Building Your Restaurant's Foundation, provides you the framework to build a solid business plan, which is key to persuading investors to part with their cash. It also covers how to choose the right location to attract your target customer base. And finally, this part educates you on negotiating your lease and finding the cash needed to get you moving in the right direction.

Part 3, Setting Up Your Restaurant, discusses how to create and compose your menu, from the way the menu looks down to what exactly is on the menu. It moves in to how the front of the house should be created, how the bar should be set up, and how you should design the back of the house.

Part 4, An Owner's Role in Management, gives you all the information you'll need to hire and train staff and purchase the necessary supplies. You'll learn how to run your office, understand the costs of doing business, and find out how to market your restaurant to pack the house nightly.

Part 5, Running Your Restaurant, will mentor you in how to give your restaurant the foundation to inspire your staff and distill a clear warm message that makes the guest feel good about coming there. You'll learn how to run a safe and clean restaurant and how to manage and motivate your employees to ensure they succeed.

Finally, we've included appendixes with a glossary full of helpful terms and resources you can look into for extra help should you need it. We've also included wonderful pre-opening and operational checklists you can use to help keep you on the track to succeed

Extras

Throughout this book, you'll find sidebars that will guide you in learning to start up and manage a restaurant. You'll find important information that reveals additional facts and issues you may encounter as you plan and run a successful restaurant.

DEFINITION

In these sidebars, you'll find definitions to help you understand terms that are used in the restaurant business.

POTENTIAL PITFALL

Pay special attention to these sidebars, which warn you about common mistakes and misconceptions about the restaurant business.

SMART MOVE

These sidebars provide extra facts and important notes that explore nuances of the restaurant business.

Acknowledgments

Growing up Italian, Sunday meals were the quintessential example of seamless collaboration. My family is largely to thank for my inspiration. My grandparents' ability to cook up the weekly Sunday feast, all while entertaining us, was the first spark. Then there was my dad's unorthodox advice to follow my heart and not worry about not having a safety net. My mom would immediately write back to every critic who uttered a discouraging word. My wife has taught me that we really do need 11 different mustard varieties in our fridge to live a life rich with flavor.

I would like to acknowledge the person who first gave me the opportunity to work on the world stage, design guru David Rockwell. Thanks also to Elizabeth Keyser for giving me this incredible opportunity to share my experience and knowledge.

—Jody

It takes a lot of smart people to write an *Idiot's Guide*. Thank you to Jody Pennette who shared his decades of experience in the restaurant business, and described it in such lively language. Thank you to my acquisitions editor Janette Lynn, development editor John Etchison, agent Marilyn Allen, and husband Michael Mordecai for his insight and encouragement.

—Elizabeth

Trademarks

All terms mentioned in this book that are known to be or are suspected of being trademarks or service marks have been appropriately capitalized. Alpha Books and Penguin Random House LLC cannot attest to the accuracy of this information. Use of a term in this book should not be regarded as affecting the validity of any trademark or service mark.

An Introduction to the Restaurant Business

A restaurant has two sides. Like theatre, there's a stage, a set, a performance. Behind the scenes in the kitchen, there's more action and drama (and flames). To be a restaurateur, you'll have to manage the hundreds of details of both.

We'll start by figuring out why you want to start a restaurant. A lack of understanding about the *business* of the restaurant business puts many first-time restaurateurs on the path to failure. So to begin with, we've got to separate emotion from business.

We'll talk about the contemporary market. How relevant you are to the contemporary market-place is far more important than worrying about your competition. We're going to help you through the hard work of really figuring out your restaurant concept. Once you clearly define your concept, all of the other parts—the name, décor, menu, and more—will fall into place.

By the end of this part, you'll create a mission statement, and from that a more detailed concept statement that fills in the details visually. In addition, we'll explain what you need to do to start your business entity and run an enterprise.

Why Open a Restaurant?

In this chapter, we're going to look at your motivation for starting a restaurant, and separate emotion from business. We're going to talk about what personal qualities restaurateurs need, as well as the skills required to succeed.

The restaurant business is more than a business, it's a life. We'll discuss the commitment it takes to launch and run a restaurant and the challenges it entails. There's no more rewarding career than working in the restaurant business, especially if you follow the right track to success.

In This Chapter

- Determine why you want to open a restaurant
- Discover personality traits and skills you need to open a restaurant
- Learn about the commitment, challenges, and rewards
- Find out what it takes to succeed in the business

Why Should You Start a Restaurant?

Restaurants are, at heart, a business devoted to pleasing people. Restaurants evoke emotions. They feed, quench, seduce, soothe, or excite their guests. For an entrepreneur, opening and running a successful restaurant can be a rush like no other. However, understanding the balance between commerce and creativity is essential for an owner seeking financial success.

> **DEFINITION**
>
> The word **restaurant** comes from the French word *restaurer*, meaning "to restore." Restaurants were first referenced in print in Paris in the late 1700s.

Restaurants are the most mercurial of small businesses. Yet there's no other industry that people march into with so little experience or preparation. Rather than start with a business plan, beginners leap in head first and are often fueled only by passion, excitement, or ego.

The words "let's open a restaurant" inspire a rush of hope and energy. Once you experience the rush of starting a restaurant, it's hard to stay away. Every day is new: the gleaming tableware arrives, the bar is installed, and the beer taps are primed and set in place. The chefs are experimenting with new dishes in the kitchen, and the sound system is starting to pulse. It's very exciting.

There's no denying that a certain romance has gilded the frame and misted the picture of working in restaurants. In movies, beneath a halo of gleaming copper pots, a handsome, charismatic chef wearing an expensive Oxford shirt casually chops carrots on a thick marble counter. The chef sips wine as his assistant, dressed neatly in a Martha Stewart-like apron, and arranges and rearranges a bowl of giant South African strawberries.

Unfortunately, the professional restaurant kitchen is far less glamorous, and far more volatile and ego-driven. It's a high-pressure cauldron, where our chef, wearing thick rubber-soled shoes and a food-splattered apron, sweats profusely as he orchestrates the preparation of dishes at a table for 12. The shrimp hits the hot pan. The sherry ignites. The garlic is burned and the chef swears in two languages.

The first thing to figure out is, why do you want to start a restaurant? What are your goals and aspirations? Take a pen and paper and write down your top five reasons for wanting to start a restaurant. Let's do it right now.

Far too often, the decision to open a restaurant is purely emotional. People don't consider the overall commitment required. They don't think about it from a business perspective. Your emotion should fuel your business, but use your business sense to keep an eye on the bottom line and make your restaurant successful.

Look at your list again and ask yourself, are your reasons emotional or business based? Are you caught up in the romance, the dream? There are a million reasons why people should not open a restaurant. Here are the top five reasons not to start a restaurant:

1. My hobby is fine dining. I know good restaurants.

2. My passion is cooking for my friends. I'm really creative.

3. I want to open a little bistro just like one I ate in while in Europe.

4. I love the Caribbean—if I had a restaurant I could live there!

5. I've got a great idea for a franchise that could go nationwide and make millions.

Now look at your list. Any overlap? Let's take a closer look.

It's funny the way enjoying dining in restaurants tends to build our confidence that we're experts in what makes a good restaurant. But a good restaurant, no matter how subjective the view, isn't necessarily a successful one.

Few dining locations have been more successful than McDonald's. But does that make it a good restaurant? What makes a good restaurant is utterly subjective. Experience in dining out doesn't mean you know how to start and run a successful restaurant, let alone a good one.

Your love of cooking and getting creative in your own kitchen isn't enough experience, either. So you've mastered the art of cooking boeuf bourguignon, and friends around your table say it's better than what's served at your town's top fancy French restaurant. But before your mind starts spinning out the fantasy of owning your own bistro, with its warm tone of ochre on the walls and the way the candlelight will make guests' faces glow … STOP!

Remember, cooking and managing a professional kitchen requires solid business skills. A successful restaurateur's focus is always on the dollar—purchasing and keeping an eye on inventory, price points, and profit margins. And opening and running a restaurant requires even more business skills—combining skills and abilities in finance, management, team leadership, marketing, customer service, equipment maintenance, and more. Without these skills, your best boeuf bourguignon will be lingering in a lonely dining room.

Right Brain vs. Left Brain

There's a right brain/left brain struggle in running a restaurant. The right side of the brain thinks about the magic of the experience, obsessed with flowers, music, and lighting. The left side thinks of maintenance, organization, and systems. That's why many successful restaurants and restaurant groups are collaborative ventures. Chef Jean-Georges Vongerichten and restaurateur Phil Suarez come to mind. Suarez has a great background in advertising, video production, and deal-making. He's teamed up with Vongerichten, who excels at training a kitchen staff to flawlessly execute his recipes. Together, they've created some of New York City's most talked-about restaurants.

An entrepreneurial spirit and attention to detail and discipline are essential for success in the restaurant business. If you're not disciplined, you could be out of business in six months, yet not even be aware of that fact for a year. You can lose a lot of money, and a whole lot more.

New restaurateurs go out of business because they don't treat the restaurant like a business. Restaurants can be profitable if careful attention is paid to controlling costs and managing details. If this is in your nature, then opening a restaurant is a good platform.

 **POTENTIAL PITFALL**

> If attention to detail is not in your nature, learning to pay attention and manage the details can be difficult and costly. The restaurant business may not be for you.

Personal Qualities

Personal qualities are important, too. Having a natural inclination for nurturing others is a good start. This is the hospitality business. Pleasing others, and getting pleasure from it, is the core of what restaurants must do.

You also really need to understand what a restaurant is and how it functions. Restaurants are like families. Getting your family all moving in the same direction can be the ultimate rush. If that fuels your passion, you've got the quality of a restaurateur.

You know you're a restaurateur if you can smile while grinding out a busy night with a staff short one worker, and a dishwashing machine that won't drain.

The moment of truth is when the last few guests are leaving, thanking you for a wonderful time. That's the ultimate goal. It's that moment, and afterward, as the tired staff begins to straighten up the dining room, the manager counts the till, and the sound of laughing as stories are told of the night, fills the empty dining room. If that fulfills your soul, if that's what you strive for, you're ready to start a restaurant.

Restaurateurs require a wide bandwidth of skills:

- An obsession with detail
- People skills
- Management skills
- Business skills

- Budget analysis

- Financial budget management

- HR practices

- Maintenance skills

- Cleaning skills

- Collaborative skills

- An aesthetic sense

This range is why teams are so important in restaurants. You need a range of skills and experience to execute a synchronized performance with perishable inventory, an uncertain number of guests, and a staff who often have little professional commitment.

SMART MOVE

Clogged drains, toilets, and grease traps will break your system. Keep on top of the maintenance. And more importantly, know how to fix problems yourself when an emergency crops up.

Time Commitment

Starting and running a restaurant takes a major commitment of time. It's hands-on work in a constantly changing environment. Restaurateurs work hard 18-hour days and weekends. Forget about spending the holidays with your family. And don't expect to go on vacation for at least a couple years.

Pre-opening and the first several months of operation will require the greatest commitment of your time as an owner. If you invest in this time wisely by finding the highest-quality staff and training them in your systems, which we will teach you in this book, you'll be able to run a successful restaurant and make a decent living. And have a personal life.

First you must lay down the track properly, so that following it becomes rote, and the food, service, and culture you want to create accurately reflect your aspiration.

SMART MOVE

An owner's time onsite is directly proportional to the amount of training and the quality of staff they've invested in up front. Hire high-caliber chefs and general managers who can lead their respective teams in harmony.

Doing It for the Money

If you want to start a restaurant because you think it will provide a stable annuity, think again. The margins are slim and the costs are unstable. Labor costs are the most difficult to manage. It changes nightly, depending on the volume of sales and number of hours worked. In addition, overhead can be a silent profit killer. It contains many line items: insurance, utilities, and linen costs to name a few. Remember, a restaurant is a business with a basic limited revenue stream.

A profit margin of 20 percent is a model of perfection. For each dollar made in sales, 80 percent covers the total cost of running the restaurant, and the remaining 20 percent is profit. We'll discuss profit scenarios and budgets more in Chapters 5 and 16.

It's very important for the owner to be directly in charge of the financial management of the restaurant. You've got to keep an eye on food costs, labor, overhead, and much more. This is a business. Never forget that your purpose is to make a profit. Your financial goal is to reap a 20 percent profit. To achieve that, you need to set up good systems and have the discipline to follow them.

> **SMART MOVE**
>
> You don't need to know how to cook to be a restaurateur. In fact, not cooking will give you more distance and the ability to analyze whether a dish is turning enough profit to be on your menu.

Achieving Success

Jody's first restaurant was a failure. He had dropped out of college and toured the country with a rock band. Then his father lured him back east with the idea of opening a restaurant. His father was a creative director at an ad agency and he loved restaurants and design. So he started renovating a place while Jody took a university course in institutional food service.

Jody and his father opened The Stone House in Greenwich, Connecticut, in the 1980s. It was beautiful and busy, but it failed—in just nine months. Why? Because they didn't have the experience of managing the expenses and the day-to-day dynamics. They were also too trusting, and people took advantage of them.

The restaurant had lost money and was closing. Jody's father asked him what exactly he had learned in that food service course, which wasn't much.

So his father hired a tutor who was a consultant from Restaurant Associates, a premier national food-services company that starts and runs restaurants and caters events at places like the Kennedy Center. Jody learned that apprenticeship was a more effective teaching model for him. In fact, apprenticeship is the traditional form of teaching in professional European kitchens.

Jody had passion and a ton of entrepreneurial spirit, but no business foundation. So he started working in chain restaurants, including one of the largest bakery-cafés in Canada. He had been a rock 'n' roller, and his creative spirit chafed against the sterile corporate uniformity. But he soaked up all the knowledge he could. There was a lot to learn about the systems that allow restaurant owners to manage everything from inventory to plate cost indexing—the keys to making a profit in this industry.

Everything else Jody learned about the restaurant business came from working at restaurants. He started off managing other people's restaurants, and then opened his own. He learned a lot from his mistakes. This book will share with you the lessons he learned and how you can prevent making the same mistakes.

You Can Do It!

If you haven't worked in a restaurant, you'll be at a slight disadvantage because you haven't experienced the systems in play. You haven't seen or used the equipment behind the scenes. Educate yourself. When you go to restaurants, watch the way the front of the house works. You can also ask a local restaurateur if you may observe how the back of the house works during service. You'll have to stay out of the way.

The main skill you will bring to your restaurant is management. You need to lead your team to accomplish your vision. Your job is to make sure this happens profitably.

Make no mistake, this is a volatile industry, filled with egos and emotion. You will experience almost every scenario, learn so much from your own failures, and cautiously celebrate your triumphs … always keeping in mind that "you're only as good as your last chicken salad."

The Least You Need to Know

- Your commitment to your restaurant business is more important than your passion for food.
- A good restaurant is one that consistently delivers the promised experience, profitably.
- The sooner you educate yourself in what you don't know, the more profitable your restaurant business will be.
- To build your dream of managing a successful restaurant, you must watch every penny.

CHAPTER 2

Defining Your Market Relevancy

A successful restaurant starts with a great concept, but simply having a great concept isn't enough. It must be relevant to your market, which can be intensely local. A great restaurateur is constantly learning lessons and making discoveries about markets.

In this chapter, we'll talk about doing market research, defining your target market, and understanding your target market's dining habits in order to develop a concept that meets the market's needs.

In This Chapter

- Why being relevant is key to success
- Why competition is less important than relevancy
- How to research demographics and trends
- Knowing how your concept reflects current trends
- Determining your restaurant's target market

Market Relevancy

Relevance is a mantra, the key word for sustainable success. Relating to your market and reflecting the modern lifestyle is critical in creating a lasting relationship with the consumer.

The internet has flattened the world. These days, consumers immerse themselves in food, chefs, cooking, and the latest restaurants. Chefs are like rock stars. Closer to home, farmers are our rock stars. Farm-to-table, organic, and sustainable are some of the local trends. We all have our short list of dining discoveries we love to turn our friends on to. What are the places you tell your friends about? What are the places you go back to again and again?

Those places reflect current dining trends. Maybe they serve made-from-scratch pizza fired in a seasoned wood-burning oven, or fish tacos with spicy mango salsa, or craft beer with a pub menu replete with house-ground, hand-formed hamburgers and raw and vegan offerings.

Competition

People love to tell you that 90 percent of all new restaurants fail. Actually, 30 percent of restaurants fail in their first year. Failure is often attributed to competition, but other restaurants aren't always the cause of a new restaurant's failure.

SMART MOVE

An important part of your boots-on-the-ground market research is gathering information on how much restaurants in your area are charging. You should know the upper threshold for prices in your location.

Don't worry about your competition. That's not to say you shouldn't *know* your competition. But it's far more important to think about whether your restaurant concept is relevant to the contemporary marketplace and its consumers than to wonder and fret about what the other guy is doing.

Relevancy Is Local

Understanding your market is key to your success. Jody lives in Greenwich, Connecticut. What's relevant to Greenwich? You've got a world-class audience, people with Manhattan cachet. They're smart and well-traveled, but they're not flashy. What do they want? A lot of them want the friendly welcoming atmosphere of the local country club on Thursday nights and hearty food like a good prime rib. The club makes its members feel like members. It makes them feel at home.

The people who go out to restaurants want the same thing the people who go to country clubs want. They want to be made to feel welcome.

For example, Jody helped start one of the most successful new restaurants in Greenwich, named Gabriele's. It's a high-end Italian steakhouse that's packed every night. The key to the place is Tony, who greets everyone at the door and makes them feel important. On his night off, however, there's a built-in 30 percent deflation to the experience of dining there.

The key to success is to make the customer feel welcome from the time they step inside your restaurant.

Learning from Mistakes

The biggest lesson Jody ever learned about market relevance was also from one of his biggest mistakes. A famous Latina singer and her husband started a flashy and fun club/restaurant in South Beach, Miami. It harkened back to the Ricky Ricardo era of the big band music in Cuba. It was a great concept, and a lively place. Jody partnered with her to create more of these clubs elsewhere. The business venture was a failure. Why? Because it turned out what works in South Beach doesn't work in Fort Lauderdale.

These clubs failed because the idea wasn't relevant to Fort Lauderdale's market. The customers in Fort Lauderdale came from places like New Jersey, not Havana. They weren't interested in heavy Cuban food. They didn't have a history of eating Cuban food, and didn't understand the culture beyond the veneer of mojitos, Cuban sandwiches, and hand-rolled cigars, so they weren't likely to eat it regularly.

> **POTENTIAL PITFALL**
>
> Latin food has become increasingly popular; however, the contemporary diner is unlikely to want to eat completely authentic Latin food. For example, few diners want to order Mexican menudo made with tripe (cow's stomach) or the barbecue skewers of chicken hearts that are popular in Brazil. Contemporary American diners prefer steak.

On paper, the concept of a fun Cuban club/restaurant seemed like a "can't miss" restaurant. But relevancy is everything. The brand was relevant in Miami—the epicenter of Cubans in America. However, just 25 minutes away in Fort Lauderdale, the concept wasn't relevant at all.

Matching Genre to Market

Restaurateurs who have successfully mined the Cuban theme, such as Jeffrey Chodorow with his Asia de Cuba restaurants, riffed on the concept of a contemporary South Beach nightclub atmosphere, combined with modern Latin cuisine. Dinner is theatre, and drinks such as Brazilian caipringias (sugar-cane rum muddled with fresh limes and syrup) and mojitos filled with fresh mint transport urban professionals in a cold city to a warm tropical climate.

A Modern Latin menu can include ceviches with Asian influences, such as shrimp in ginger-coconut-lime broth. The trend of health-consciousness can be incorporated with Rick Bayless, of Chicago's Topolobamba, Mexican-inspired sautéed kale and black bean tacos topped with toasted pepitas—pumpkin seeds. Even classic French pairings such as foie gras and apples could be Latinized with tropical fruit.

Chef Doug Rodriguez, considered the father of Nuevo Latino Cuisine, who opened Patria in New York City in 1994, is Cuban-American. He opened Alma de Cuba in downtown Philadelphia with restaurateur Stephen Starr in 2001.

The famous dessert is a cake in the shape of a cigar, complete with paper wrapper, and a matchbook made of some sort of sugar concoction. The waiter lights one of the faux matches, and the scent of browning sugar wafts over the table. Tableside displays of fire are traditional in French cuisine. Think Crêpes Suzette. This is how a restaurant surprises and delights guests.

These are examples of how contemporary restaurants transport customers to some imaginary place, a warm climate where the drinks are refreshing, the staff is welcoming, and glamour is in the air. People come to a restaurant to enjoy life.

More Lessons

Understanding local traditions is important to being relevant to the market. When Jody contemporized a tired and Americanized genre, Chinese, he opened eco-friendly organic Chinese restaurants in two markets, in Westchester, New York, and Greenwich, Connecticut. These markets turned out to be very different from one another, and offer lessons for the beginning restaurateur. Ten miles isn't far geographically, but it can be a world apart, culturally.

His goal was to bring a bright, fresh approach to a genre that was dwindling because of the American audience's awareness of wellness and health. In Greenwich, the clean, all-white, contemporary design and health-conscious menu got an initial burst of curious customers. But it didn't last.

The lesson: The locals, though well-traveled, didn't have a tradition of or passion for Chinese food.

In Westchester, however, the genre resonated with the consumer. There was a tradition and passion for Chinese food. When a restaurant updates the food and environment of a beloved genre, it creates energy.

On Fridays and Saturdays, and somewhat on Thursdays, people look for experiential dining. The restaurant's design and the organic menu executed by Hong Kong chefs provided a new experience that enhanced the cuisine. The restaurant was busy Thursdays, Fridays, and Saturdays.

However, contemporizing a genre can sometimes cause a disconnect with the consumer. Westchester consumers were used to engaging with Chinese food in a specific way. Sunday was the big day and evening for Chinese food. The old-school Chinese restaurants, with their red banquettes and bastardized food, are informal places, and Sunday is often about casual dining, wearing your sweats to the restaurant and then going home to watch a movie. This contemporary Chinese restaurant wasn't a sweat-pants kind of place.

The lesson: As you explore how you will contemporize a food genre, think about how consumers are used to experiencing it; when do they eat it, how often and is it casual or fine dining?

Drinking habits are another area to explore. Because Jody was appealing to the health-consciousness of his Greenwich consumers, he included fresh-brewed teas, and beer and wine. In Purchase, New York, the restaurant had a full bar. He quickly learned that most Purchase customers didn't drink. Whether there should have been a full bar and special cocktails in Greenwich became a matter of much debate with his managers. That's how it goes in the restaurant business—everyone's got a lot of opinions.

The lesson: Understand your target audience's drinking traditions.

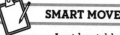

SMART MOVE

Avoid neighborhoods that are too quiet, where the majority of potential diners are over the age of 60. In places like that, everyone has dinner at 7:30, and your restaurant's a ghost town at 9. That doesn't work. A restaurant needs turnover from the moment it opens to the time it closes.

The lessons of these two nearly identical restaurants show how intensely local markets can be, and how important it is to really understand your target market, their dining and drinking habits, and traditions. Jody decided not to change the Greenwich restaurant's drinks program because the drinks were not the issue. The food concept did not engage the consumer in that market. He closed the Greenwich restaurant and began targeting new markets and locations for the concept.

Takeout

Many people would rather not cook on Mondays, likely due to the bustle of the weekend before. For many, Chinese represents takeout, but you need to know your market to know what sort of takeout restaurant works in the area.

For example, Jody's Chinese restaurant offered takeout in Greenwich. However, delivering to the mansions of back-country Greenwich turned out to be a nightmare. Far away from the restaurant's location, these mansions were off winding roads and locked behind enormous iron gates. Deliverers would have to buzz and wait, then go through the hoopla of opening the gates, which were guarded by a giant growling dog. Then the delivery guy would be afraid to get out of the car.

Jody turned to serving the corporate community, where takeout turned out to be a better bet with standing orders of dinner for up to 60 people every week.

Finding a night to close to save labor costs one night a week can be a challenge in a Chinese restaurant. It's really hard to choose. Sunday is the biggest Chinese night. Monday's a big takeout night. Tuesday and Wednesday, it's an alternative to a full-on dining experience.

The market has many nuances. You must know your market and its nuances when choosing what type and where your restaurant will be located.

Adapting to the Market

In addition to recognizing the market's nuances, you also have to be open-minded and flexible, without diluting your concept. Your plan must be flexible enough to contour to the terrain of the market, which will have peculiarities you might not have anticipated.

> **POTENTIAL PITFALL**
>
> Service is a problem in secondary markets. Finding a reliable and professional staff is difficult. Limiting service by having less formal contact with guests or by having counter service is a model for getting a powerful food concept across to this market. You won't be undermined by bad service and turn-over by limiting your service. The concept hasn't changed but the delivery model has, making it more stable. Restaurants can manage customer expectations-customers will stand in line at places where the service is grumpy and hurried, but the pizza rocks.

When adapting your concept to the market, start by looking for high-visibility and small-footprint spaces, with smaller square footage and lower rent, such as those near train stations. Locate your takeout restaurant where highly educated, affluent people are willing to pay more for the higher-quality takeout.

Note, you should always start with developing your concept, then think about the market relevancy. Then, and only then, can you start thinking about your location, and fit the location to your restaurant's concept. Don't start with the location. (We'll talk about location in depth in Chapter 6.)

Market Research

This is your industry. You must know the trends. This doesn't mean we want you to fit yourself into trends, because what you really want to do is find a way to express your own unique vision.

Understand your market. Know the region's history, and understand its prevailing trends, what has worked, and what hasn't. Know about the various parts of your town or city and what's important to its citizens. How long have local politicians been heralding the revival of the riverfront? Has the commercial-residential vision of the local developers brought more young professionals to Main Street?

To do demographic research, we suggest you visit the town. Go sit at an outdoor café and watch the people. Walk the streets, and look at cars. Are they Toyotas or BMWs? Look at the stores. Are there recognizable brands or are the stores independent? Are people walking on the streets? Are they shopping? Are they carrying coffee? Do they have disposable income?

Check out which restaurants are busy and which ones aren't. When you go into a restaurant, sit near the waiters' station where you can overhear conversation. You can pick up plenty of information about the local restaurant scene by listening to waiters. Also, talk to the bartender and ask about the restaurant. You may find out that brunch business is really busy with lines out the door and that Mondays are dead. The staff tells the truth, while owners will paint a falsely optimistic portrait.

SMART MOVE

Start building a profile of the people in your target market. Keep doing your espionage. Look at who is dining out. Who are the regulars? How many nights do they go out? Are they families, friends, or singles? Gather enough information to understand who they are, what they do, and where they do it.

Official Story

You can get plenty of demographic information from your town's website. Most towns have departments of economic development that create town profiles available on their websites. Keep in mind, however, that the data is usually two to three years out of date. Town profiles usually include:

- Population

- Projected population growth

- Median age

- Breakdown into age distributions

- Major employers

- What towns residents commute to

- What towns workers commute from

Keep in mind, there isn't a perfect way to process this information. Knowing that the median age of the population is 41 and the median household income is $74,728; that 70 percent of the population is white, 24 percent is Hispanic, and 6 percent is African American doesn't tell you what the dining scene is. You need to narrow it more by focusing on what segment of the dining market you're targeting. You need to revisit your concept.

Say your concept is New England seafood. There are a whole bunch of questions you need to ask yourself about the genre of New England seafood. You'll also need to do some research to answer these questions about your restaurant concept. Do not fear—there's a wealth of information out there on restaurant trends, from restaurant trade associations, consulting firms, organizations like the Small Business Association, and yes, even blogs.

To determine how relevant your concept is, ask yourself the following questions. (Insert your concept for the seafood concept.)

- How popular is seafood?

- Has it grown in popularity?

- What are the dining trends in seafood restaurants?

- How do those trends reflect contemporary lifestyles?

- How has seafood fit into the local lifestyle, and how has that changed or remained the same?

- When you think of how New England seafood has changed, can you place those changes as part of a larger movement?

As you build the answers to these questions, you will begin to understand your target market and whether your concept is something diners want.

Market Bandwidth

Next we'll look at the seafood restaurants in your area. Look at the market bandwidth—the range of offerings in terms of price and sensibility. The list of local seafood places will range from a shack overlooking the harbor that fries frozen clam bellies to the mid-level casual seafood house chain at the mall to the expensive high-end place people go to celebrate anniversaries and graduations. You will plot the local seafood restaurants and see where your restaurant falls into the bandwidth.

Good Enough to Steal

Jody knew his organic Chinese restaurant was speaking to the contemporary market because so many people in town stole the components and opened their own "healthy Chinese" restaurants.

They thought all the organic restaurant did was tout fresh, high-quality ingredients. Owners would steal the menu and then hire a designer who puts up reclaimed wood and fancy light fixtures with Edison bulbs. It's a contemporary look, but it doesn't speak to the changing culture of the genre. They chose to copy our menu without paying attention to how to execute the concept. They didn't succeed because they couldn't execute the idea. They couldn't manage all the minutia of the business.

Creating a restaurant concept that's relevant to the market is a craft. People ask, "Are you afraid someone will steal your concept?" We each have our own technique. Five people can play the same song on the guitar and none will ever sound the same. It's better to follow your natural style than to follow someone else's version.

The Least You Need to Know

- A great concept can thrive in one market but fail in another.
- Conduct market research by walking around your city or town, eating in restaurants, and watching people and their consuming habits.
- Understand how your food genre has or has not adapted to contemporary dining trends.
- Don't worry about competition; it's less important than market relevancy.
- Other restaurateurs may try to steal your concept, but your execution of the details of running your business will help you succeed.

Distilling Your Concept

In this chapter, you'll learn how to develop your concept. We'll lead you through a brainstorming session that will help you gather and then parse your thoughts into two paragraphs to create your draft mission statement. You'll refine it further as you test your concept against the contemporary local market. How relevant is your concept? You'll refine your mission statement further.

Next, you'll create a storyboard with all the supporting elements. This is a visual task, so you'll use photos to create either an online bulletin on Pinterest or a PowerPoint presentation. Start collecting images by category, menu graphics, music, uniforms, tableware, signage, and décor. As you do this, your concept will come more clearly into view.

In This Chapter

- Refining your restaurant's concept
- Condensing your concept into a mission statement
- Testing your concept's relevancy
- Choosing your restaurant's elements
- Building and presenting your concept statement

From there, you'll build your restaurant concept statement, which is a visual-heavy presentation that expands on your mission statement with information on the food, décor, and target market, and why this concept will appeal to your market.

The Concept

What is a restaurant concept? Your restaurant concept is the core idea of the business. It's the story behind the experience you're going to give your customers. The concept encompasses the food/cuisine; how it's served; and whether your restaurant is quick, casual, family style, ethnic, hip, urban, or elegant. It's expressed through your design, menu, and name.

Your concept is vital. It's the soul of the restaurant and its message—your core belief about what your restaurant is going to be. Before you take any action to open a restaurant, you need to think about and take time to distill your concept.

Finalizing your concept is hard work. Most people just want to skip ahead to the fun stuff. "We'll have our artist friend paint a mural!" Forget it. The gorgeous mural, the perfect neighborhood, the amazing young new chef you've discovered—they're all great ideas, but they must support your concept. If you force together a bunch of good ideas that have no cohesion, the guest will likely have a hard time defining exactly who and what you are.

> **POTENTIAL PITFALL**
>
> There's no surefire way to create a fail-safe concept. Even restaurants with great concepts can fail if they don't stack up enough positives—which are all the things we'll talk about in this book, such as watching food costs, keeping an eye on financials, running weekly inventories, and setting up systems to thwart theft.

Your concept touches your customer's senses. It's what the customer sees, hears, and smells, and how they're welcomed, treated, and fed. Today dining out is treated as a form of entertainment, and restaurants make it a theatrical experience. No, we're not talking tired mystery dinner theatre.

New York City's Times Square has restaurants designed to transport guests to a medieval Japanese ninja village. It has restaurants designed to look like spaceships. A beginning restaurateur doesn't have the resources to create that type of extravagance. Someone who hasn't gotten their feet wet in the industry should never dive headfirst into a multimillion-dollar enterprise. No matter how humble your restaurant, you should always think about the experience you'll create, the show you'll put on, and the place you'll take your guests.

Creating Your Mission Statement

You need to figure out your restaurant's story and its message. Stating "This is my passion" isn't enough. Your belief that you make the best burger ever isn't enough, either. It's a funny thing about being the best. It's not as important as some people think it is.

You're going to play with your restaurant's mission statement. It's a clear, concise, and specific description of your business strategy. It states your restaurant's *raison d'être*—its reason for being. Note that word "strategy." A mission statement shows how your idea is going to succeed in business. It's not, however, an in-depth business plan, which we'll discuss in Chapter 5. Right now, you're simply working on the concept.

Start by sitting down with pen and paper. The goal is to create a two-paragraph description. In the beginning, start by jotting down words and phrases instead of full sentences. If you're a visual person, you might brainstorm by sketching. The first step is to scribble down words or sketch images that come to mind as you walk through a series of questions to help you form your ideas.

We'll begin with a "what?" question. Remember, this is a process. You don't have to get it right out of the gate.

Food

What is your restaurant going to serve? What experience will your customers have?

Possible answers could be New England seafood; Southern comfort food; vegetarian, raw or vegan; Brazilian steakhouse; Cajun; Turkish takeout; breakfast and lunch deli; Israeli street food; kosher; Italian American; Northern Italian; New American; Japanese ramen; or Irish pub.

These answers fall into genres. It's pretty simple, but somehow when people start thinking about the kind of restaurant they want to open, they complicate it. One man told Jody, "I want to start an eclectic Mediterranean restaurant." Jody asked him, "Have you ever said, 'I feel like having eclectic Mediterranean tonight'?"

A chef wanted to start a restaurant that would serve his "inventive cuisine." He was going to serve dishes like "a sous-vide, biodynamic egg nestled in an emulsion mushroom foam." Jody told the chef it didn't matter how amazing that egg might be, from what free-range hen it was laid at what farm, how bright orange the yolk, how firm the white, and what 12-hour sous-vide technique the chef discovered to produce the perfect consistency of yolk that would ooze at the pressure of a fork. No matter what far-out chemicals the chef discovered that would suspend his foraged woodland mushrooms into a foam that would dissipate on the tongue—leaving a trace of woodland essence—only $\frac{1}{10}$ of 1 percent of potential customers would want that.

However, is there a way that the chef's idea can be profitable? Is there a foodie culture in his location that will support a restaurant based on his gastro-molecular cuisine? How often are people going to want to eat it? These questions might not seem as delectable as the chef's special Egg in the Woods dish, but they're the type of questions his concept must stand up to.

> **SMART MOVE**
>
> Create a storyboard of images that expresses the experience of dining at your restaurant. Online design sites abound. Pinterest is a great resource for creating an online bulletin board for gathering and sorting images. Then thin out your images and create a storyboard in PowerPoint or other presentation program.

Service Style

There are a number of service styles, such as buffet, self-serve, counter order, and sit-down. There are four primary types of service: fine dining, casual dining, fast casual, and fast food.

Fine-dining restaurants are the highest priced. The cuisine is complex, with numerous steps and processes taking place over several days. The cooks may have received culinary training and the servers have worked in a fine-dining establishment. Service may be more formal and a dress code and reservations may be required.

Casual restaurants offer less complex food with table service. Reservations may or may not be required and a dress code rarely is enforced. Casual restaurants are more family-friendly. Menus include more items than fine-dining restaurants. The menu might include many types of pasta and several chicken or seafood preparations. A buffet of cooked items, held warm over steam trays, may be a part of this type of restaurant as well (though they're seen less frequently in contemporary restaurants).

Fast casual restaurants offer menu items similar to fast food but with higher-quality or healthier ingredients. A fast-food place may offer a hamburger, but a fast casual restaurant might offer a hamburger of grass-fed beef on a fresh-baked bun with hand-cut sweet potato fries. There's no table service at these restaurants.

Fast-food restaurants offer the fastest service and lowest price. The décor is simple and there's takeout and/or drive-through service. Many fast-food restaurants are franchises of a larger brand. There's no table service and the servers (cashiers) and cooks usually have little experience.

Your Special Approach

The next question is "What is your restaurant's unique take on preparing your type of food?" How are you going to make this genre contemporary?

Say your concept is New England seafood. How will you prepare and serve it in a way that distinguishes your restaurant from others?

As you brainstorm about this, jot down some words and sketch a few pictures of what you think about it.

Your notepad might reveal a drawing of a fish, crabs, and a boat. The words you write could be: locally caught, sustainable, lively, ginger, hot pepper, Thai basil, today's food, fresh, healthy, New American, touch of Asian and Latin, crudo, salsa, ceviche, sea-to-table, local fishermen, and local oyster beds.

Now, let's put those words into a sentence: "My restaurant's approach to New England seafood is sea-to-table, local and sustainably caught seafood, cooked in a fresh, healthy New American style, with Asian and Latin flavors, including a raw bar."

Your Customers

Your next question is "Who?" The answer to "Who?" isn't you. It's your customers. Who are they? Brainstorm and jot down some words again: Seaport tourists; businessmen; families; locals; people who want healthy, fresh, locally caught fish; foodies; and local food people.

Now, put those words into a sentence: "My customers will be drawn from the tourists who come to the aquarium and locals. The downtown business brings a lot of workers and travelers downtown and will draw an after-work and dinner crowd. It will also draw locals."

  POTENTIAL PITFALL

A sign you haven't defined your target market is when you have too many target markets. A beginning restaurateur's enthusiasm may make her think everyone will want to come to her restaurant. The happy hour crowd and family dinner hour are two different markets with different needs altogether.

When you review the sentence about the restaurant's target market, you discover you need to examine this a little more closely. Tourists, families, locals, and business people are separate markets, with different needs. Aquarium tourists are mostly families with children. Convenience and proximity are important to them. They visit for lunch and dinner. The business crowd normally eats lunch during the week and congregates during happy hours after work. The happy-hour crowd and families dining with children don't mix. Families with school-age children come on weekends, when you will do your busiest lunches. You will want to do more marketing research on the dining habits of the business people and locals, who visit your restaurant market more frequently.

Product Value

The next questions are, "What are you going to bring to your customers? What will you do for them? What value will you offer them? How will you make their lives better?"

Once again, write down the words (or sketch images) that come to mind: fresh, healthy, now, great quality, seasonal, wake them up, exhilarating flavors, good feeling, friendly, clean, happy, and homemade pie.

Now, put these thoughts into a sentence, "I will provide my customers with a bright and friendly environment where they can eat healthy, freshly caught sustainable seafood made with seasonal local fruits and vegetables."

Tonight, Let's Have ...

There are only so many customers. What makes you think you're going to be able to steal a customer from an existing restaurant? What will draw the customer to your place?

This question tests your idea against the local restaurant market. Start by writing down the names of the restaurants in your local market that serve seafood: Cecil's Fish 'n' Chips, The Clam Shack, Asia Sushi Bistro, Captain Morehouse's Lobster house, The Sandpiper, and so on.

What words come to mind when you think of these places? Fast food, frozen fish, fried food, grease, broiled dinner, old, tired, great view, boring food, sushi, fresh, quiet, old-fashioned seafood restaurant, and worn carpeting.

From these words, a sentence starts to evolve: "Most of the seafood restaurants in the area are old and tired fast-food fish 'n' chips or standard seafood restaurants known for fried sandwiches made from frozen fish. Our sit-down restaurant will appeal to the contemporary customer's desire for fresh and healthy food. Our fish will be fried in olive oil and breaded in crisp carb-free almond flour. We'll freshen the old standards like the lobster rolls by transforming them into lobster tacos. Raw fish and sushi is a growing market, and we'll offer *crudo*, ceviche, and sushi appetizers of sustainably caught or raised fish."

> **DEFINITION**
>
> **Crudo** is Italian raw fish. Traditionally served like tartare, which is chopped and seasoned, today crudo takes a leaf from Japanese sashimi, with thin slices of raw fish. Contemporary Italian restaurants top crudo with sea salt, fresh spices, and olive oil.

Notice how your core menu is starting to develop. Composing a menu is a process, too. We'll delve into the details of creating a balanced, tested, and profit-yielding menu in Chapter 9.

Guest Experience

What will the guests' experience of your restaurant be like? How will you contemporize the look and experience of eating New England seafood? How will you transport your guests through this experience?

Dining out is entertainment these days. It's not what you do, but the way you do it. The way you do it depends on your target audience and the service style of your restaurant. No matter the level, imagine that you're creating a movie set design.

Close your eyes and imagine walking into your restaurant. What's the first thing you see, smell, and hear when you come through the door? Who are the first people you meet? Who are the other customers? Design your picture.

Making Money

How is your restaurant concept going to make a profit? Remember, this process you're working through is about creating a product you will bring to the market.

Think about the hours you'll be open, meals you'll serve, your price range, and what prices other restaurants are charging. Lunch isn't usually a big money maker. However, depending on the number of seats and concept of your restaurant, your takeout business could be a huge contribution to your daily sales. Be sure the items on your takeout menu travel well, and will deliver a minimally diluted takeout dining experience consistent with your concept. In addition, make sure your takeout business doesn't interrupt the experience of your dining-in customers. Guests waiting for takeout should be blocked from the view of the dining room or have a separate entrance.

Common Good

Some mission statements talk about what they'll do for the community, the environment, or the world. If social or environmental wellbeing is central to your concept, put it in your mission statement and be faithful to your promises. Keep your credibility, because word spreads when you don't. If you say you support local agriculture and you use Farmer Sally's kale but you don't, you can bet she's going to hear about it, tell her friends, and it'll end up all over Facebook.

As you start to write about your restaurant's philosophy, you might find yourself so steeped in the process you've been working through that the sentences will seem to flow smoothly.

> "My sea-to-table restaurant will promote local fishermen and serve sustainably farmed fish. It will educate the consumer about extinction, overfishing, and what fish they shouldn't eat."

Whoa, that sentence is a bit of a bummer. "Educate"? "Shouldn't"? Those words don't inspire. This sentence needs to be rephrased in a more positive way.

> "My sea-to-table restaurant will support the work of local fishermen and sustainably caught or raised fish. We'll promote the best, freshest, seasonal seafood and re-introduce forgotten local favorite fish."

Now that sounds more positive and interesting.

Your Mission Statement, Draft 1

Now string together all the sentences you've written and see what you've got, then edit it. Cut out any extra words. Read your draft mission statement aloud, and edit out more unnecessary words.

Next comes the hard part: read it aloud to a few trusted friends, family, or colleagues. Listen to what they say. Don't explain your concept. If there's a common denominator in their comments or something that's not working for them, be open-minded and try to figure out a solution in your mind. Put it down on paper. You need to smooth your mission statement's rough edges so your concept is concise and clear.

 POTENTIAL PITFALL

Don't argue with your advisors. People usually get defensive when their ideas are criticized. Try to separate useful comments from useless comments. Separate business from emotion.

Eventually, you'll hone your mission statement into something simple, such as:

> "Bring to market a family-friendly, high-quality New England seafood experience using local, sustainably caught and raised seafood and a contemporary eco-friendly American service culture and design aesthetic."

Creating a Storyboard

Restaurants are visual mediums as well as mood-inducing spaces. To help you brainstorm the look of and guest experience in your future restaurant, create an online bulletin board using sites such as Pinterest or search online restaurant design sites and copy pictures into a PowerPoint presentation. Once you know what your concept is, all the elements should fall into place.

Find pictures that express what coming to your restaurant will be like. Only you know the type of food you'll serve. How will it be served?

Your Name

Don't put pressure on yourself to come up with the perfect name right away. Finding a name that fits your restaurant concept is a process. You don't need to know your restaurant's name when you set up your LLC. Your LLC can be named anything. It needn't be the same as your restaurant name.

The right name for a restaurant has a way of suddenly appearing and being just right. It can be a word or words that capture your concept and your spirit. Brainstorm with your clever friends. Make lists, do a play on words, and create word associations (but don't be too cute). The connotation should be positive and related to your concept.

Great Names

Dinosaur is the name of a beloved BBQ restaurant chain that started in Syracuse, New York. What do you associate with dinosaurs? Big bones. It's a good name. Contemporary barbecue restaurants have great names such as Blue Smoke in New York City. A place named Mesquite promises a different experience than Al's Barbecue Pit.

Eponymous names work when the name has been used so long it's a revered brand, like the 90-year-old Pepe's Pizza in New Haven, Connecticut. The pizza was so famous that the family decided to open outlets throughout the state and into New York.

Eponymous restaurants work for the famous, such as Jean-Georges in New York City. Eponymous names signal the serious intentions of the chef-owner. When a classically trained chef puts his name on his restaurant, it signals he's proud of what he's doing.

Names don't work when they relate to a personal event in your life—an event or place that has nothing to do with your restaurant's concept. If you're opening an Asian Bistro, don't name it after the Scottish highlands where you honeymooned. Don't name your restaurant after your dog. (Though of course it didn't hurt a dockside restaurant in Martha's Vineyard, whose Black Dog logo became a summer status statement.)

Signage

You need to examine your name in terms of signage. How big is the size of the sign your town zoning department will allow? How well will your name fit on that sign? The letters need to be big enough to be read clearly from cars passing on the street. A long name will require smaller letters and will be less legible. One- and two-word names (one to three syllables total) have a contemporary feel.

Name Rights

Run a check on your name to make sure it's not trademarked. We know a guy who figured he got off easy when a company came after him saying his restaurant's name was infringing on their trademark. Why did he feel like he got off easy? Because he was able to change the last letter of his restaurant's name from an "a" to an "o." His restaurant's name is now grammatically incorrect in his native Italian, but at least he didn't get sued—and changing the name was inexpensive and easy for his customers to absorb.

The lesson of this story is to do research first so you don't end up dealing with threatening letters from lawyers. That kind of stress pulls your attention and energy from the daily management of your restaurant.

With the advent of Google, all restaurant names are likely to appear as trademark infringement since you're now listed with every other joint in the world instead of within your local county. You can't easily protect a name or brand in a market where you don't do business. The goal is to be mindful of local places, brands, and names and to be sure you haven't borrowed an identity along with a similar name.

Keep in mind that your trademarked name, logo, and/or tagline are your intellectual property. Your restaurant's name is an asset. There's always the chance you could sell your restaurant or expand the concept, but that's years down the road after you've made this new restaurant a success.

Concept Statement

You now have all the material you need to put together your concept statement. The concept statement brings together all of the aspects of your restaurant. You can create it in PowerPoint, using plenty of images to illustrate the mood and feeling (cozy? sexy? vintage? authentic? eccentric?) of your future restaurant.

The components of a concept statement include:

- The type of restaurant
- Food theme
- Design theme
- How it's unique
- The target market
- Why customers will visit your restaurant
- The restaurant's name

Looking at your storyboard, you can start to sort through images to find images that best illustrate the following restaurant elements:

- Décor
- Lighting
- Menu
- Service
- Location
- Size
- Seating
- Bar
- Hours

Remember, your concept must work in a specific location in a specific space. When you find that place, you're going to have to be very careful with money, because you're not likely to get your hands on enough for construction, design, and start-up. In Chapter 6, we'll talk more about figuring out how many tables you can fit into a space, how you can estimate average check per seats to determine if your restaurant concept can succeed on or off Main Street, and whether your customers will go out of their way to find you.

The Least You Need to Know

- Do brainstorming exercises to define your concept.
- Condense your concept to a one- to two-paragraph mission statement.
- Collect images that express the look and mood of the experience you want your guests to have.
- Your restaurant name should evoke your concept—or at the very least, convey to the guest a sense of what to expect.

CHAPTER 4

Licenses and Legalities

Your restaurant needs to be safe. Your customers need to be safe. And you, the restaurant owner, need to be safe. That's what this chapter is about, really. Yes, you'll be filling out forms from A (alcohol) to Z (zoning). But don't worry, the restaurant industry is easily ushered through the process of procuring the permits and licenses to run a safe and legal establishment.

Most of the laws governing restaurants are local. They vary from state to state, county to county, town to town, and even specific parts of town. If you're an independent sort, you might wonder why there are so many rules. The answer is that municipalities (and businesses) need safely constructed buildings that aren't fire traps. Towns and cities want restaurants where the food won't make people sick.

In This Chapter

- How your local liquor laws could affect your business model
- What permits you need and how to make getting them easier
- How to set up your business entity
- Types of insurance you need to protect your assets

Your local government website is the go-to site for the details of what's required for restaurants at your specific location. Along with ways to make the permit process easier, we'll show you how to structure and set up your business, prepare to pay employee withholding taxes, and take care of the IRS's tip allocation form. And we'll tell you what kind of insurance you need to protect yourself, as well as your personal and business assets.

But first, let's get down to drinking. Laws, that is.

Know Your Local Liquor License Laws

There's an old restaurant adage: "You make your money on the booze." In a full-service restaurant with sit-down dining and a bar, alcohol makes up 35 percent of your total sales. Alcoholic beverages are high-profit items. The profit margin is about 75 percent.

Liquor licensing laws have a dynamic effect on your budget. They vary from place to place. Some states have a fee-based system; others have an ownership model. Depending on where you live, you could pay a yearly license fee in the hundreds of dollars or buy a license for hundreds of thousands of dollars.

Some towns or counties, such as parts of Martha's Vineyard in Cape Cod, are "dry." They don't allow alcohol to be sold in stores or restaurants. Most dry towns allow customers to "bring your own booze" (*BYOB* or *BYO*). No-alcohol policies and BYOB scenarios cut the high profit alcohol brings to a restaurant's bottom line.

> **DEFINITION**
>
> **BYOB** or **BYO** are acronyms for "bring your own booze" and "bring your own." Some restaurants that don't have a liquor license allow guests to bring their own wine. The restaurant charges a corkage fee to cover the cost of the goods and services to serve the wine.

But some restaurateurs choose to open a BYOB anyway. In Philadelphia, the high cost of purchasing a liquor license has spawned a hip BYOB restaurant scene. Young chef-owners opening a BYOB can enter the market without the financial burden of buying a license. Even in cities with reasonable annual licensing fees, some restaurateurs open BYOBs. Customers love them because it lowers tabs. That can keep a restaurant's seats filled. But be warned: customers wince when corkage fees are more than a token amount.

Fee-Based and Commodity Licensing Model

In places like Boston and Florida, a liquor license is a tangible asset. Most states issue affordable new licenses by lottery, and they are limited by quota. Calculate the odds: a dozen new licenses a year and a lottery. No one in their right mind bases a business on that.

The alternative is to buy a liquor license on the open market. Scarcity determines the price. A distorted inflated market grows for this asset-based commodity. The cost of buying a liquor license could range up to $500,000, depending on the state and county. Often, an old tavern can have value beyond its business enterprise because it owns a license.

There are professional brokers who handle the purchase of a liquor license, and some financing companies will hold the license title in escrow as collateral. Buying a license should be handled through a broker—it's an expensive purchase and laymen are at a disadvantage. Typically, brokers are attorneys who specialize in obtaining liquor licenses. The attorney-broker runs a title check, and makes sure there are no liens or encumbrances on the license. You don't want surprises—like finding out the last owner still owes $30,000 to a liquor vendor. Make sure the license applies to your geographic location. Often, licenses are not transferable to a new site.

A fee-based liquor license is an easier proposition. In places like New York and Connecticut, a fee is charged every one or two years. The range can be relatively nominal, $1,200 to $2,500 a year. It's a lot less expensive than buying a liquor license.

Classifications

There can be different *classifications* of liquor licenses, such as live entertainment or cabaret, which permit dancing.

> **DEFINITION**
>
> Municipalities issue liquor licenses according to **classifications** or classes, which are categories of establishments where liquor is sold and carried away or sold for consumption onsite. A classification such as tavern might indicate an establishment in which alcohol but no food is served.

These classifications affect fees. Some states have restrictions that are enforced through zoning. For instance, you might encounter rules that an establishment selling liquor can't be within 1,500 feet of a school or church or an existing establishment with a liquor license.

Often, municipalities have exceptions for enterprise zones. Enterprise zones are areas targeted for economic growth. Tax breaks are offered to local businesses. Keep in mind most municipalities are intent on keeping their commercial districts from turning into Vegas overnight.

The classification of restaurant or café can impose restrictions, too. Some states require a separately allocated bar area with the view and access restricted. For instance, the opening cannot be more than six feet and the barrier wall must be at least six feet high with four feet being solid and the remaining two feet being diaphanous (covered with plants, sheer curtains, etched glass, etc.). Minors must be able to enter the restaurant, eat in the dining room, and use the restroom without having to come into direct contact or open view of the bar.

A café license doesn't require a separation between bar and eating area, but no one under drinking age may enter the premises without a guardian. This is something to consider if you have a family-style dining concept.

Knowing your local liquor code is vital. Do an internet search to find your state alcohol control board. Their websites define state liquor codes and provide links to local county and town codes. You need information to answer the following questions.

Local Liquor Law Checklist:

❑ Is alcohol allowed to be sold in your town and location?

❑ Are there any specific zoning laws that restrict liquor licenses, such as proximity to a church, school, or other businesses?

❑ Are liquor licenses issued by yearly fee or must you buy one in your location?

❑ What are the classifications of liquor licenses and how do they affect building regulations?

❑ What are the costs of liquor licenses in your location?

❑ Could your restaurant thrive if it were BYOB?

There's a ton of rules, regulations, requirements, and restrictions associated with liquor laws. On your state's website, you should be able to find the associated fees and downloadable application forms.

Streamlining the Permit Process

"Code" is the word used at the zoning, building, fire, and health departments. Your restaurant must be "code compliant" before they'll let you open your doors to the public. Zoning is the local government body that determines the intended use of the location. The building department must approve the specifications of materials and methods, such as details like the thickness of insulation and the number of electrical outlets. The fire inspector makes sure your space follows fire prevention codes. Fire departments also inspect commercial buildings several times a year.

Health Codes

Town and city governments regulate food service establishments to ensure they're safe places to eat and drink. Health codes vary, but all require safe handling, proper storing and preparation of food, and employees practicing good hygiene. Restaurants are required to have a food service establishment permit that states they've met all the federal, state, and local health requirements.

Some states require that two people from your restaurant staff take a state food handling course to be certified. It's recommended that the restaurant owner take the class for his or her own edification and to make sure this knowledge stays when staff changes. If the owner can't take the course, the manager and chef should.

A yearly food establishment service license is also required. Each new owner must apply for a permit. They aren't transferrable with the premises.

The building and fire departments will determine that all the components of your plan meet safe building and fire-prevention codes. Inspectors from building, fire, and health will review your progress and sign off when it's complete.

Contacting your local town hall departments in the planning stage is essential to avoid surprise complications further down the road. They'll give you parameters to follow.

It's always best to go along with their requirements rather than try to convince them that you're "special." People love to find places with *grandfathered* conditions—those that existed before local zoning codes were established. Local zoning boards make some exceptions for certain "pre-existing" conditions.

Let us say this loud and clear: safety violations are never grandfathered.

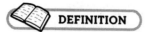 **DEFINITION**

> **Grandfathered** is used to describe conditions that existed before zoning laws were implemented, and so are allowed to continue despite not conforming to current laws. For instance, a restaurant that has been running since 1920 in a neighborhood now zoned for one-family residential has been grandfathered.

We recommend that beginners start restaurants in spaces that have been operating as restaurants and are up to code, or will require few alterations to meet code. Remember, every time ownership of a restaurant changes hands, local officials review the plan and can require you to upgrade to current building, fire, and health code and Americans with Disabilities Act (ADA) requirements.

You can greatly simplify the process of opening your restaurant if you're careful not to modify an existing restaurant space beyond decorating and signage.

Signage, by the way, can be one of the most time-consuming parts of the process. Often, architectural review boards and zoning must approve your plan for a sign. Signage is a strictly enforced code item. The linear street frontage of your building is part of a formula used to calculate how many square inches the sign can be. There are rules governing how tall each letter can be, based on the size of the total sign.

Colors are monitored. Some municipalities have "light blight" restrictions in downtown areas.

Sometimes, even if your sign meets all the measurements and regulations, you may still have to defend it before a city board. A space that never was a restaurant requires some exploration. Can you get a liquor license there? Will your zoning board approve it as a place of public assembly? This process could drag on for months. And that's *before* you start your expensive and time-consuming build-out, which town officials will want constructed to current code.

Historic Properties

Historic designation is a potential hornets' nest. Many older buildings like banks and firehouses make cool venues, but if they're registered as historic, the modifications you're allowed to make could be limited. Landlords think historic designation adds value but actually it diminishes it, and in some parts of town it can be very restrictive.

ADA Requirements

The Americans with Disabilities Act (ADA) requirements are a body of legislation governed by local municipalities, and they require some understanding. The zoning department will review your plan to, for instance, make sure the aisle ways between workstations and customer areas allow easy access for people in wheelchairs. In some areas, such as Los Angeles, bar heights must allow a wheelchair bartender and a wheelchair guest.

In older construction, external access by ramps possibly might be given a pass as a "pre-existing condition" under a grandfather clause. But in a new development, installing external ramps for access by the disabled is non-negotiable.

Prevent headaches and budget blowouts by finding a property that has been operating as a restaurant and is up to zoning, fire, and health codes, or will need few upgrades to be compliant with building, fire, and health codes.

POTENTIAL PITFALL

Avoid real estate or sites that will require getting variances, official exemptions, and permission to vary from zoning regulations. Variances are available in some cases, but the approval process can be long, expensive, and painful.

If you choose a space with lots of code violations or one where you're starting from scratch and doing a complete build-out, you're starting with some big question marks. What you discover behind the walls can blow your budget, your schedule, and your mind.

Local Zoning, Building, Fire, and Health Departments

When you're dealing with zoning, fire, and health departments, you don't call the shots. But these folks are not your enemies. You're going to have an ongoing relationship with your local fire and health inspectors. So find out what they want, and give them what they want. If they find a violation (and it seems they always will), fix it ASAP. The repercussions of not fixing violations can be severe. You could make your guests sick with food poisoning. You could be sued. You could lose your business license.

On a more minor scale, it's bad publicity to get a bad health inspection report. These days, a customer can easily find out if the staff at their favorite restaurant is washing their hands. Many town websites post restaurant health department ratings.

It can be frustrating. Just remember, behind each form and each official, behind each violation (punishable by fines and court action if not remedied), is the intent of creating a safe environment and a safe community. Sure, it can seem that they go overboard sometimes. But it's never a good idea to argue or get in a fight with your zoning, fire, or health inspector. We all walk the line sometimes, especially when we're new to the process.

SMART MOVE

Use your professional team, your lawyer, builder, architect, or designer, to take the emotion out of dealing with town officials. Hire professionals who work in the town frequently. They're familiar with the process and the people at town hall. That makes the process a lot smoother.

There's often a mutual respect between the town hall team and the area's professionals. The combination of an architect and designer presenting a well-thought-out plan to a government panel such as the zoning board of appeals can lessen scrutiny. Colors and interior sketches can help to bring officials to an emotional place. They want their town to thrive. However, the floor plan schematic will ultimately demonstrate the code compliance they're looking for.

External patio permits are often issued seasonally and they require displacing interior seats so as to not increase overall capacity. This happens when parking spaces determine seating rather than it being determined solely by square footage. Capacity formulas are set according to interior space and available parking.

The dynamic of getting the fire department to allow more seats per square foot and a lower number of allowable seats per parking spaces means you must build in a fixed-capacity design based on displacement. You don't want to leave broad open areas that you could be inclined instantly to fill in with seats after you've been granted a *certificate of occupancy (CO)*.

> **DEFINITION**
>
> A **certificate of occupancy (CO)** is the official document a municipality will issue to your restaurant once you've passed final inspections from the building, health, and fire departments. Once you get that CO, you can open for business.

There's one old trick that almost every busy restaurant has used. That's having a seating plan to pass requirements and slowly adding seats to fill in as needed. Local fire inspectors know this, and usually they'll give you a little slack—as long as you leave clear space at exits and don't create an obvious hazard by overcrowding.

Application requirements vary, but most include the application form, a nominal fee, scale drawings, the name of your contractor and his license number, and certificates of insurance for workers' compensation with the property owner listed as the certificate holder.

Ultimately, no matter what the stage of planning and construction, you have to demonstrate the code compliance they're looking for.

Permit Expeditors

In a metropolitan market, the cost of hiring a permit expeditor is well worth it. Permit-expediting companies take care of all permits needed to get your building and space within all city codes and laws.

An expediter can cost in the range of $2,500 to $7,500 in New York City, but it's a slam dunk. They take care of it—it's a game they know how to play. They know Jim at the city's zoning desk. If you go it on your own, and you're unfamiliar with the people, culture, and requirements, your application could be denied. A delay caused by a permit denial can push you off course. Permit expeditors will also find and remove any violations and represent you in zoning court. However, it's better to find a space that doesn't have violations.

Structuring Your Business Enterprise

You will have to set up your business's legal and operating structure. For restaurants, a limited liability company (LLC) is the business model of choice. LLCs have many benefits:

- They offer protection from liability.

- They're taxed at the owner's individual rate instead of the corporate tax rate.

- Losses offset income from other sources.

- They're easy to set up.

Most restaurants form an LLC. It protects personal assets from liabilities incurred by your business. LLCs can be made up of one or multiple members. When there's just one member, it's taxed as a sole proprietorship. Benefits include being compensated through distributions of the profit, which are taxed at the owner's individual rate.

Business profits and losses are treated as "pass-through"; members report profits on their own taxes. Losses can be used to offset income an LLC member gets from sources other than the business.

The federal government doesn't tax LLCs, but some states do. All LLCs must file tax returns. A single owner files a sole proprietor tax return. Multiple members file as an S Corporation. Profits are taxed at a corporate rate of 15 percent. Members are considered self-employed, which means they're required to pay self-employment tax contributions toward Medicare and Social Security. The LLC's entire net income is subject to this tax.

Depending on what state you live in, LLCs are issued by the state attorney's office, department of commerce, or another government entity. You'll find the forms and instructions on their website. Even if you use a lawyer, which is recommended, familiarize yourself with the components of an LLC:

- Choose a name for your business.

- File an article of organization.

- Draw up an operating agreement (if there are multiple members).

- Get a federal tax number in order to start the LLC.

Federal Tax ID

The federal government requires businesses to get a federal tax identification number (called an Employer Identification Number, or EIN). The IRS assigns the nine-digit number to business entities operating in the United States. It's how the IRS will identify your business and tax reporting. You can apply for a federal tax ID online at apply-gov.us/tax-id/?gclid=CIreyc7fr8ICF UQV7AodTmQAyQ. It's a simple process. If you need assistance, you can pick up the phone and speak to an agent in their office.

The Taxman Cometh

Tips your employees get from customers are subject to withholding tax, and employees must claim all tip income, including tips you paid to them for charge customers and any the employee got from the customer directly.

Point of Sale (POS) systems are sophisticated. Your POS system can be your best friend and record tip information if you use it properly.

> **DEFINITION**
>
> **Point of Sale (POS) systems** are computer programs that act as the central nervous system of a restaurant. The system manages table orders, kitchen order tickets, and guest checks; processes credit and debit cards; keeps track of inventory; and runs detailed financial reports.

Your POS system will calculate and keep a record of tip allocations. Employees are required to report tip income using Form 4070, "Employee's Report of Tips to Employer," due on the 10th day of the month after the month the tips are received. This statement must be signed by the employee. If the monthly tips are less than $20, no report is due. We tell our employees that if they report less than 10 percent on tips, they must be doing a really bad job as a server to get tips that low. They should report *at least* 10 percent.

The IRS has forms employees can use to keep track of tips. For complete information go to the IRS's Restaurants Tax Center at www.irs.gov/Businesses/Small-Businesses-%26-Self-Employed/ Restaurants-Tax-Center.

Withholding

As the employer, you're required to collect income tax, employee Social Security tax, and employee Medicare tax on tips reported by employees. You can collect these taxes from an employee's wages or from other funds he or she makes available. But the best advice is to hire a payroll service.

A payroll service will make automatic deductions from your employees' paychecks. That will prevent a danger—a restaurant owner dipping into payroll deductions to cover expenses. Everyone says they'll never do it, but it happens again and again. It causes a lot of headaches come tax time.

If you own a large food or beverage establishment, meaning you have more than 10 employees working more than 80 hours on an average business day, you'll use Form 8027, "Employer's Annual Information Return of Tip Income and Allocated Tips" to report employee tip income. A worksheet for determining whether a business meets the criteria listed above is included in the Instructions for Form 8027.

The best resource on restaurants and taxes is from the horse's mouth itself, the IRS's Restaurants Tax Center. Don't expect your accountant to wave a magic wand. Be prepared to ask useful questions during meetings with your accountant.

Insurance

Restaurants can be dangerous places, with flames, knives, boiling liquids, and alcohol in a high-pressure, fast-paced environment. However, many restaurants actually overinsure. There are four types of insurance a restaurant owner needs:

- Property insurance
- General liability insurance
- Liquor liability insurance
- Worker's compensation

Most states require liquor liability insurance for any establishment holding a liquor license. Yet many restaurants overinsure for liquor liability. If your insurance broker is offering you extra coverage for liquor liability, evaluate the cost/benefits. The notion you'll be sued every time a person who drinks in your restaurant does something stupid … well, let's examine it.

A 200-pound man comes into the restaurant. He's coherent and articulate, and you serve him one drink. It's the drink that puts him over the edge. He leaves the restaurant unnoticed, and drives his car into a tree. The point is, there's no scientific way to measure someone's sobriety when they come into your restaurant. A restaurateur will be sued only in the event of gross negligence. Instead of buying extra insurance, put time into training your manager, bartender, and waiters to manage noticeably intoxicated guests and facilitate safe transportation home.

Business interruption insurance is another thing for which we don't recommend increasing your monthly payment. A lot of people are spooked after years of storms, hurricanes, and week-long power outages. After Hurricane Sandy, Jody's restaurants were out of power for days and lost a lot of food. He put in a claim with his insurance agent and received a check.

> **SMART MOVE**
>
> Instead of increasing your overhead costs by overinsuring, reduce risks by training your staff to promptly address any issue that creates a potential liability, such as mopping up spills.

Instead of business interruption insurance, invest in an alarm system on your walk-through that will tell you when power's gone off. It should go to you, your manager, and chef's iPhones. If you get that message, get down to the restaurant and flip the circuit breaker. If it doesn't go back on, bring in dry ice and protect your food.

The cost of an entire restaurant package, with general liability and workman's compensation, can average about $25,000 per year. You'll see state restaurant associations offering links to insurance. Look at those offers carefully, and don't subscribe to an expense you can't control. Insurance should be considered one of those constants in your overhead budget, like your rent.

Our theory is you want to first build your business into something worth protecting before you spend a lot of money protecting it.

Be Honest

You'll be estimating sales and payroll, but don't lie. The days of cash and scamming are over. Everyone's wired, all information is available. In the electronic age, it pays to be above board. You don't want to be audited. You don't want the audit to come back with a walloping number of outstanding taxes you need to pay, plus penalties. You can't get away with it.

It's good to create a "Black Belt Team" of professionals who have higher skills and experience when they're needed. There's a host of folks who can help you make your way through the thicket of licenses and legalities, most importantly your lawyer, insurance broker, accountant, and payroll service.

Don't hire professionals to manage something just because you don't understand it. Hire them because they can devote more time to doing it correctly with their advanced skills and experience. That's worth paying for and needs to be part of your operating budget. When you're working with your team, remember that you're the leader. You're paying the salaries of your lawyer, architect, builder, and designer. Never let a consultant intimidate you into doing something that compromises your restaurant concept beyond recognition.

The Least You Need to Know

- The laws governing building and running restaurants are intensely local. You need to research liquor licenses; zoning, building, fire, and health department codes; and ADA regulations on your city or town website.

- If your state uses the ownership model for liquor licenses, work with a license broker or real estate agent who specializes in restaurants.

- Work with, not against, your local zoning, health, and fire officials and members of regulatory boards.

- Rely on your builder, architect, and designer to make presentations and pull permits at town hall.

- Hire professionals such as an accountant and insurance broker who specialize in restaurants and payroll services.

Building Your Restaurant's Foundation

Now that you've defined your restaurant's concept, it's time to create a business plan. All the work we did in Part 1 will come into play here, as we discuss drawing up budgets to open and run your restaurant, and how to manage costs and make a profit.

Then we'll talk about finding the right location for your restaurant concept. Yes, your concept determines your restaurant's location—whether you need to be on Main Street or are better off a couple blocks off Main, whether you can be in an off-the-beaten-track location or need to grab drive-by traffic. You'll also get lots of tips on negotiating a lease.

Finally, we'll talk about where you're going to find the money to open your restaurant. It's nearly impossible for a new restaurant owner to get a loan from a bank. Where else can you find the money? We'll talk about a range of options, and we'll help you avoid traps.

Creating a Solid Business Plan

Managing a restaurant is like having a teenager. It can be unpredictable. It misbehaves. That's why you need a solid and realistic financial plan. A strong plan will put you in the position to be prepared for any misbehavior your "teen" surprises you with.

A financial plan is your foundation for sustained success. It shows how you will generate a profit and pay back your investors. And, by the way, you *can* pay back your investors within the first year or two, if you follow your sound financial plan.

Here's an example. An average suburban restaurant with 80 to 100 seats, aspiring to do $2 million in annual sales, has the potential to yield a $400,000 profit. That's 20 percent of the pie. Say the restaurateur's investors put in $500,000 for the capital budget. Your operating budget profit will allow you to pay back your investors in a couple years *and* fund your reserve account. That's the best-case scenario.

To create a realistic financial plan, you need to understand basic restaurant math. Don't worry, we're going to make it easy. It's more detailed than difficult. And we're going to share the worksheets and forms we've created to help you through the process.

In This Chapter

- Why you absolutely need a business plan
- Understanding budgets, expenses, and profits
- How to draw up a realistic financial plan
- Putting your business plan together

Setting Your Capital Budget

A capital budget details how you're going to spend the money you need to get your restaurant up and running. It's the most misused tool in creating a new restaurant business. But it's vitally important. Setting a realistic budget to open your restaurant creates a solid foundation for the business. What's a realistic capital budget? One that allows for delays, such as when your contractor is missing, the electrician can't come until next week, and your painters can't start on the exterior until the rain stops.

You might also have unforeseen renovation costs and soft costs such as recipe testing, pre-opening training, and utility deposits. And most importantly, your budget needs to include a working capital reserve to cover six months' operating expenses for worst-case scenarios such as a rough winter of major snowstorms, when customers stay home and business drops.

> **SMART MOVE**
>
> It's a myth that a restaurant won't make a profit until year three or four. You can make a profit in month one—if you follow a well-crafted business plan.

That said, few restaurateurs set realistic capital budgets. They don't fully fund their restaurants, and that sets their business on a shaky foundation. All too often, restaurateurs find themselves dipping into the operating budget to cover the final renovation bill. Or even worse, they're dipping into employee payroll tax withholdings, a practice that is illegal. It happens way too often. It's a bad business practice, and it's not going to make you happy come tax time when you're scrambling to come up with those funds.

The Operating Budget: Your Moneymaking Plan

You can start your business with a $100,000 investment or you can spend millions, but the people who succeed are those who start out with a good income stream. This is where the operating budget comes in.

Your operating budget lays out the projected costs and sales of food and liquor, labor, and overhead. This is your profit. Food and liquor average 30 percent of sales; labor averages 35 percent; and overhead averages 20 percent, which includes 7 percent for rent. That's 85 percent—the remaining 15 percent is profit. The ideal profit margin is 20 percent of sales. Plan to make a good profit.

Food and Liquor Profit Formula

Typically, food costs are 30 percent of sales. Liquor costs are 20 percent. Depending on the mix of food to alcohol, the blended total could be 25 percent of sales.

That means it's essential that you make a profit by building menus with high-profit items you sell a lot of. Say a hamburger costs you $1 to produce and you sell it for $4. Your food cost is 25 percent. Your menu price points will vary, and include higher price point items such as steak. A steak costs you $10 and you sell it for $20. The food cost is 50 percent of sales. You've just put $10 in the bank.

The utopian model for average food and beverage costs is 20 percent. A 25 to 30 percent blended food and liquor cost is an ideal target range. It's essential that you stick to the formula you establish in your operating budget. We determine our food price points by doing yield tests, pricing out the cost of ingredients, adding *wrap-around costs*, and knowing the threshold for price in the market.

> **DEFINITION**
>
> **Wrap-around costs** represent the items you give away such as salt and pepper, ketchup, lemon wedges, or a cotton candy surprise at the end of the meal.

You must keep an emotional threshold on prices. Even if your restaurant is high-end and known for being expensive, don't be greedy. Don't slap your guests in the face with a $15 tab for desserts when everyone else is charging $10.

Wine pricing is critical, too. As the bottles get more expensive, the profit margin shrinks. If you buy a bottle for $50 and sell it for $125, you've made a $75 profit. That's a 150 percent markup. When you sell a $6 bottle for $6 a glass, that's a 300 to 400 percent markup.

Strategy comes into play with wine. For low-priced wines, don't choose those everyone knows, such as Santa Margherita pinot grigio. Your guests know how much it costs; they see it in the liquor store or supermarket, and they'll resent your markup. Instead choose a more obscure pinot grigio. Put three of them on the menu, priced at $19, $26, and $35. People don't want to seem cheap. They always choose the middle-priced wine—so make sure it's a high-profit bottle.

Testing Food Cost Profits

After the first 30 days, we run a test to determine the profitability of each item on the menu. The POS system tells us how many of every menu item we've sold in the last 30 days. We set three categories: profitability, popularity, and production (how difficult or time-consuming it is to make). Then we grade the dishes from 1 to 3.

For instance, firecracker spring rolls are popular, so they get a 3. In addition, they're profitable, so they get a 3 for that, too. However, they're made from scratch, so they get a 2. Add that up and the spring rolls have an 8 out of a possible score of 9. They're staying on the menu.

We do that for every item and re-examine every one that scores 7 or below. It's a useful exercise because it helps take the emotion away from the dishes.

You also have to keep an eye on your chef, the creative genius. Chefs are artists who rarely understand profits. He or she wants to step outside the menu you've established. That's when your food formula goes out the window. This might indulge your chef's ego, but it's not good for the business system. Say he creates a roasted maple-syrup pork belly dish. It tastes great, guests love it, and the waiters are recommending it. But your chef and waiters are shooting the restaurant in the foot if this dish scores 5 on the profitability, popularity, and production (PPP) test.

We manage this by having our chefs create eight or nine specials they'd like to add to the menu, and cost them out. If we put them on the menu, we run them through our profitability, popularity, and production test. The results determine whether the dish stays or is chopped from the menu.

Managing Labor Costs

Labor is the most volatile cost. A restaurant requires lots of staffing, with contingency plans based on holidays, weather, or promotional events such as restaurant week. You need a deep roster of staff.

Once we create a staff schedule, we cost it out, including payroll taxes. We project the sales number for the week and manage the labor to be 30 to 35 percent of sales. For instance, if we project $35,000 in sales, the labor budget will be $10,000.

Once you set your staff schedule, don't let your manager knock it off course. Don't let your manager send a bartender or waiter home early because it's a slow night. Keep your staff busy even in slow times. You can use the downtime for training. Send home the staff who can't make a sale, such as hosts, busboys, and runners. A bartender only needs to sell one drink every hour to pay for all the cleaning he can perform. Employees standing around doing nothing have a negative impact on morale, and that's when your employees get into trouble and cost you money.

Overhead: The Unknown Enemy

Overhead is a vast category encompassing internet connection, insurance, grease trap service, utilities, rent, bookkeeping, and bank fees. It should add up to 20 percent of sales. That includes rent, which is 7 percent of sales. Once you set your overhead costs, don't relent. Your business success is based on setting as many fixed costs as possible.

Here are examples of overhead categories and the expenses associated with them:

Overhead Categories and Expenses

Category	Expense
Rent	Includes taxes and common area maintenance charges
Utilities	Phone, internet, wifi, cable TV, gas, electric, water, and sewer
Repairs & Maintenance	Pest control, grease trap cleaning, and supplies
Marketing	Reservation system, advertising, marketing, public relations, special events, menus, and uniforms
FOH Supplies	Tableware, linens, and takeout containers
Administrative	Taxes, insurance, credit card fees, banking fees, office supplies, and professional fees (includes your accountant, lawyer, etc.)

The restaurant business is a game of shaving pennies wherever you can. It means making decisions about what overhead expenses your restaurant can do without. Why do you think so many contemporary restaurants have bare tables? Because it removes the expense of washing linens.

Putting Your Business Plan Together

You know why future restaurant owners need a business plan? To remind themselves that it's a business! Now that you have an overview of the expenses of running a restaurant, we'll show you how to put the components of a business plan together. These days, business plans aren't the dry, black-and-white documents they used to be. We create PowerPoint presentations and make liberal use of visuals to get the look and feel of our concept across. A business plan can be as short as 8 pages or as long as 40. Your business plan is the tool that will show potential investors your business is going to succeed.

Cover Page

The cover page should contain an image that embodies your business concept. It should be attention-grabbing, something the reader wants to look at—something he or she will want to eat. The name of your restaurant and company name also should appear on the front page. The cover page should make the reader desire to know more.

Table of Contents (TOC)

The table of contents lists all the major headings and subheadings your business plan will contain.

Executive Summary

The executive summary has two parts: a short, concise two- to three-sentence encapsulation of you and your business experience and why you will succeed at this business. Keep it fact-based and write in an active voice, stressing verbs and containing few adjectives.

"cb5 is a boutique restaurant concept firm that has developed more than 300 dining establishments around the globe. After hand-crafting inspired dining concepts for clients for 18 years, cb5 has elected a single model that they galvanized and blueprinted, making it ready for a multi-unit rollout."

The second part of the executive summary is your restaurant's mission statement. This is one sentence that describes your restaurant concept. It states what you will provide your customers and shows why customers will choose your business over another.

"Bring to market a sophisticated high-quality modern organic Tuscan trattoria, a menu produced by authentic Tuscan chefs, combined with a contemporary eco-friendly American service culture and design aesthetic."

Business Concept

In this section, you'll go more in depth into your business concept. Start with a historical sentence or two about the type of cuisine your restaurant will be serving. Include what it is, where it came from, how it changed over time, and most importantly, how you will make it relevant to the contemporary market.

"Americans have carried on a long love affair with Italian food. As its popularity grew, more Americanized versions of classic Italian dishes evolved and soon an entire genre of cuisine "Italian American" was a staple from coast to coast."

You want to show the reader a snapshot of the contemporary market. How have other cuisines changed over time in this country? How have perceptions changed? Have they changed in ways that are testament to their sustainable popularity? The answers to these questions should make the reader realize there's a new way of thinking about food and your restaurant encapsulates this new way of thinking/dining.

"The foodie culture is creating a demand for a healthful return to authenticity of this grand, but often bastardized, cuisine."

Bolster your argument with five or fewer quotes from reputable sources regarding the growth and acceptance of your restaurant's cuisine.

"There are more Italian restaurants in the state than any other type, according to the Zagat Restaurant Survey."

Market Analysis

You're going to show why your restaurant concept will work. Create a list of all the restaurants in your geographic area of interest. Mark each restaurant that serves the type of cuisine you'll be serving. Note if your market area is saturated with your particular type of generic cuisine.

Break down each restaurant in your cuisine group by service type (high-end full service, casual full service, takeout/delivery only). Then rate each restaurant on a sensibility scale. Sensibility factors are things today's consumers are concerned about such as healthy, fresh, clean, organic, local, and sustainable. This shows how each restaurant is fitting in to the new way the cuisine is perceived, and it's called market bandwidth. You can create a graph using Price and Sensibility as your *X* and *Y* coordinates showing readers how your restaurant will fit into the market.

You can also create a market share pie chart breaking down the variety of restaurant types for your cuisine in your geographic area. They should include high-end, full-service, casual full-service, and takeout/delivery only. The chart should show how your restaurant concept is poised to fill a gap in a growing market.

Management Plan and Organizational Plan

This section answers the question, "Who are we?" You want to stress that you have the experience and skills to launch and run this venture. Unless a chef is a business partner, don't single out the chef. If there's a certain type of chef that's central to the concept (juggling hibachi chefs, for instance), describe that. If you have a strong business partnership that's central to your concept—you've teamed up with a company making fresh pasta—show how that will make your concept more profitable.

"Plenty of restaurants claim to offer "authentic" cuisine and will typically overpromise on their concept. Jody Pennette, who has opened more than 300 restaurants around the world, knows American consumers want more than 'authentic'; they want healthful too."

Marketing Plan

The marketing section can include branding; and images of the menus, table settings, uniforms, and the restaurant space. Remember, a restaurant's look is a marketing tool. Location can be as well. In this section, you want to show your plan to draw people to your restaurant.

Financials

This is where we get into the nitty-gritty, all-important topic of money. You'll figure out how much it's going to cost to start up, and how much money you expect to make daily, monthly, yearly, and over three years. These figures are the benchmarks for your future business. They'll also show how you can pay back your investors.

Start-Up Cost Projections

Prepare your capital budget starting with your initial investment, detailing all of the startup costs associated with your restaurant, such as construction, equipment, furniture, professional fees, training, recipe development, and the opening party Be sure to include a working capital reserve to cover six months of operating expenses and a reserve for renovation overruns.

Pro-forma Income Statement

A pro-forma income statement is a projection of your business earnings. In accounting, the income statement shows whether the business earned a profit. The basic formula is Sales - Expenses = Profit. Restaurant math is calculated differently, as you can see in the following table.

Restaurant Math vs. Accounting Math

Income Statement			Income Statement		
Restaurant Math			Accounting Math		
Daily Sales			Daily Sales		
	% of Sales	**Daily Average**		**% of Sales**	**Daily Average**
Sales	100.0%	$4,761.90	Sales	80.0%	$4,761.90
Expenses:			Expenses:		
Food & Liquor	25.0%	$1,190.48	Food & Liquor	25.0%	$1,190.48
Labor	35.0%	$1,166.67	Labor	35.0%	$1,166.67
Rent	7.0%	$333.33	Rent	7.0%	$333.33
Overhead	13.0%	$619.05	Overhead	13.0%	$619.05
Profit	20.0%	$952.38			
Total Costs	100.0%	$4,761.90	Total Costs	80.0%	$3,809.52
Profit	0.0%	0.0%	Profit	20.0%	$952.38

In restaurant math, the net income or profit is included as an operating expense of 20 percent.

In this restaurant math scenario, profits above 20 percent are realized at a much higher rate of return since your rent and overhead have already been covered. That's where you really start making money.

Prepare your projected income statement in three ways:

1. Daily for each day of the week with a total and average daily sales.

2. Monthly for each of 12 months with an annual total.

3. Annually with projections going out three years. All of these will be used as benchmarks when your POS system is spitting out the income statements of *actual* data. The numbers in the business plan are the numbers you'll need to hit when you start doing business.

Timeline/Growth Plan

You should show that your restaurant is going to make a profit when it opens. Unless you're a seasoned restaurateur, don't start spinning out plans to expand and grow. We suggest beginning restaurateurs focus on showing that their restaurant will make a profit immediately. One timeline an investor will be very interested in is seeing how his investment will be repaid Your LLC's operating agreement will include a section on the allocation of profits and losses.

"Profits shall be allocated in the following order and priority: (i) first, in proportion to any deficit Capital Account balances, until such deficits are eliminated; and (ii) second, to the Members pro rata in accordance with their respective Percentage Interests until the balance in each Member's Capital Account is equal to the amount of each Member's Adjusted Capital Contributions; and (iii) third, any remaining Profits shall be allocated among the Members pro rata in accordance with their respective Percentage Interests."

Contact Page

The final page of your business plan should contain your contact information. It's better to put it on the back page rather than the front, because you want the cover page to be clean and uncluttered.

The Least You Need to Know

- In "restaurant math," expenses and profits are calculated as a percentage of sales.
- A business plan is more than a necessary tool for selling your concept to investors—it establishes the financial benchmarks your restaurant will need to hit to make a profit.
- Work up a realistic capital budget that includes contingency funds for unforeseen renovations and enough money to keep the restaurant running for six months.
- Create your business plan as a presentation and use visuals to get the feel of your concept across, and charts and graphs to illustrate market analyses.

Choosing a Location

Like so many aspects of starting and running a restaurant, finding the right location is part art and part business. Finding the best site for your concept and market requires a lot of subtle factors coming together. At the same time, it requires unemotional analysis, math, and spreadsheet skills.

We're going to look at the relationship between restaurant concepts and destination, and we'll show you how to avoid common mistakes and how to find a site that charges affordable rent. In addition, we'll discuss the importance of parking space.

Then we'll help you do the math to understand the relationship between rent, square footage, seat numbers, and average check per customer. You'll learn how to estimate your profit in a given space, and the conditions you need to make the profit flow in that space.

In This Chapter

- Finding the right site for your restaurant
- Leveraging your concept: destination and traffic
- How important is plenty of convenient parking?
- Can you make a profit in this space?
- How your monthly rent stabilizes cash flow

Find a Site Relevant to Your Market and Concept First

There's an order to finding a location, and it doesn't begin with location. It begins with concept and market. Don't start with an emotional attachment to a location and space. Falling in love with a building shouldn't be the beginning of your plan to start a restaurant. Your concept will determine the best location for your restaurant, and affect the amount of rent you'll pay.

Concept

Defining your market and concept is the first step in starting a restaurant. Once that relationship has been evaluated, a restaurateur looks at location. The guiding question is, "Am I bringing the right restaurant to the right vicinity?"

This next level, analyzing the location, relies on a balance of factors that relate to your concept and how well-defined it is. Building a concept to back-fit into an existing space is a different and less credible model.

There's a reason we stress having a strong concept that's related to your market—because it can make the location part of the equation and become a stable factor that will benefit your bottom line.

The Relationship Between Concept, Location, and Rent

Your concept plays a big role in how people will find your restaurant. We call this *destination* vs. *capture*.

> **DEFINITION**
>
> In restaurant terms, **destination** means that people will leave their homes deliberately to visit your restaurant. **Capture** refers to attracting people who happen to be walking or driving by.

If your restaurant is truly compelling, it's destination-worthy. Folks will seek you out, even in the rain. A strongly defined concept can be leveraged: customers will travel to experience your menu, style, and reputation. (And they'll set out for your restaurant knowing exactly what they want to eat.) The good news is that with a strong concept, you don't have to be located in the higher-rent districts in town. A strong concept can equate to paying lower rent.

A lot of people get this wrong. Restaurateurs who have a strong concept feel they need to be located on Main Street. But actually, that usually isn't the case. They'd be better off a block or two away, where rents are lower. Away from the main drag, they might be able to find a free-standing building or more interesting architecture. Parking is probably more easily accessible there, too.

But take caution: a location too far on the outskirts can be out of sight and out of mind. One of those "We always forget about that place. Next time." Remember, today there's so much noise out there on the internet and social media that it's not easy to get people's attention. It's not like the old days when everyone in town saw the ad you put in the local paper.

The less-defined your concept, the more you need to be in a place of high traffic. Suppose your restaurant is a friendly, casual American tavern. That's the kind of restaurant that wants a central downtown corner—a location where people will fall in the door. Note that you'll pay more in rent, but you'll have greater exposure and capture more hungry passersby circling the block, looking for a place to restore themselves with food and drink.

> **SMART MOVE**
>
> When you're looking at potential sites, consider your audience and the concentration of dining options in that area. Walk around; go into restaurants; look at their menus, food, and prices; and see what kind of business they're doing.

Your concept and location will also affect your overhead and staffing. A destination restaurant needs an investment in a good communication and reservation system. For the less-defined concept on Main Street, your focus will be on service flow—getting your customers in and out.

So what it really comes down to, what you really must think about, is how much value a location will have for your concept.

Genre and Location

Let's look at some restaurant concepts and think about the best place for those restaurants to be located. A steakhouse is an expensive restaurant with a limited menu. It speaks of power and indulgence. Steakhouses are also one of the few businesses left where the customers may still have expense accounts. Who are your customers? They'll be mostly business people and executives—and some regular folks blowing the lock off their wallet to celebrate a special occasion.

What's the best location for a steakhouse? Morton's The Steakhouse locates its restaurants in the heart of cities. Many are ensconced within the solid steel and glass structures that are home to the biggest names in international business. In Chicago, Morton's markets itself as being on the "Gold Coast" and close to many upscale hotels.

Now imagine you're opening a restaurant that will feature lots of salads and light, healthy food. It's a menu that appeals to women. You might look for a Main Street location near shopping, a space with an atrium and natural light that will draw the ladies who lunch and dine, according to market research.

> **POTENTIAL PITFALL**
>
> Thinking about paying $70 to $80 a square foot to rent space near upscale shopping? That's not a draw for your dinner customers. Your hours aren't in alignment and the streets are likely to be deserted at night.

Students and young urban up-and-comers prefer a raw edge to their dining experience. New music trends and contemporary ideas about organic farming and eating local foods are important to them. A traditional steakhouse in this market would be too stiff and old school. On the other hand, in a bustling midtown area filled with business, a gritty Soho-style café might not have the sense of power or energy required to make a statement. It's about sizing up the idea to the target audience.

How Important Is Parking?

It might surprise you to hear that parking isn't a make-or-break for a restaurant. If the thought of having to find parking dissuades your guests from coming to your restaurant, you don't hold enough of their interest. When Jody opened Lolita, a dark, sexy tequila bar and restaurant still going strong in Boston, the concept was compelling enough to make customers figure out the parking. The Lolita experience—dark, loud, with upscale Mexican street food—created such an opiate of good feelings, customers had to come back. They still are.

If you're opening a family restaurant, parking is more of an issue. SUV-driving customers unload caravans of children, adults, strollers, toys, and travel packs. They'll need convenient parking to do that.

> **POTENTIAL PITFALL**
>
> Be aware of perceived parking issues, but don't let that put the brakes on settling on a location that works for your restaurant concept in more important ways. People always complain about parking, but they always find a spot.

Parking accessibility is not the same as lack of parking. We all know plenty of bustling Main Streets with on-street parking that sucks. However, customers know it, and they know where the municipal parking lots are, and the side streets where parking is free. That's the sport of it. Many people have no issue with paying a meter to park. Parking meters that accept debit cards are plentiful nowadays, but lots of folks still keep a bag of quarters in the glove compartment just in case.

Ethnic restaurants can be destinations. Think about a steaming hot bowl of pho, the herb-filled Vietnamese rice noodle soup. When people get the craving, they're willing to drive through gritty urban streets or to a strip mall in desolate outskirts to get it. They won't give up on parking, even if they have to circle the block to find a free space. People will deal with the lack of convenient parking to eat what they're craving.

Valet Parking

Valet parking is cultural. It's common on the West Coast, but not as common on the East Coast. If your restaurant is on the East Coast and you're the only place in your area that has valet parking, it's likely to make your guests uncomfortable even if you offer it for free—which you should if no one else in your area provides it.

A valet charge can rub customers the wrong way. They'll dwell on it and hold it against your restaurant. Restaurateurs often hire a valet service, but we don't recommend it. The service is just going to charge you more for hiring the same kid most people would hire to work for tips.

Instead, hire your own valet, a staff member who becomes an ambassador for your restaurant. He'll greet people as they pull up in their cars. His headphones keep him in touch with the hostess desk. If someone without a reservation pulls up, the valet can immediately let the guest know if there's a table or a seat at the bar where he can order dinner or have a drink while he waits. It's hospitable, and it keeps customers flowing in.

Can Your Concept Make Money in This Space?

There's an important equation that can help you evaluate your location and whether your restaurant model will work there.

As you remember, you're aiming for a 20 percent profit margin. That means you'll make 20 cents for every dollar in sales. Never forget how slim the margin is in the restaurant business.

Let's do a little back-of-the-envelope calculation. First, we're going to gather some numbers about your proposed restaurant location and do some simple math. We'll walk you through each part:

1. Total square footage

2. Back-of-the-house square footage

3. Dining room square footage

4. Number of seats in the dining room

5. Average check per seat

6. Monthly rent

These figures come together in a formula that will help you run the numbers on various scenarios and see if they'll work to create a profitable restaurant.

Let's start with square footage. When you look at a possible space for your restaurant, keep in mind that typically a third of the total square footage is allocated to the *back of the house* that will run the restaurant.

 **DEFINITION**

> The **back of the house (BOH)** includes the kitchen, prep areas, storage, receiving, office, and restrooms in the restaurant.

Subtract one third from the total square footage to estimate the square footage of your dining area(s).

How many seats will fit into your dining room? The number of seats a restaurant has is determined by the type of restaurant it is. The square footage range for a sit-down restaurant is 12 to 15 square feet per seat. That rises to 20 square feet per customer for fine dining. Banquet restaurants are economical, fitting a lot more people at 10 square feet per seat. (That's why they're so popular today—they save landlords space and make customers feel cozy or intimate.)

The average check per seat is an important number. To estimate the average check per customer of your future restaurant, role-play ordering with your family and friends. Hand them your sample menu and ask them to pretend to order a meal as they would if they were in your restaurant. About 8 to 10 people will give you a good sense, but place your guests in the moment by telling them the occasion, such as it's lunch, dinner, dinner with family, dinner on a date, or girls' night out.

Try to mix it up to get the best data, and you'll come up with a realistic idea of the average check. Your estimated average check per customer might be $30 to $40, more or less, depending on your concept.

We'll talk more about *triple net* (*NNN*) in Chapter 7, when we get into the nitty-gritty of negotiating a lease.

 **DEFINITION**

> **Triple net (NNN)** means the tenant will be solely responsible for all the costs associated with the space being rented above and beyond the base rent. The original three item categories that made up this title were net real estate taxes, net building insurance, and net common area maintenance (CAM).

Breakeven

Now we're going to figure out the breakeven, or the point where your expenses are covered and your profits begin. You need to establish the bare minimum sales threshold. You also need your fixed overhead numbers—the expenses that aren't relative to sales, such as rent, insurance, and key salaried staff such as the general manager and the chef. These are the fixed costs you carry whether you're open or not.

Then build a mock schedule based on the minimum number of staff needed to adequately serve guests in a style consistent with the concept. For example, a coffee shop might only have a counter person, server, cook, and dishwasher. A trendy café likely needs a host, but on slow nights the manager can double. The café needs a bartender and servers, but on slow nights they can get by without a busser or runner.

Cost out the mock schedule and add in the elements that are fixed—the costs associated with owning the business even if a hurricane closed your restaurant for a week.

Fixed Costs: Overhead

Fixed Cost	Monthly	Weekly
Rent	$10,000	$2,300
Insurance	$2,500	$575
Manager	$5,200	$1,200
Chef	$5,400	$1,250
Total fixed overhead	**$23,100**	**$5,325**

Since we know payroll is 30 to 35 percent of sales, and we already are spending $2,450 in salaried positions, we're projecting that $16,000 in sales per week is our breakeven number.

This leaves $3,150 for staff. That's only $450 per day if you're open 7 days. Waiters average about $7 to $9 per hour (in our neck of the woods). Even on a slow night, you'll need two waiters on 7-hour shifts, which is $120 per day, plus a 12 percent *benefit multiplier*, which adds up to $135.

DEFINITION

A **benefit multiplier** is the factor you multiply the labor schedule total by to arrive at a good estimate for the total payroll liability, including taxes, worker's compensation, insurance, and tips.

This leaves $300 per day for the kitchen, with cooks making around $80 to $125 per day, and dishwashers $80 per day. You're at your minimum. The manager will also have to greet people, answer the phone, and pitch in—but can't tend bar too, so now you have to go above the payroll threshold and add another $100 per day for a bartender to staff your restaurant minimally.

Next, we add the minimum salaried staff expenses.

Staffing	Monthly	Weekly	Daily
Cook	$3,000	$700	$100
2 waiters (1 per shift)	$4,100	$945	$135
Bartender	$3,000	$700	$100
Dishwasher	$2,400	$560	$80
Total	$23,100	$2,906	$765

Now we'll look at variable expenses. We know that overhead should be 20 percent of sales. At $16,000 per week, that gives us $3,200 for overhead. We need to subtract our fixed overhead weekly costs of rent and insurance ($2,875). That leaves us with only $325 for variable costs such as linens, credit card charges, phone bills, and printing. You can see that when your sales are lower, the overhead cannot be covered by the aspired-to 20 percent because it can be devoured by these types of expenses.

So let's try sales at $16,000 per week. Fixed overhead is $5,325. Overhead is $16,000 multiplied by 20 percent ($3,200), less rent and insurance ($2,875) and $325 per week for variable costs such as linens, credit card charges, phone bills, and printing.

Now we'll see if our $16,000 breakeven figure is correct. We'll add up our weekly costs of goods—our food and liquor expenses—with labor and overhead. Our costs of goods will be higher when we're using this minimum model because of waste and spoilage. Overhead represents our ($2,875 fixed costs plus our $2,000 non-fixed minimum).

Minimum Expenses to Reach Breakeven

Costs of Goods	$4,500
Labor	$6,400
Overhead	$4,875
Total	$15,775

Breakeven at $16,000 in sales per week is achievable.

If you have 75 seats in a site that costs $10,000 a month in rent and your average check per seat is $40, you'll need to fill an average of 400 seats per week to break even. To be in the model of a 20 percent profit, you'll need to fill 825 seats per week. Ask yourself if that's a reasonable number of guests to expect. Think about the flow of guests throughout the day, evening, and week. Think about turnover. At suburban restaurants, weeknights can be "soft," meaning they attract fewer guests and have lower sales. But on weekends, the restaurants are packed at lunch and tables have at least two seatings a night.

To make a 20 percent profit according to this scenario, your restaurant will have to do $33,000 in sales per week.

Now imagine your restaurant is a small Mexican place where the average check per person is $20 and, based on your rent, you need $20,000 in sales per month to break even. Your place is 3,500 square feet, and after allocating one third for the back of the house, you have room for 65 seats. At an average of $20 per check, it's really going to be tough to get beyond the breakeven point. This is the reality that makes it really difficult for the little restaurant where the food is great, but there are only a couple of seats. In that situation, the owner is going to need to maximize takeout and catering, or have a hot bar scene.

The Waterfall Effect

After the break-even point, a restaurant strives for what we call the Waterfall Effect. This is the incremental increase in profit that will help you build a cushion, which will help you survive a snowy night and will create financial success.

To help understand this dynamic, imagine two scenarios. In one, 200 people descend upon your restaurant to eat at 8 P.M. It would be hard to make money if those conditions occur nightly. To feed all those people at once, you'd have to build a big kitchen and have a big staff.

Now imagine you have a 75-seat restaurant and are turning tables three times a night. You're making big money. All your costs—labor and overhead—are static, except for food. That's when you've hit the waterfall. The waterfall is when the weekly income surpasses the fixed nature of labor and overhead, so the margin of profit is based upon the cost of product—which gets lower and better for the restaurateur because all the product is used and waste is low.

SMART MOVE

You don't pay your cooks by the chicken. Maximize your profit by keeping kitchen staff efficient and productive.

Places with big bar scenes can create a kind of waterfall with a lot of wine and bar sales.

Restaurant sales can vary depending on the time of year for reasons such as weather or school schedules. Sales can also dip on certain days. Some restaurants are slow on Mondays and Tuesdays. Lots of restaurants try to lure people in on Mondays with half-priced bottles of wine. However, Jody's staff discovered another way to solve the issue, which made the water (profits) pour.

Jody had a very successful restaurant that was serving dinner to an average of 600 people per night. That average reflected the super-busy weekends and slow Mondays and Tuesdays. Everyone on staff kept asking, "How do we make Monday and Tuesday better?" Everyone was throwing around lots of ideas. Then one of the guys said, "We have a two-hour wait with beepers Saturday night. Why don't we streamline our production so we can serve more people?"

The team analyzed the menu and determined what was time-consuming to make, and how to simplify making the food by looking at what could be made ahead of time. Jody and his manager re-evaluated the labor costs, the back of the house, and the front. They added staff—hostesses, servers, and bussers—and trained them to graciously and professionally move the people and the food. Once the team implemented the efficiencies, they were able to reach 1,000 *covers* per night. Yes, they nearly doubled production by re-examining systems and processes. This sustained the restaurant for five more years until the lease expired.

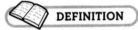 **DEFINITION**

> **Covers** refers to the number of people filling the seats in a restaurant during a shift, such as dinner. "We were slammed Thursday. We did 300 covers."

Sometimes trying to turn Monday into Saturday isn't worth the effort or expense. Your rent cost stays the same every day. So maximize a day such as Saturday, which is more popular with hungry customers searching for good food.

The Least You Need to Know

- Never choose a location before considering other factors. Choosing your location follows defining your concept and market.

- A strongly defined concept can be leveraged when you're seeking a location. You can get away with paying less rent because your customers want to come to you.

- Ample, easily accessible parking is less of a hurdle than you might think.

- Run the numbers to figure out how many seats the location will hold, the average check per seat, the minimum sales you'll need per week to cover your costs, and how many customers you'll need a week to make a 20 percent profit.

Negotiating Your Lease

Your monthly rent will be your most stable overhead cost, a reliable cost that can help maximize profit. Most commercial leases are for 10 years, with two 5-year renewal options. Locking in a rent that isn't more than 6 to 7 percent of sales is essential for financial success.

In Chapter 5, you learned the equation to use to see if you can make a good profit in a space. Now we'll help you negotiate a good lease by teaching you about commercial lease strategy points and tips on negotiating with your prospective landlord.

In This Chapter

- Why leasing is best for beginners
- Tips on working with real estate brokers
- Benefits of taking over an existing restaurant
- The basic terms of commercial leases
- How to negotiate a smart lease

Should You Lease or Buy?

We don't recommend buying to first-time restaurateurs. Buying a building, and investing in real estate in general, is a completely different endeavor than starting a restaurant. Buying takes such a significant financial and managerial commitment that it distorts the equation for a beginning restaurateur.

Think about it—an investment in a building is huge. Let's say the building costs one million dollars, and the capital investment in your restaurant is $300,000. The investment angle doesn't hold up. If you have that much doubt about your restaurant's prospects to back up a $300,000 investment with a million-dollar real estate deal, maybe you should re-evaluate your plan to open a restaurant.

An exception would be if you already have significant experience investing in real estate, or if you're a restaurant veteran who has good financial backing. In that case, buying a building can be a great asset to back up the volatile nature of the restaurant business over the long term.

Working with Real Estate Brokers

Work with experienced professionals who specialize in commercial real estate, know the land-scape, and have worked with restaurateurs. Your sister-in-law or her cousin just became a realtor? Sorry, but you don't have time to help her make her first commission. You're looking to make a long-term financial commitment, and you need a seasoned professional. Don't let your goal be sidetracked by helping newbies who need a break. It may sound cold, but this is business and you've got a lot at stake.

POTENTIAL PITFALL

Don't let a real estate agent rush you or push you into a property that doesn't work with your business model. The agent's goal is to close the deal quickly. Take enough time to make an informed business decision.

Okay, you've found a commercial real estate broker who has been in the business a long time, and knows the territory, players, and history. Give them a profile of what you're looking for and the business terms you can live with. Remember, your broker is really just a facilitator. And remember who's paying your experienced real estate broker's commission—the property owner. Your broker's interest is in making the deal and getting his or her commission. You need to be your own advocate and make sure you don't compromise to the point where it knocks your business model off course. You've got to watch your own back. That means read, analyze, and understand the entire lease. There's no such thing as a "standard" lease.

The Ins and Outs of Commercial Leases

There are two basic designations of property: residential and commercial. Most of us are familiar with residential leases for apartments and houses. Commercial leases are a little more detailed. They have additional charges you don't see in residential leases, the triple net (NNN) charges you learned about in Chapter 6.

Commercial rent is based on dollar-per-square footage annually, and NNN is based on a percentage of that. It's usually between 5 to 10 percent of the rent. For example, if rent is $50 a square foot, NNN might range from $5 to $15 per square foot per year. Costs vary depending on whether you're a tenant in a free-standing building or one of a dozen tenants in a strip mall. In the latter case, your portion of NNN would be calculated by dividing your restaurant's square footage by the property's square footage.

Calculating NNN Charges

Rent	$50 per square foot
Space	1,000 square feet
NNN	$10 per square foot
Annual Rent	$50,000
Annual NNN	$10,000
Total Annual	$60,000
Total Monthly ($60,000/12)	$5,000

Terms to Know

Triple net indicates that the monthly rent includes property tax, insurance, and common area maintenance (CAM). Tenants pay for the upkeep of shared areas. This can include parking lots, walkways, utilities, security, and property management.

Usually these charges are estimated annually, and that figure is divided over 12 months and added to each rent payment. At the end of the year, the estimate is compared to the real expenses. You could be given a credit or a bill. When you look at restaurant spaces, ask the landlord what happens if repairs are suddenly needed. Will the landlord cover them or expect the tenants to come up with the cash? Once you become a tenant, avoid maintenance surprises by staying apprised of what's going on in the building and any repairs that are needed or are underway. The landlord should always be responsible for roofing expenses; it's his building, and if the roof's leaking you can't operate and pay rent.

SMART MOVE

To make sure NNN charges won't surge, examine the property. Ask the landlord for his maintenance operating budget and capital budget forecast. Ask to see the records of the most recent three years of charges.

Unscrupulous landlords have been known to increase CAM fees to help cover vacancy costs by suddenly adding fees to rent.

There are legitimate ways NNN can increase. Property taxes are passed along to the tenant (you). That means if your renovations add and build value to the building, the town or city will place a higher tax on the property. (Check with your local economic development bureau and other public-private partnerships devoted to increasing business in your town to see if there are any tax abatements.)

That said, as much as restaurateurs have to mind their pennies and be frugal, the truth is accelerated CAM or property taxes rarely make or break a restaurant. The equation for success is to stack up as many positive fixed decisions as you can, such as signing a lease for rent equal to 6 to 7 percent of your sales. It's one of the biggest numbers you'll live with for years, so negotiate well.

These days, rental increases should be in the 2 to 3 percent range annually. That means by the end of five years, you'll have to bump your prices 10 percent to meet this rent increase. In the past, during times of inflation, landlords could increase rents sharply. Some leases state that increases will be tied to the consumer price index (CPI). Check to see that the proposed increases in your rent are in line with your local CPI, which can be found on the Bureau of Labor Statistics website.

Protect yourself from an open-ended lease. A lease is a way of putting bookends on the deal. Don't sign anything for which someone can suddenly change the numbers.

Negotiating Points

As you negotiate, keep notes on everything the landlord agrees to, and make sure these points make their way into the lease in writing.

Following is a list of additional points to try to get on the lease. We'll discuss them in more detail later.

Lease Negotiation Points Checklist:

❑ Include rent abatement during the build-out and permit process.

❑ Contingency in the event zoning use changes prevent opening a restaurant or getting a liquor license.

❑ Exclusive use: ask the landlord not to lease to the same type of restaurant as your raw vegan place.

❑ Assignment: Your right to transfer the lease to a new tenant is a valuable asset you might want to sell 10 years from now.

Your lease should not include the term "in sole and absolute discretion of the landlord." You want the word and spirit of "reasonable" included.

Sometimes you can negotiate with your landlord to let you start off paying a lower rent, such as 6 percent of your sales, with the promise it will rise to 7 percent when the restaurant exceeds minimum sales. It's a way to incentivize him; it makes him want your restaurant to do well.

Try to negotiate a two- to three-month abatement in paying rent to cover the time you're making investments and improvements to the property. Use your limited capital decorating budget on things that express your concept. Don't start renovating bathrooms. Instead, paint, resurface, and redecorate. Use what you have. It can take an experienced eye to see the diamond in the rough and how color, texture, and consignment store lighting can transform a space. Even people who have a good eye, who've picked up a lot of knowledge about restaurant interiors over the years, rely on interior decorators to express their restaurant's concept.

SMART MOVE

An unrented space is a landlord's greatest expense. Landlords are motivated to give deals to tenants who show the ability to commit to a 10-year lease and create a thriving business.

Other Incentive

In addition, you should try to get the landlord to include a Tenant Improvement Allowance (TIA). TIA is the funding a landlord may or may not provide a restaurant to spend on the renovation or development of the space. You can also ask for a Furniture Fixture and Equipment (FFE) allowance, which refers to money a landlord might provide to help with furniture, light fixtures, and equipment.

Key money is what a restaurateur pays either the departing tenant or the landlord to take over the space and an FFE.

Don't buy equipment you don't need. Only buy equipment if it's a good deal, is in good shape, and will work to express your restaurant's concept. For instance, the fancy new ice machine the departing tenant installed produces the ice spheres and pebbles that will help define your bar program. Ask the departing restaurateur or the landlord for a written schedule of what's included in the key money. That schedule will be attached to the lease. You don't want to assume you have the ice machine and then sit down to sign the lease and discover the machine was leased.

> **DEFINITION**
>
> **Key money** is an amount of money a departing tenant or the landlord will request from an incoming tenant in return for the furniture, fixtures, and equipment they are leaving behind. Make sure to confirm in writing who owns what before you pay anyone. A Uniform Commercial Code (UCC) search will help disclose any filed liens. Many states have online UCC lien searches.

Jody recently paid key money for the first time. He paid it because the guy selling the restaurant had a kitchen set up with good equipment that worked perfectly for Jody's restaurant concept. He wanted the space and equipment, and the key money sweetened the deal for the departing restaurateur.

Restaurant leases are long, because restaurateurs often need a lot of time and money to earn a profitable return on their investment. The classic idea is it takes four to five years to create a solid business, and then you make money for five to six years. After that, you decide whether to renew your lease or sell it. Your lease is a tangible asset, and a lease with five or more years on it can be sold. Remember most commercial leases state that options to extend the lease become void if the tenant stops paying or falls behind on rent. It's worth negotiating a clause to restore the option upon payment of the arrears.

Condition of the Space

Your lease will specify the condition the premises will be in when the landlord turns over the key. Whether you're taking over an existing restaurant space (the path recommended for new restaurant owners), renovating, or doing a new build, your lease should specify what equipment is included, and note all electrical, gas, HVAC systems, fire sprinklers, and ADA accessibility.

To check on the condition of the equipment, refer to the tags that note when they were serviced recently. Kitchen service providers will come in and make sure ovens are calibrated, and give you an inexpensive consult on the condition and outlook of the equipment.

Run specs by your local health department. Often they'll want to look at your menu and know how you'll be cooking items. They want to know how your restaurant will control fire and grease. If your health inspector decides you need to extend your exhaust hood 6 inches around the cooking line, and expand the exhaust hookup, that's an expensive proposition. It could throw off your capital budget.

New Construction

New construction is often delivered in what's called *vanilla box* or warm lit shell.

> **DEFINITION**
>
> **Vanilla box** is a term that usually indicates the landlord will bring basic utility services and plumbing access to the space and cap them. He'll finish the ceiling and cover the walls in sheetrock. This is also sometimes called "warm lit shell."

Make sure the space has adequate gas and electric power. A strained electric service will cause issues. Imagine if all the lights in your restaurant were to dim every time the soda gun compressor kicked on. Gas power usually isn't an issue unless there's been an extreme change in use of the space, such as it was built to be a card shop and now it's a restaurant. To determine whether the system will deliver the high heat a restaurant stove needs, track down the spec cut sheets for your equipment online, or go through your kitchen equipment sales and repair service. It can be expensive to upgrade a gas line to a restaurant.

In some areas such as Aspen, where natural gas isn't available, kitchens are fueled with propane. That makes high-heat cooking a challenge. Jody learned that the hard way when he started a restaurant there. No one told him you can't get as high a heat with propane as with natural gas. When the chef started testing recipes, they didn't turn out right.

If he'd known about the propane problem, Jody would have built the stove to compensate, but now, after the fact, retrofitting the stove was costly and pushed the restaurant off schedule. And the food never was as good as he had originally planned.

You never know what unexpected disasters can befall a restaurant space. There was a well-known sushi restaurant in a gorgeous mountain resort, which moved into a historic house that had been renovated by digging space for a new kitchen beneath the building. Here in this land of open, screenless windows, bugless nights, and cool mountain air, came an unexpected problem. The renovated restaurant smelled intensely of fish, and that wasn't a good thing. The owners had to install an expensive ventilation system to fix this unforeseen problem.

Before signing a lease, verify that the infrastructure can support your restaurant's needs.

Infrastructure Checklist:

- ❏ Gas
- ❏ Electricity
- ❏ Plumbing
- ❏ Ventilation

Everything on this checklist has the potential to cost several thousands of dollars to bring up to code. Discuss any concerns with your local building, health, and fire departments.

Existing Space

A beginning restaurateur is wise to find a space in which someone else has invested in restaurant infrastructure. When restaurants go out of business, the improvements are often retained and secured by the landlord. Listen to word on the street about restaurants that are not doing so well. Look for restaurants that are going out of business in your desired location. And then bide your time.

As a restaurateur goes out of business for financial reasons, he falls behind on rent. He can't afford to pay it. During his first wave of denial, he'll try to sell the restaurant for what he invested in it—but it isn't worth that much. In the second wave of denial, the restaurateur tries to sell his furniture. But it has little value. At this point, it's just a bunch of used furniture.

The value in the restaurant space lies in the infrastructure—the kitchen hood, grease trap, stove, and walk-in refrigerator or freezer. If you can get these without having to invest your own money, you'll be in better shape. Buying brand-new grease traps and hood vents doesn't bring a return on investment. Depreciating equipment on taxes is done over a protracted period. You need to ride it a long time to get your investment back.

The savvy potential restaurateur looking for a restaurant space waits it out while the first owner gasps his final breath and the landlord takes back the space. The landlord will probably throw in the tables and chairs with the deal, and with some creativity you can repaint, reuse, and *upcycle* what's left behind.

> **DEFINITION**
>
> When you **upcycle,** you take a particular item and refresh its look. For example, you can take a worn-out chair and repaint the wood, then add new upholstery to create a piece that can be used in your restaurant for years to come.

Once you find the space within your desired location, a space that has the bones that are compatible with your concept and that's either closing or has closed, you'll have to give your landlord two months' security deposit to secure the place. Make sure your accounts are in order. There's no quicker way to tank a real estate deal than to hand over a security deposit that's no good.

Rent Abatement

If you're renovating the space, try to negotiate a period of free rent or a rent abatement period during the amount of time estimated to perform the renovations. Landlords are usually agreeable to this because the time is being used to add value to their building. Typically, all permanently installed items such as stoves and walk-in refrigerators remain the property of the building owner unless otherwise specified in the lease.

In the lease, these terms are called lease commencement and rent commencement. What Jody usually does is tell the landlord to give him 90 days or until the day the restaurant opens, which-ever comes first. If the restaurant opens sooner than 90 days, he starts paying rent opening day. Don't try to take advantage of the landlord. By having your concept complete, you start prepar-ing your new restaurant before you sign on the dotted line. During the due diligence period, in which you've tied up the space with a deposit (which is almost always refundable), you can explore the details. From the moment the 30-day due diligence period begins, your team needs to get busy.

Once you sign the lease, you've got to finish renovations and open the restaurant by the time the first rent check is due. A budget can be ruined before the restaurant's doors open if construction issues cause delays.

Few landlords are willing to include a contingency clause that allows you to cancel the lease if you can't open for business or have delays. The only case for making headway with a landlord on canceling a lease is a situation such as you aren't able to get a liquor license due to certain conditions relating to zoning or change of use. However, it's part of the real estate broker's job to vet that. In that case, you should be able to walk away from the lease. Rent abatement is the proper way to deal with the time required to get your restaurant up and running.

Exclusive use—a clause in the lease stating that the landlord will exclude or limit competing restaurants in the same complex—is a tough bargain. It isn't easy to get landlords to agree to exclusive use unless you have brand recognition. For example, Dunkin' Donuts can require a landlord not to lease to another coffee shop in the same shopping plaza. If you don't have the power of a big chain restaurant, don't worry too much about exclusivity. Your landlord wants to keep his real estate rented and earning income. And it's to his benefit not to allow direct com-petitors who would knock current tenants out of business. Your successful restaurant is a benefit to his shopping center.

Assignment—your right to sell or transfer your lease to another—is an important negotiating point. It's an exit strategy that, depending on the success of your restaurant, could put you in a position to make money or staunch the debt if you close down the business.

Many times, the deal is predicated on the landlord formally accepting the new tenant. He has to grant the assignment to the new tenant. Sometimes, if the landlord thinks the former tenant has a stronger track record, he might ask to hold the former tenant on as a security guaranty.

The landlord might ask for some type of protection if the new tenant doesn't complete the terms of the lease. Jody prefers a "good guy" guarantee. It states that if he decides to close the busi-ness and is unable to assign it to another tenant, he'll guarantee that from one year to the day he returns the keys, he'll pay rent. But if the landlord can't rent the space to anyone else within six months, Jody is done. There's something seriously wrong with a commercial space that stays vacant longer than six months.

The Least You Need to Know

- Signing a lease that's 6 to 7 percent of your projected sales is one of the smartest long-term business agreements you can make.
- Leasing an existing restaurant space is recommended for first-time restaurateurs.
- Work with an experienced commercial real estate broker, but do your due diligence.
- Be familiar with the terms and the terminology of commercial leases so you can negotiate on FFE, TIA, and rent abatement.

CHAPTER 8

Finding Your Cash

There are many ways to fund a restaurant, except the most traditional way—walking into your local bank and asking for a loan. In this chapter, we'll show you how to seek what's called private equity funding, investments from your business, social, and family networks.

We'll also show you the private equity funding formula, the rate at which your investors expect to be paid back, and give you tips on managing your investors' expectations (free meals on the house?). We'll also look at whether "crowdfunding" is a viable option for funding a restaurant.

Financial traps abound for the restaurateur, and we'll show you how to watch out for them.

In This Chapter

- Why banks rarely finance restaurants
- Where to find your funding
- Does crowdfunding work?
- How to negotiate an agreement with investors
- Tips on managing your investors
- How to avoid financing traps

Where Do You Find Your Cash?

Banks are reluctant to fund what they deem a high-risk business. High-interest loans are available through the Small Business Association (SBA) and national loan companies specializing in restaurants offer high-interest loans. Restaurants are better off with investment capital than loans. Restaurants have an uncertain cash flow and margins are slim. Established restaurateurs are better candidates for loans, as they have a track record and know what they can afford to pay and when.

If you don't have a track record in the restaurant industry, it will be difficult to find an investor. Chefs have an easier time—they have a marketable skill and a reliable track record.

Alternative financing is the path restaurateurs must take, and it can be tricky to navigate. Most restaurants are funded by family, friends, personal savings, and business partners. If you have a strong enough business plan, you might be fortunate enough to raise private capital from an outside investor.

Another investment scenario involves sweat equity: two investors—one with cash, the other without. Say a chef and his buddy want to open a restaurant. The chef has talent, experience, and a great concept. His friend has never stepped foot in a restaurant kitchen, but he's inherited money. If they both agree on what is fair up front and put it down in the operating agreement, it can work. Once again, you must establish the value that each person is bringing in advance.

A restaurateur who isn't a chef is likely to rely on friends and family for funding, and go in without enough capital. In the restaurant industry, you can open owing everyone and cross your fingers until it hopefully all falls into place. The restaurant industry's fatal flaw is the ease of entry, and hence the high fatality rate.

Investors are typically found through business or social connections. If you've got the outgoing personality of a restaurateur, you probably meet people all the time. Pull out all those business cards everyone's always giving you. Start reconnecting with colleagues, alumni, people you've played sports with, and people whose kids have gone to school with yours. Start hanging out where people with investment money hang out. It's not always the fanciest place in town. They might be gathered around the bar at the casual tavern across from the train station.

SMART MOVE

Be ready to answer the question, "What do you need?" from a potential investor. Know your concept, market relevancy, and numbers inside out. Follow up on any interest by sending potential investors your marketing materials.

We're big believers in the power of family, teams, community, and working face to face. But we certainly expand connections through business networking sites such as LinkedIn and social networking sites such as Facebook.

People looking to invest often get the word out, but if you need money quickly they'll often take advantage of the deal. It's important to take your time, to go into business with the right person, for the right reasons. This is going to be a long-term relationship. Find investors who share the restaurant's vision and concept (yet again, having a good concept is important). If the investor shares the vision, it helps align expectations. That's important.

Private Equity Funding Formula

Restaurants aren't actually such a crazy place to invest. During the last economic downturn, restaurants were outperforming Wall Street. During times when the real estate and stock markets are more stable, restaurant investors are scarce. People invest capital in places where it will be safe and earn a decent return.

There are investors out there with portfolios of restaurant investments. They spread out their risk by investing varying amounts, which could range from $10,000 to $50,000. But novice restaurateurs will have difficulty gaining the interest of a savvy investor.

There are several formulas for private equity funding, but a good working model is called the 80/20. This model allocates 80 percent of all profits to be directed to retiring the investor's capital infusion, and 20 percent of profits to be distributed to the equity base of members according to their percentage of ownership.

Once the investment has been recouped, the equation inverts. The investor retains 20 percent equity and 80 percent is distributed according to ownership stake. Investors like this because their investment is given a preferred return. It's prioritized until they're risk-free. Most investors seek a 20 percent or better return on investment (ROI) in restaurants because they're high-risk propositions.

Your LLC's operating agreement is the tool that governs your agreement with investors. It will state the percentage of ownership and how income and loss will be allocated.

POTENTIAL PITFALL

Don't let capital budget cost overruns infect your operating budget. Operating agreements should state that profits will *first* be allocated to retire any deficit in the capital account balances. This helps contain capital budget overruns.

The operating agreement will outline how decisions are made, and how limited the investor's role in running the restaurant will be. Investors want to limit their liability, and they need to be careful about their involvement in the business. If they sign checks or are involved in financial decisions, they have an incumbent liability regardless of the LLC status. Letting them know that is also a way to check any over-involvement of "silent" partners.

Managing Investor Freebies

Often, people invest in a restaurant to enjoy the sense of "I own this place." It can be intoxicating, and it's one of the lures a restaurateur uses when creating an investment group. Several friends from overlapping social circles will all take a small piece, lowering the risk. The risk for the restaurateur is that it can make a group of people feel like they have unlimited access.

The best way to manage their visits, expecting free meals and drinks for themselves and their friends, is to establish a policy up front in the operating agreement. Jody gives each investor a house credit, which can be produced as a credit card with their name on it. Programmed with a monthly amount, it can be swiped through the POS system. These investor credit cards encourage investors to visit and bring their friends. And they can pay the pre-agreed amount without having to get into an uncomfortable issue. The meal credit card is a good way to keep them happy and avoid giving away the house.

All investors want, really, (along with having their investment paid back) is to visit the restaurant and be welcomed warmly by management and staff. Make them feel like they belong, but don't start a pattern of giving out freebies; your business partners should understand that affects the bottom line.

Family Funds

Raising money from family can be hard because there are mixed expectations. They want more consideration as family, and you want more, too. Jody has experienced the good and difficult sides of having family invest in his restaurants. Keep family and business separate, unless you have no other choice.

It's easy when the restaurant is a success. You repay your family's investment. Everyone quadruples their money. Everyone brags about the place. You're a hero. It's fun. Holidays are a joy. Then they ask if they can invest in another of your restaurants.

The second restaurant struggles. Everyone sees that as an opportunity to bring their opinions to the table. They're trying to help and improve the situation. But their doubt and lack of confidence creates tremendous stress for you as the owner of a new restaurant. Everyone seems to have forgotten about your success with the first restaurant.

In Jody's family, relations rubbed raw when he purchased a new car, using a nonrelated income source, his consulting business. Family investors whispered, "How can he drive a new car when he hasn't paid us back?" That's the kind of thing you're up against with family investors. They have emotional involvement. Business people and savvy investors understand that business models follow different paths.

POTENTIAL PITFALL

If you ask an investor to wait too long to recoup their investment, you're unwittingly inviting them to look over your shoulder. That brings secondary opinions to all decisions made about expenses. And that brings stress. Paying back your investors is a line item in your income statement.

Investment from family works best when the business is compartmentalized, but that can be hard to do. A family investment should only be considered when the money at stake isn't needed for any imminent purpose. They need to know that they could lose their money. The motivation should be to support each other and know you're investing in one another's futures because you care.

Responsible Selling

You're filled with enthusiasm about the restaurant you want to create, but remember not to overpromise and oversell when you try to intrigue investors. You're going to be held to your proclamations.

Pitching a restaurant investment opportunity to your family requires setting realistic expectations. Don't be a salesman, but instead act as an objective businessperson. Present your business plan. Share your pro forma budget and goals honestly.

Just as you would with a nonfamily private investor, you need to make sure your expectations are aligned. You need to manage your investors' expectations. Your operating agreement will outline the terms of repayment. Never pledge a fixed amount of return. There are many unexpected things that could upset your grand plan for success. Make certain your investors are prepared to let their money take this voyage without needing a certain amount back in a fixed amount of time.

If your father-in-law invested in your restaurant and it's doing decent business but hasn't met its projection, and he hasn't been repaid a dime, then you go out and lease a new car, Thanksgiving dinner could be pretty tense.

Crowdfunding

It's been a hot topic ever since the advent of Kickstarter, the online funding source where people stage campaigns to raise contributions for projects. The reality is, it's difficult to raise enough money to open a restaurant through *crowdfunding*. The average successful campaign raises less than $10,000, according to Kickstarter's website. It's quite rare for a restaurant startup to raise $100,000 through crowdfunding. Most individual contributions are small, and they usually come from your existing social and business networks.

> **DEFINITION**
>
> **Crowdfunding** is an online source of raising funds for projects, businesses, and artistic enterprises. Kickstarter is the most well-known site, and sites such as Foodstart and Equity Eats specialize in raising funds for entrepreneurs in the food service industry.

Creating a crowdfunding campaign is a full-time job. Successfully funded projects (only about 40 percent of projects *are* successfully funded) often have a great video (the better the video, the better your chances for funding). You'll also need to create a program of prizes and incentives, which could range from a free dessert to dinner at the chef's table, depending on the amount of the contribution. The cost of prizes and shipping the prizes is time and money. (Hint: don't choose heavy prizes!)

It's a gamble. If you don't reach your goal, you don't receive any money. Say your goal is $30,000, but you only reach $27,000. You don't receive anything.

The upside is that even if you don't raise enough money, or *any* money, crowdfunding can be an effective way to bring attention to your project. You might reach investors with real money to invest in your project.

Crowdfunding campaigns work for smaller food projects. They've been used, in conjunction with grants, to repair restaurants damaged by hurricanes. They've been used along with grants to start a family farm. They've been used to raise short-term cash to keep a restaurant going. Crowdfunding is a tool, and you'll have to evaluate your needs to see whether it's worthy of the investment of time in relation to the cash it will bring in and the potential for bringing you to the attention of an investor. It's a capital-free, time-heavy investment.

Leasing Equipment

You can reduce the amount of start-up capital you need to raise by financing a portion of the business. You can lease equipment such as dishwashers, ice machines, and coffee brewers. You can even lease a POS system. But remember that the 20-percent slice that's yours in a strong profit model will have to carry the finance charges. You could be better off buying used equipment rather than financing new.

> **POTENTIAL PITFALL**
>
> Never sign any personal guarantees in any contract, including equipment leasing. Read all contracts carefully, and put a big "X" through any paragraphs that state you will be personally liable. Remember, your LLC is designed to protect you from being liable for your restaurant's debt.

Financing Traps to Avoid

The biggest mistake you can make is not starting out with enough money in your capital budget, and not having a contingency plan for the build-out cost and time overruns and any unforeseen circumstances. Your capital budget should also include six months of working capital. These are the hallmarks of all good business plans. Finding yourself short on cash is what leads to the following traps.

Cash for Credit Card Receipts

One snare many restaurant operators trip on is accepting cash in advance for future credit card receipts. Once your restaurant has been open a month, you'll probably get an offer from what's known as a factoring company. They're financial institutions that offer high-interest loans, which they'll deduct from your restaurant's future credit card sales. Part of the agreement is that you use the factoring company's credit card processor.

Depending on your existing credit card receipts, these companies might offer loans in hundreds of thousands of dollars. The terms can amount to *usury*. It can collapse a business instead of saving it.

 **DEFINITION**

Usury is the practice of lending money at unconscionable or exorbitant rates. Illegal high interest rates can be masked under different labels to avoid scrutiny under the law.

Why would restaurant owners get involved with a perilous loan? They need a cash infusion, and banks won't lend to them. Actually, the premise of these types of loans isn't so bad, if followed correctly. But they're rarely used in the proper fashion. The smart way to use this type of financing is if there's a return on the investment.

Say you accepted this cash loan to add an exterior patio and eight extra tables for patrons. You use the profits from these tables to pay back the high-interest loan quickly. This requires discipline. You'll need to judge whether this is an opportunity to increase your profit margin over time.

More often, taking these loans leads to disaster. We've seen a lot of restaurateurs take the cash and buy a sports car or a boat. They want to project an image of success, but it's an artificial success.

Now they've got a shiny red car, and a significant piece of critical cash flow is being deducted from every receipt. The restaurant owner is really in trouble. Restaurants are a cash-flow-sensitive business, and these types of deals are usually preying on the weakness of an owner in denial that his restaurant model isn't performing well. As a restaurant owner, you need to have an accurate sense of your profitability. It's essential to all decision-making. Sadly, too many owners don't understand their restaurant's finances, and they don't start looking into the finances until too late.

Personal Lines of Credit

We can't say it enough times: don't sign anything that makes you personally liable. Don't accept personal lines of credit.

Don't mortgage your house. Restaurants can be like quicksand. Find investment money that can be lost and life will go on reasonably well. Knowing your home is at stake is stressful. And it can lead to making poor, pressure-driven choices. When you run a restaurant, you need to keep a cool head.

Built-in Credit

It's not a model for financing, but the restaurant business has a built-in line of credit that can be put to work, if you use it carefully. Vendors usually establish a 7- to 30-day credit term. This means you can pay them back after you've sold the food they've sold to you. Liquor companies often give a 30-day window, too.

> **POTENTIAL PITFALL**
>
> Staying on top of your financials, your profit and loss, on a daily, weekly, and monthly basis is essential. You'll be prepared to pay your vendors on time. It's good business, and a sign that your business is doing well. When bills are unpaid, word travels.

But beware: when a restaurant isn't managed properly, this credit line can be abused. The restaurant world is full of stories of lauded New York City chefs sued by vendors—$100,000 owed to their meat purveyor, $50,000 to the vegetable guy, and $75,000 to the liquor vendor.

A restaurant's payroll is issued a week behind. The restaurant business has a built-in positive cash flow. That's just as long as you didn't undercapitalize the build-out and start drawing from the operating budget to pay the plumber. That would be a big mistake; it's criminal in most states not to cover payroll.

If you open with just a little cash reserve, you can feel some comfort in the fact that you get a gentle build-in to the payment cycle. Once in the stride, it's perpetual—the interest-free loan is a one-time benefit that's sustained until the end of the business lifecycle.

Sales and Payroll Tax Trap

One dangerous trap is your accrual of sales and payroll tax in a fiduciary capacity—the money withheld from your staff's checks. This money is not yours. IRS penalties for not paying the sales and payroll taxes are high. And it's actually a misdemeanor, a criminal infraction, in most states.

The problem is that too often, restaurateurs treat it like a reserve piggy bank. We strongly suggest you set up a separate account for tax deposits, with no checks or ATM cards attached to it. Strictly deposit the sales and payroll taxes each week. Better yet, hire a payroll service that automatically deducts the amounts from employees' paychecks, and files and pays taxes on your behalf by deducting from your account weekly.

Restaurateurs can get into a lot of trouble by not paying taxes. The stories splash across news outlets—12 armed agents from the IRS's criminal investigation unit swarming into a restaurant in an affluent part of the city, and removing boxes of evidence of the restaurant's sorry financials. You read stories of chef-owners who owe $2.5 million in taxes, and their friends say, "He didn't do it out of malice. He was driven by optimism and creativity. He was convinced he could turn his business around."

Setting Up a Bank Account

Pick a bank that has a few convenient local branches and offers multiple levels of service, such as wire transfers, bank checks, and payroll accounting services. You want a bank that doesn't charge for making cash deposits. (Yes, some actually do.)

You want a bank with great customer service—a place where the tellers make change on a Friday afternoon without rolling their eyes. Keep in mind, these days so many people pay with credit cards that restaurateurs have to bring cash in so they can pay out the tips each night.

The Least You Need to Know

- Most beginning restaurateurs raise capital from friends, family, and friends of friends and family.
- Private investors will expect 80 percent of the restaurant's profits until their capital investment is completely repaid, and then they'll earn 20 percent of the profits.
- The best way to avoid financial traps is to start with enough money in your capital budget and have a six-month contingency operating budget.
- Manage investors by having clear and realistic discussions, the same expectations, and an operating agreement that delineates roles and responsibilities.

PART 3

Setting Up Your Restaurant

It's time to compose, design, set up, and lay out the parts of your restaurant. We'll start with creating a working menu that reinforces your restaurant concept, and show you how to take that forward through the development process with your chef to what we call the "blueprint." Every aspect of a dish will be tested for profitability. You'll also be given some tips on channeling your chef's creativity.

We'll talk about your restaurant's physical space; how to set up the front of the house, the bar, and the back of the house; and how to keep all your equipment and the premises clean and working.

Composing Your Menu

In this chapter, we focus on putting together your restaurant's menu. We'll show you how to create a menu that speaks about your restaurant. The menu is part art and part commerce. The lists of delicious-sounding dishes, and their prices, reflect the recipes and plates you have created, tested, and standardized so you can make a profit and your restaurant will be successful.

In addition, we'll discuss how to test the costs of the items on your menu. And finally, we'll talk about how to create the physical menu, and its components and design.

In This Chapter

- Creating a menu that tells a story
- How to create a well-balanced menu
- How to cost-test your menu
- Streamlining and "blue-printing" your menu
- Designing and creating the physical menu

Your Menu's Story

Your menu is so much more than a board of fare, a list of items and prices. It's more than just a message about what kind of restaurant guests can expect. Your menu tells a story. It's a guide to the experience that's about to happen. It's a map for dining in your restaurant.

The menu also reflects your hard decisions about your restaurant's concept, and your work with your kitchen team to refine, test, and blueprint the menu. It's the food your place is based on, which has to taste good and make a profit.

Your menu says a lot about you. It brands you, markets you, and reflects your image.

Think about how we glance at menus in restaurant windows, quickly assessing the restaurant and deciding whether we will go inside. Potential customers quickly view all sorts of menus— the 100-item small-print menus taped to the window of the quick Chinese takeout, a gilded twig-framed menu on handcrafted paper with tonight's menu in a fine handwritten script, the sun-faded menu offering "Mama's famous meatballs," or a sidewalk blackboard offering a three-course "prix-fixe" lunch for $14.99.

Setting Your Working Menu

You've already determined your food concept, now stick with it. You must stay with your style. Stay relevant to your point of view about good cooking and dining. If you've got an Asian restaurant, don't put a burger on the menu just because it's popular.

Entrées are typically more true to the concept. Starters can be more experimental.

SMART MOVE

Decide whether your restaurant and concept are best served with composed plates (starch and vegetables) or à la carte (a main ingredient, garnished). In the à la carte scenario, sides can be suggested by the server.

The small-plates trend has taught contemporary diners that each dish doesn't need a starch and vegetable. On the opposite end, large, shared, family-style plates are popular. If your concept is shared plates, think about the guest experience. Soup, for instance, is not an item people share— unless they're quite intimate.

Balance

Less is more in restaurants today. The quantity of items on your menu should be limited, with each bringing a distinctive flavor profile.

As you build your working menu, you'll create a list of dishes that balance several factors. It begins with balancing how the cooking methods are spread out over time and space. You need to have dishes prepared in advance but also some that are ready to be cooked at the last minute. You'll balance cooked and raw ingredients. You may balance traditions and trends. On the plate you'll balance color, texture, and taste. An important consideration is the balance of the work and execution in the kitchen. If everything on your menu was sautéed, for instance, it would cause back-ups in the kitchen.

Kitchen Cooking Stations:

- Cold dishes

- Fried foods

- Sauté

- Oven

- Stove

- Grill

Some kitchens have a microwave station. We don't use them in our kitchens.

If everything was cooked at one station, food would be coming out too slowly. Guests would be hungry and cranky. Balance the cooking methods on your menu. Make sure your kitchen can keep up with the busiest of times. You want to spread your menu among cooking stations and you need to spread them out over time. Some dishes can be slow-cooked, others served cold, others grilled *à la minute*.

> **DEFINITION**
>
> The French term **à la minute** is used frequently in American professional kitchens. It means food that's cooked to order. Examples might be a grilled steak, a sautéed chicken breast, or deep-fried calamari.

One, Two, Three

Begin by breaking your working menu into smaller parts. Think of it as three acts, with a beginning, middle, and end. An Italian meal begins with sparkling wine with appetizers, followed by pasta, and then the main dish.

Whether you think of it as appetizers, entrées, and desserts, or the English's less romantic starters, mains, and puddings, divide your menu into three acts.

What are your three main acts? How are they broken down within your contemporary take on the type of cuisine you're serving? Your first act could be broken down into appetizers, soups, and salads.

Food Choices

Today's dining customer wants choices. You can build in freedom within your menu to give choices to, for instance, vegans, vegetarians, gluten-free, and people with food allergies. You want to allow your guests freedom to customize their meal without stepping out of your genre. That's one of the reasons the small plate trend is so popular. (Plus, it introduces a lower range of prices.)

Today's restaurateur is wise to think of contemporary diners' interests in health. Vegetarian options are required. Remember, too, that at the same time there's an interest in health, there's also a focus on flavor that can supersede it for most diners. Bacon has never been more popular. There was a time when bacon was practically considered a public enemy, filled with the killers: fat, salt, and nitrates.

Today, contemporary chefs get kudos for smoking their own bacon and curing their own hams, and there are plenty of nitrate-free cured meats out there. The foodie culture has encouraged these two sides of dining—health and indulgence—which is another factor in the balance on your menu.

Beverages

Your drinks program should be in the spirit of your restaurant concept. Mediterranean restaurants pour the wines of South America, Spain, and California by the glass. New American restaurants shake up cocktails with craft-distilled spirits and fresh juices. A vegetarian sushi house could feature retro sake bombs made with Pabst Blue Ribbon beer.

If your concept was a New Southern restaurant, what classic drinks would you want your bartender to contemporize? A muddled mint julep? Plays on Southern Sweet Tea, Arnold Palmers, and Kentucky Bourbon on the rocks (extra-large ice-cubes)? It's the same as for food. Take a genre, and make it contemporary, relevant, and more interesting.

Apply the same three-act metaphor to your drinks program. Imagine how the guest is going to experience your restaurant from the beginning of the evening on.

You'll run your drinks menu through the same paces we're going to talk about later on for streamlining and blueprinting your menu.

Refining Your Menu

The next stage is what we call "cook-throughs." That's when the chef and cooks get together in the kitchen and create the dishes. We want to make sure dishes can be executed repeatedly with the same results.

SMART MOVE

Most people order the same thing every time they go to a restaurant. Success in the restaurant business has been built upon an ossobucco and polenta dish that stayed popular for 20 years. That's a blessing and a curse for a chef who will have to make it the exact same way for decades or face mutiny from his customers.

Yield Tests

What we're doing during this process is building up data for every dish we serve. We then use this data to help create spreadsheets that keep a firm control over spending.

We created an inventory template we use to order and cost out every item used in every recipe in every plate. You'll find more information on the components of this multipage spreadsheet in Chapter 16. It's vital that you begin to build up your data and test your recipes *before* you open. Bring the laptop into the kitchen, and if you need administrative staff to enter the prices, hire someone to help.

You want your executive and sous chef involved in costing from the beginning, especially if they're young Culinary Institute of America (CIA) grads. They probably have visions of sugar plums in Maine juniper red wine sauce dancing around their get-famous-quick impatient young minds. The main thing they need to learn is how important repetition and consistency are in keeping food costs in line. You can't have your chefs changing things up; it will throw off your carefully crafted cost framework.

So often, restaurants can be derailed by enthusiasm. A chef is excited about a new kind of mushroom. You need to ask some questions: How are you going to pay for it? What costs are you cutting to cover those mushrooms, and how much of a profit will be made on that dish?

Refining Dishes for Plating

Cost, however, isn't the only consideration here. As you analyze each dish, think again about how the dish balances ingredients, flavors, colors, and textures. Keep thinking of ways you can refine the production of the dishes and streamline the production.

Real-Time Testing

Your first set of willing guinea pigs are your stakeholders. Your second (and sometimes third) will be family and friends. A beginning restaurateur will find value in doing two family and friend dinners.

Tasting with Stakeholders

Investor dinners are usually for six or eight investors and their husbands or wives. For the restaurateur, it can be one of the more vulnerable nights, coming as it does so close to the anxiety-filled days of opening. The restaurateur must control the experience. Let your guests know that this evening is a celebration, not a panel on the food, service, and atmosphere. It's not to get their opinion on the food. It's not to take a poll or a thumbs-up or thumbs-down on the dishes. It's really more about sharing an almost-finished product.

Of course, they're going to give you their opinions anyway. Restaurant investors often want to show off how much they know about food and wine, and sometimes they're bulls in a china shop, but you have to defer. Deal with meaningless criticism, such as "I don't think you should serve potatoes with that," by using misdirection. Bring attention to another unique aspect of the potatoes. "Did you notice how they were served in cones the way they are in Belgium?" This will divert investors into talking about their European travels.

In the days before opening, your staff gets raw. Everyone's been working around the clock. Your chef's frazzled. Your investors and their significant others probably don't realize how sensitive everyone is at this point. So try to make them feel like they're at an intimate dinner party—where you wouldn't critique the food. Let everyone order what they want, but push the conversation away from the food.

> **POTENTIAL PITFALL**
>
> Don't get defensive if your investors start criticizing the food. Prepare your chef to put on his Teflon suit, and let any comments roll right off. You don't want your chef to quit before opening because his ego was bruised at an investors' dinner.

The investors' dinner is an opportunity to test your systems and equipment under the pressure of performance with a small audience. Your investors are probably not going to understand the real purpose of this event. Remember, movies have one director. A menu needs one, too.

The Physical Menu

Whether your menu is a chalkboard, iPad, or traditional card, is a decision ruled by your concept. For the beginner, we recommend designing a menu that can be easily printed on card stock at either your local printer or on your own printer. (Though, quite frankly, for the hassle and time of dealing with a fussy printer, you're better off spending the money to have it printed professionally.) Do scope out the closest printer to your restaurant. There will be times when you're happy it's around the corner. Plus, doing business locally makes you part of the community, sharing in the collective spirit of the neighborhood. There's a good chance you'll be adjusting your menu in the upcoming month, so don't go nuts thinking you're getting a good deal on a bulk printing.

Words

Words on menus are important, and studies by linguists have useful lessons for restaurateurs. A linguistics professor who studied 6,500 menus (that's 650,000 dishes) discovered that the longer the words in the menu, the higher the price of the dishes. He determined that each additional letter added 18 cents to the cost of the meal.

Professor Dan Jurafsky, in *The Language of Food: A Linguist Reads the Menu* (W.W. Norton), also found that the types of words reflect prices, too. Extra descriptions like "tasty," "delicious," and "world famous" are used in restaurants with lower prices. Less expensive restaurants often offer many choices. Think of diner menus, booklets of laminated pages and color photos, offering Gourmet Burgers, Value Favorites, Greek Delights, and Our Famous Cream Cheese Cakes.

Some words, however, add value, such as references to provenance, or the place where the food was grown or raised. Spices and exotic names add value, too.

Menus need to be consistent in the point of view and in the language. They also must be accurate.

Accuracy

Accurately describe the food you offer. If it says the meat is roasted, the meat should be roasted. If the menu says a salad has pomegranate seeds in it, be sure not to substitute dried blueberries. If the menu says it's organic, be sure it is. Deliver the meal you promised. Promise a meal you can deliver.

A menu should be consistent in its style, or the way words are treated. Don't spell the same word more than one way on your menu.

Ethnic and Foreign Words

Be consistent in your use of ethnic and foreign words. Don't slip in and out of an ethnic style (Reggiano Parmigiano vs. Parmesan, for example).

If you're using foreign words to get across the feel of your restaurant and the expressions aren't familiar, you can provide a pronunciation guide and definitions. But don't underestimate the knowledge of your customers; it can be a turn-off in many markets. If you have a contemporary Mexican small plate concept, there's no need to give the pronunciation of tacos.

But if you use the word *antojitos*, you could provide the pronunciation and definition on the menu. "Antojitos (ahn-toh-hee-tohs) is a word used in Mexico for street food, little snacks, nibbles, or appetizers." Reading that definition makes people want to snack, doesn't it?

> **DEFINITION**
>
> **Antojitos** means little snacks, cravings, or nibbles in Spanish. It's a term used in Mexico for street food. Small plate restaurants use the term in the appetizer section of the menu.

Language Style

The formality or relaxed quality of your language reinforces your concept. A contemporary New American menu might have a section called "Snacks" or "Nibbles" or "From the Fields."

As for naming dishes, you should keep it simple. The name should tell the diner what the dish is. Some restaurants turn locals into regulars by naming dishes after them. Once again, it all ties back to how the name relates to expressing your restaurant concept. Start looking at menu names. One dish was called "Angel Kisses" on a bistro menu. It sounded like a dessert, but it was gnocchi in a garlicky sage-butter sauce. Garlic and kisses don't mix for many customers.

More important than names are descriptions of the food listed on the menu. These descriptions should capture the flavor profile, rather than list all the ingredients, which can be tedious rather than evocative. Listing an unexpected ingredient piques the diner's interest. You can make note of common allergens such as peanuts if they're used as a garnish. People with allergies often ask about ingredients.

What a Menu Should and Shouldn't Do:

- It shouldn't provoke laughter (knowing irony, yes; mockery, no).

- It shouldn't be full of typos.

- It shouldn't be pompous—make it real.

- It should make the guest crave eating and drinking the restaurant's fare.

It's a cool idea to have the forager or fisherman come to your restaurant's back door. To have a backyard farmer offer you rabbits. To have your hunter friend bring quail and pheasant. But before you put it on your menu, realize that most health departments will not consider these approved food sources. If they find these products in your kitchen, they'll remove and destroy them, and you could be fined.

Some restaurants get away with this under the radar, but don't try it.

Furthermore, foraging for restaurant staples isn't a good route either. Some people discover foraging, and in their newfound enthusiasm decide to launch a business. They have no idea how tedious and time-consuming it's going to be, being outside digging, hunched over patches of wild dandelion and chicory.

One new forager got a newspaper to write about how he was providing foraged greens and mushrooms to local restaurants. The next thing you know, the local health inspector made surprise visits to those restaurants. Foraging is not considered an approved source of food. (Note: some local health codes make exceptions for home kitchens; others strictly forbid it.)

SMART MOVE

Noma in Copenhagen was named the best restaurant in the world for creative menus of foraged indigenous species. Chef René Redzepi's rediscovery of forgotten foods has been celebrated by chefs and it points to the desire to return to local food systems in the age of industrialized food and globalization. In the United States, food safety laws don't allow foraged food, but chefs turn to locally farmed foods for freshness and variety.

Menu Design

Your menu, the physical object that people will hold and read, reinforces your concept through the design of your logo and interior, the colors and textures, and the motifs.

Check out sites like Pinterest to see what kind of menus are out there. Google your restaurant genre to see how you can update traditional menu designs. Notice what you like and what you don't like. It's a good idea to work with a graphic designer to design your logo and menu.

The menu tells the customer how to order. It's a guide to ordering. It lets the customer know, for instance, if the menu is a contemporary take on the Southern "meat and three" meals—meat with a choice of three vegetables. The menu shows how to choose the components of the meal.

Think about how certain types of menus typify certain restaurant variations—for example, the laminated booklets in diners with lurid color photos of the food. If you're doing a contemporary take on a 1950s diner, a laminated menu with retro graphics would be appropriate.

When you think of a formal restaurant, such as a traditional French restaurant, you tend to think about a big booklet, too—one that announces its importance by its very size. The cover is leather and the interior pages are on good-quality paper, often in cream or white.

Booklets can still be used to show a serious foodie intention, but today they're often smaller. You should think carefully about the size, how your customers will hold it and use it and the information it must convey

> **POTENTIAL PITFALL**
>
> Design your menu so that it fits on the table. Imagine a table for two with two people each holding your menu. Is there room for them to lay it down on the table? Overlooking a point like this leads to uncomfortable guests who can't even see each other over their big menus. Always think about proportion.

Readability

Most designers choose design over legibility. Is the font big enough? Will your guests be able to read it in the evening when the lights have been dimmed? Who are your customers? People tend to have more trouble seeing in the dark as they get older.

Of course, Jody completely bucked this advice with his Mexican restaurant and tequila bar. The place was so dark and so loud that people brought flashlights to see the menu. The Zagat restaurant review even had a line about how you needed to text your dinner companions.

How many pages should your menu be? Beginners should start with a focused menu that fits on one page. The drink menu can be on the back, and the dessert and lunch menus can be separate.

Menu Component Checklist:

- ❏ Logo
- ❏ Categories
- ❏ Dish names
- ❏ Prices
- ❏ Descriptions
- ❏ Drinks
- ❏ Chef-Owner Name: Only include if there's a chef-owner or if the chef is a partner in the business
- ❏ Health Warning: Local health departments often require certain warnings, such as the potential harm of eating raw eggs or shellfish for at-risk guests. Check with your health department to get the exact language.

❏ Policies: Include polices such as "20 percent gratuity is added to parties of six or more." Policies can be personalized to make them friendlier.

❏ Allergies: Include allergy notices such as "Please inform us of any allergies; we are happy to accommodate your allergies."

❏ Philosophy: Some restaurants like to include their philosophy, such as "We feature pasture-raised meats."

Nutrition Claims and Calorie Counts

Calorie counts are required in some parts of the country. For instance, since 2008, New York City chain restaurants with more than 20 outlets are required to list calorie counts on their menus. This public health measure is designed to bring attention to obesity, heart disease, and diabetes, and their relation to shockingly large calorie counts on today's menus. When the Hard Rock Café started listing calorie counts, people were surprised to learn that the "healthy" salads they were ordering—with shrimp, nuts, cheese, and a creamy dressing—contained 920 calories, almost half the recommended 2,000 daily.

Portions have increased since the 1970s. Today a typical hamburger has 97 more calories than back then. Fries have 68 more, according to the Rudd Center for Food Policy and Obesity at Yale University.

If your concept is health-driven, you may want to spotlight how few calories, how many healthy vitamins, and how much fiber your dishes have. Remember, today there are apps that calculate calories, and super-healthy food-obsessed people are likely to use them.

The Least You Need to Know

- A menu uses all of its parts—design, words, and descriptions—to tell the customer the story of your restaurant.
- Think of balance when you create your menu, select your dishes and their cooking methods, and plate the dishes.
- Test each recipe to ensure it can be replicated again and again.
- The investors' dinner is your first trial run. The focus is on service and hospitality—it's not a forum on the food. It's a celebration.

CHAPTER 10

Designing the Front of the House

Finally, you're getting to the fun stuff. Design is everything. Don't tell the chef, but we think the design is just as important as the food. Design is a big part of the experience people are going to talk about when they tell their friends about your restaurant.

The design of the front of the house is tackled *after* you've distilled your concept (refer to Chapter 3) and found your location. The front of the house is designed *before* you plan your budget and funding.

In this chapter, you'll learn how to create a welcoming restaurant—a place that makes your guests look and feel good. We'll discuss how all the components—from tables, floors, lighting, to artwork—express your concept.

In This Chapter

- Creating your restaurant's look
- Using design as a marketing tool
- The basic principles of restaurant design
- Creating comfortable, flexible seating
- The importance of lighting

Bringing Your Restaurant Concept to Life

Jody is inspired by movies, and thinks of a restaurant's concept as a screenplay, and design as the set. If your restaurant were a movie, the exterior and the front of the house (FOH)—the hostess desk, the dining room, and the bar—would be the location. (We focus on the bar in Chapter 11.)

The design of the front of the house tells your restaurant's story. You've got to know what that story is, and what your restaurant's message is, before you can create your design. A good design brings your story to life.

The restaurant's style and design are inextricably linked to your concept. Your guest's personal interaction with the staff and the food will make up their experience.

Design creates energy and mood. It needs visual coherence, where all the components come together to tell the message. Restaurant design must also be practical. People need to move through this space. Food needs to be moved from the kitchen to the tables. Tables also need to be cleared after guests are finished with their meals.

SMART MOVE

If you want your restaurant to stand out, you need to do something that stands out. Jody had success with restaurants that bucked design trends, and were so cool they annoyed some people. But the target market loved the energy, and the restaurants prospered. Be bold in your choices.

An appealing design also creates an experience that gets people talking about your restaurant. Twenty years ago when Fairfield County, Connecticut, restaurants had a Pottery Barn sensibility with friendly khaki-wearing staff fumbling through, Jody created a restaurant named Baang where the sensibility wasn't an oblivious cliché. He hired restaurant designer David Rockwell, who was just emerging at the time, to create a hip, vibrant, and colorful atmosphere. The restaurant served an Asian fusion menu that was homage to Chinois on Main, the trendy L.A. restaurant. Baang's calamari salad remained a favorite for 20 years. Yes, the restaurant prospered for 20 years!

In 2010, Jody noticed that the hometown locals were bummed out about the economy even though they were still living great lives. So he decided to bring some sexy fun to town by opening Lolita Cocina & Tequila Bar. It was designed to be a hideaway for successful 35- to 55-year-olds. The design was dimly lit Mexican bordello, with red-flocked wallpaper and red glass chandeliers.

The menu was indulgent versions of Mexican street food—guacamole with lobster made tableside. It offered 150 tequilas with some at $100 a shot. This was sipping tequila for adults. Rock was pumped out on the sound system, and it made everyone feel young again. The restaurant got people talking.

Design is also a marketing tool. You need to give people something to talk about. At Bleu, Jody's upscale contemporary French restaurant, he generated a lot of buzz by installing a see-through glass door that frosted over when guests locked the bathroom stall.

Many of your guests come to your restaurant for something more than the food. They come because they like the way your restaurant looks and the way it makes them feel. A unique design confers status on your guests. Many people can't afford to hire an interior designer at home. Hanging out at a cool-looking restaurant reflects their self-image—who they are or who they want to be.

Here are the rules for Restaurant Interior Décor 101:

- Owners need to understand that commercial design is about balance and effect, whereas decorating your home is all personal choice.

- Most people over-decorate. It's like a Christmas tree that has too many ornaments and lights. You don't know where to look. Don't overdo using decorative accessories.

- Punctuate the room to draw eyes to effects that reinforce your concept.

- Lighting is a powerful design tool when effectively used to guide the guest's eye and to hide your design's weaknesses.

The beginner on a budget can re-use, recycle, and re-adapt furniture and cheap finds. However, keep in mind scale and the need for multiples to make an impact. The lights that hang over your bar, such as a row of uniform drum shades, frosted glass balls, or copper lanterns, make more of an impact if they're uniform in appearance.

Paint

Painting is a highly effective way of transforming a space, hiding a multitude of flaws, or tying disparate pieces of furniture into a cohesive whole.

The right paint color will also set the mood and make your guests glow. Choose colors with warm undertones that reflect warm light that will be flattering to your guests. (And make sure your bathroom lighting is extra flattering!)

Not having windows or sun exposure doesn't have to be a drawback. A lot of cool restaurant spaces are basements, and they play with the idea of a wine cellar or grotto. You can do a lot with mirrors and candles in a windowless space. There are many themes that will adapt to windowless spaces, such as a nightclub.

Large windows that open, such as popular glass garage doors, pose problems for restaurant ventilation systems, as the fresh air compromises the balance of the system.

Unless you have an excellent spatial sense and experience in designing, we recommend you use a professional restaurant designer. You want your restaurant to make a statement, and professional designers are not afraid to be bold. Most laymen, unless they're artists, don't have an understanding of the importance of scale. Less is more in contemporary restaurant design.

> **POTENTIAL PITFALL**
>
> Choosing paint colors is one of the most difficult decisions for an inexperienced restaurateur. It's so easy to go wrong. Walls painted shades of blues and greens will reflect those tones onto guests' faces. Blues and greens are better used as accent colors.

Before you talk to a designer, figure out what look works for your concept. Get inspiration and ideas for the design of your restaurant on online sites such as Pinterest. Start a Pinterest board for front of the house designs. Think about how you can adapt the looks that convey your concept—on the cheap.

Do some boots-on-the-ground research by going to restaurants and closely observing their components and how they work together. How does the room make guests feel? What's the flow of movement through the room?

There's no one-plan-fits-all for layout, but there are some basic rules that a first-time restaurateur can use. Avoid broad vistas. Large open-floor plans drain energy when the room is less full. The dining room should make guests want to explore and discover hidden elements. Just as in gardens, paths are always more intriguing when you can't see all the way to the end.

Private Dining Rooms

Private dining rooms add flexibility to hosting private events. They should be vantage points with some seclusion, but not completely isolated. Your target market and concept determine the size and design of your private dining room.

A popular design for contemporary private dining rooms is to evoke the look of a wine cellar. This idea also works with floor-to-ceiling glass walls, as it opens these spaces up to light, makes them feel contemporary, and creates a stage for making people feel special.

Host/Hostess Stand

The first thing the guests will encounter is the host/hostess desk. There needs to be a piece of furniture that gives the host a sense of a barricade. The host needs a place to corral the guests. When people want to get into your hot restaurant on a Saturday night, they'll descend on your host. They'll even pretend they made that phantom reservation. They'll demand they be seated. They'll try to convince you that the 10 minutes they've been waiting is actually 30.

The hostess desk is where your guests may divest themselves of their coats and packages. Depending on the level of formality of your restaurant, your hostess can take coats or direct the guests to the coat-check station, or to where they may hang their coats on a rack near the door.

In parts of the country where it gets cold during the winter, you need a place to park big, bulky coats so they don't take space in your dining room, impeding waiters or falling on the floor and becoming a tripping hazard. Many people get weird about turning over their coats, possibly due to tipping. It could be their frugality or perhaps the fact that most people don't carry dollar bills on them these days.

> **SMART MOVE**
>
> Make it easy for guests to hang their coats. Having a coat rack or hooks where they can hang their coats and keep an eye on them seems to relax many guests. They know they can leave without waiting, without fumbling to find the coat check, and without paying a tip.

Many people opt to sit on their coats or fold them into bundles and place them on chairs. However, it's better for everyone if the coats are simply hung up.

Seating and Tables

Seating should be considered as it relates to your restaurant's concept. Who will be sitting at your tables? What type of experience are they going to have? There are several seating styles for restaurants:

- Intimate
- Family style
- Groups
- Singles
- Elegant and expensive
- Raw and urban

Having a variety of tables available is best for flexibility and for avoiding a sea of tables of ambiguous design.

People like tables that aren't "floating." They don't like feeling as if they're adrift in the middle of the room. They're more comfortable with their backs against a wall near a screen or divider, or within a booth.

The size and shape of your tables varies with your concept. A cool urban downtown-style place can squeeze six to eight people at a 48-inch round table, whereas a steakhouse would want a 60-inch table. Round tables are best for large groups up to eight. They allow more exchange than a long rectangular table where conversation is limited to the people across from each other or on either side.

Linear banquettes make good use of space, fit more people, and have a cozy and hip aura that works with the contemporary lifestyle. With two-tops lined up side-by-side, you have a lot of flexibility, as you can shove tables together depending on a party's size. There are lots of options for curved horseshoe-shaped banquettes. They're more expensive, but can make a strong impact. In addition, there are less-flexible linear banquettes.

Today, tables are selected for their bare surfaces to avoid the old look and expense of linens. Be sure to give some thought to the materials available to you and how they can work to express your restaurant's concept. Look around at the tables in local restaurants. What do you see? Retro linoleum in a family-friendly 1950s burger place. Worn wood for a barbecue joint. Marble-topped café tables for a French bistro (but beware: every click of marble tables touching can cause a chip, and pretty soon nicely worn becomes old and chipped).

Communal Tables

Communal tables have been trendy for several years, as they bring a contemporary feeling to a restaurant. However, many Americans are still getting used to the idea of sharing tables. It's a common practice in Europe, but there it's done out of practicality rather than conviviality. People sharing a table in Europe usually do little more than nod and utter a greeting. They typically don't chat, they stay to themselves.

Friendly Americans, however, approach community tables differently and, sometimes, diffidently. They may feel apprehensive about sharing a table. Once settled, they're likely to interact, asking one another about the food or other restaurants. In metropolitan settings, people are more comfortable using them because they're often in their own zone with their friends, and living in the city they're more used to close quarters.

High-topped communal tables, which are more reminiscent of a bar, provide a good view of the room and their height seems to lessen the intimacy of sharing a table with strangers, which makes people more emotionally comfortable. Adding a communal high-topped table extends the ability to dine in your bar area. They're popular for brunch and happy hour, but less popular for dinner, because they can be too small and uncomfortable.

POTENTIAL PITFALL

Low communal tables are less likely to appeal to suburban markets as they seem to require an intimacy. Jody once had a 35-foot communal table in a restaurant, and no one would sit at it unless every other seat in the place was taken.

In Aspen, where the true community table was born, they'd have a table that could seat about eight set off to the side in the dining room. The locals would sit there, enjoy breakfast among their neighbors, read the newspaper, and share the table just as they shared a common sensibility.

We've seen communal tables work in real foodie restaurants. People sitting next to us at a high-topped table insisted on giving us, strangers, a taste of their food because they were so psyched about the flavors. We've watched customers ask their fellow communal diners, "Excuse me, may I ask what you ordered?" Then they ordered the same meal.

POTENTIAL PITFALL

Chair legs on carpets are a concern because they wear down the carpet when moved. Chair legs also weaken under heavy use. Chairs on polished cement flooring need plastic caps to spare damage to the floor and the chair.

A great trick with community tables is to use runners across each setting to mark the table. When people sit at a four-top, you can slide two runners together, and then use candles or flowers to place a marker between them and the next group or couple. This little trick creates proprietary space within the contiguous table and allows parties to feel more at ease sharing a single piece of real estate.

Proceed with caution and know your customer before you commit to purchasing communal tables. An empty communal table can look like—and be—a chasm in the room.

Sound Dampening

One of the side effects of bare tables and materials such as stone, tile, cement, blackboards, and framed artwork and mirrors is that sound bounces off of them. Every clatter and clink of the plates, forks, and glasses; the clip-clop of heels across the floor;, and loud voices bounce around the space. There are high-tech solutions to dampening sound, but keep in mind they're expensive.

You can, however, rely on a few less expensive tricks to help contain sound. Curtains are a tried-and-true solution. Heavier materials such as faux velvets or theatre curtains are also effective insulators. Many restaurants create curtained entryways to contain the blasts of cold or hot air from front doors opening. (Don't cover exit signs mounted over doors, though.) These treatments can add an air of drama, and create a gateway. They also focus the customer's eye. Think about where you want their eyes to travel when they enter your restaurant.

Ceilings are forgiving places to hide sound dampening elements as well, because they won't dilute the design. Acoustic panels with sound-absorbing fabric can be attached to ceiling tiles and blended into the color scheme. Framed fabric panels can also be used effectively when hung on the walls by each table. You can also put foam on the backs of artwork or mirrors to help buffer sound.

A few area rugs will also absorb sound, even on a polished concrete floor. Bare floors are the trend in contemporary restaurants, and wall-to-wall carpets seem outdated and old-fashioned. But a few area rugs will anchor seating areas. Remember, these rugs need to be shampooed every six weeks, and will probably need to be replaced every one and a half to two years.

Secure rugs with pads and double-sided tape, which will have to be replaced every other week as it will get less sticky with wear. There are also small wedge-shaped borders that can be screwed into a floor, but we think they look awful and create more of a tripping hazard.

The best solution to echoing sound is a crowded room, of course. There's nothing better than the sound of a restaurant full of people enjoying themselves.

Curtains

Lined curtains or shades are also energy-efficient, acting as an insulator to keep hot sun out during the day, and keeping windows blanketed on cold nights when your restaurant is closed. They help keep your energy costs down. Using curtains in conjunction with sheers enables the light from your restaurant's windows to entice potential customers to come in. Curtains and shades are also useful as room dividers, as well as sound dampeners. A very cozy and luxurious look is to line an entire small room in fabric.

The sight of people enjoying themselves in a restaurant from the outside—there's no better advertisement for a restaurant. Bare windows are also in vogue, and depending on your setting, you can use outdoor lighting or street lighting to take away from the black hole of a dark window.

Tabletop

The tabletop sets the tone for the experience to come. Today, less is more. The old-school formal dining model was lots of silverware, several glasses, and a *charger*. Chargers just seem unnecessary in most restaurants today. They're removed once guests are seated.

> 📖 **DEFINITION**
>
> **Chargers** are large decorative underplates, used as part of a formal service. They're plates that are set on the table when guests sit down, but food is not served directly on them.

There's a school of thought that believes by setting the table with wine glasses, you'll nudge the guest into ordering wine. But there are better sales techniques than hoping the guest will order wine. Plus, it will save the server the trouble of taking the unused glass from the table, which must be rewashed because the guests may have sneezed or touched the wine glasses.

Since tablecloths are less common in restaurants due to the expense of laundering them, placemats are often used to prevent silverware being placed on a bare table, which is a sanitary concern.

Napkins are another tactile and visual expression of your story. The farm-to-table movement has brought a lot of blue-striped cotton dishtowels to the table, and the soft cotton has a homey feel. Some restaurants use black napkins to prevent their business clients from getting white fabric fibers on their dark suits.

Flowers and Candles

Placing flowers on tables during the day and candles at night used to be the rule of thumb. However, these days you must be mindful of your real estate. Cluttered tables make people order less as the meal progresses. Candles bring warmth and light to the table. Votive candles are the go-to favorite, but restaurant operators often use tea lights, which look less sexy and burn out quicker.

The key to votives is to clean the vessel after every use. Here's a tip: put a drop of water in the vessel before placing the candle in. It will make it easier to pop out the candle later. Don't put votives through a dishwashing machine—the wax will gum up the machine. Make sure your dishwasher guy understands this.

Keeping wine and water off to the side in a community ice bucket is one way to save room on the table, but the guests are often apprehensive about whether all their wine was poured. They like more control over their wine.

Plants

Plants are difficult. They need good light and maintenance. They were leaned on heavily when design was more benign. Today, plants harken back to the 1980s, unless they're thoughtfully introduced as design and not just filler. Too many restaurants have cheap, poorly maintained plants, and that's a sad sight that doesn't inspire confidence in the customer. An ailing, dusty plant is the exact opposite of the intention of bringing green life into your restaurant.

Sculpture and Art

Sculpture and art should be selected only to reinforce your concept, not just to cover a wall. Keep your restaurant concept and design in mind when purchasing and placing these pieces. You want them to add to the restaurant's décor, not look so jarring that the guests can't focus on the food.

Restrooms

Avoid visibility of the restrooms from the dining room. Build a screen-style portal to block that view. The beginning restaurateur will do well to not change any major plumbing (moving pipes in the bathrooms, for example). Replace toilets if they need replacing. Put the focus on the sinks, mirror, and lighting. You can create a dramatic focal point, reinforcing your design concept, at the sinks. Make sure there's enough counter space for women to place their purse, makeup bag, or hairbrush while touching up their makeup. Attractive colors that keep with your scheme and flattering light are very important in restrooms. You want your guests returning to the dining room feeling confident and relaxed.

> **SMART MOVE**
>
> Bathrooms must be kept scrupulously clean. Have your managers check the bathrooms throughout the night. They can keep checklists to ensure everything is clean in the bathrooms. Nothing ruins a guest's experience more than a dirty bathroom.

We prefer using paper towels to the hand-drying machines that blow hot air. Lately, there has been a trend toward using cloth hand towels as an upscale touch. Some thought needs to go into balancing the costs of cleaning those towels against benefits to your target market and the atmosphere you're creating. There are higher-quality paper towels to match your market, and recycled options if your concept is eco-friendly.

Outdoor Seating

Customers greet outdoor seating with joy. It instantly conveys a message of relaxation and enjoyment. Note that outdoor seating must be contained within a solid barrier if alcohol is served. A canopy or trellis with retractable canvas is a great way to provide the perfect open-air ambience and provide protection should there be a sudden downpour.

When booking reservations, don't accept them for outdoor seating. Let customers know they can request an outdoor table from the hostess when they arrive. That gives you more wiggle room if the weather changes.

On a busy night as you seat outdoors, you'll need to keep a few open sections indoors if the weather is at all precarious. This move will save you grief if all of a sudden a lot of wet guests descend upon the host looking for an indoor table to finish their dinner.

Lighting

Lighting can create magic and mood. It's what makes the room glow, makes faces look more attractive, and makes the food look appealing .Lighting is best placed from the side, as overhead lighting is harsh. Overhead lighting floods the room, and it doesn't evoke joy. Underlighting, particularly the strips of task lighting under the bar, creates a shadowy effect. Bartenders often remove those lights.

There are three kinds of electrical lighting: ambient, task, and accent. You may also have natural lighting.

Ambient lighting is general lighting from chandeliers, wall-mounted sconces, and the big drum shades popular in many contemporary restaurants. Ambient light softens as it reflects from the ceiling, casting a background glow. The areas that need illumination are key design effects. Candles bring warmth and soft light to the table.

Task lighting illuminates your workstations such as the host/hostess desk or servers' station. It provides your staff enough light so they can ensure your servers are filling customer requests accurately, whether it's placing an order or retrieving a fork.

Accent lights draw the eye to decorative elements. Make sure decorations express your concept, whether it's a statue of Ganesh, the elephant-headed God and namesake of your Indian restaurant; a framed wall of moss in your vegetarian and vegan restaurant; or the black-and-white photos of *La Dolce Vita* that decorate your hip pizza parlor. To be effective, accent lights should be about three times the brightness of the ambient light.

Natural light is always great. It makes people feel good, unless it's glaring, hot, or shining in their eyes. If the sunlight's coming in too strongly, window tinting is a subtle way to diffuse it. If an outside streetlight or glaring sign invades your restaurant space at night, sheer curtains can be an effective way to allow enough outside impact while quieting down the light.

All lighting should be on dimmer switches. Dimmers are essential for adjusting the mood to the time of day and the restaurant's energy. Managers need to be careful not to dim the lights too abruptly. It creates a shock wave in the ambiance. Be careful not to dim the interior lights too fast and make the inside darker than the natural outside twilight. Doing so paints the room in a depressing sepia tone.

Server Stations

Server stations should be unobtrusive and spread out, so there's no back-up or cluster when waiters need to use them. Separating the POS stations from the *busser reset consoles* is also smart because they have different uses. Wall-mounted POS systems are now available, which can help save space.

> **DEFINITION**
>
> **Busser reset consoles** are pieces of furniture that hold what bussers need to reset the tables—glasses, napkins, silverware, plates, etc. Today many restaurants use cool pieces of furniture for consoles and server stations.

Music is an important part of the dining experience, and yet another expression of your concept. Jody likes to customize a soundtrack for each restaurant. Think of the music as a movie soundtrack, and consider customizing one that fits your concept. It will underscore and amplify your restaurant's story. Place speakers strategically. A subwoofer built into cabinetry or the wall can be a very effective means of bringing high-fidelity sound and presence to the room without blasting music that drowns out guests' conversation. Crossover and flown speakers are the best mix of equipment to give the room a pulse that keeps guests energized.

Flown speakers are mounted on wall surfaces so they can be closer to guests' ears. High-ceiling spaces with speakers mounted on the ceiling need the volume turned loud to reach guests' ears, and then the sound in the room becomes too loud and distorted.

A crossover is a technical sound frequency disbursement component that sends the bass frequency to the bass or subwoofer and the mid- and high frequencies to the flown speakers. This creates a nice pulse you can feel and is a great way to add music to the dining experience.

Turn up the volume when the room is empty and lower it when the restaurant is full. Most restaurateurs get this wrong. They turn down the music when the room is empty and turn it up when the room is full. Music gives an empty room energy—it must be kept in balance.

Takeout

Takeout can be profitable if it works with your concept. People don't cook as much as they used to, and many people live on takeout. If you plan on this being a significant part of your business, you should create a separate entrance or waiting area just for that. If, for instance, you offer takeout pizza as well as a sit-down dining room and bar, having a separate entrance ensures the relaxed atmosphere of your dining room is not disturbed by the anxious energy of people waiting for their wood-fired brick oven pizza.

The Least You Need to Know

- Less is more in contemporary restaurant design.
- Linear banquettes and two-top tables make for the most efficient and flexible use of space.
- Painting is the most cost-effective way of transforming your space and furniture.
- Curtains are tried-and-true sound dampeners.
- Determine the look that expresses your concept, and work with a professional restaurant designer.

CHAPTER 11

Setting Up Your Bar and Beverage Systems

In this chapter, we'll discuss how to merchandize and stage your bar and draw guests into it. We'll talk about how to make your bar a comfortable and hospitable place for guests to drink, eat, and socialize. We'll also talk about some of the recent trends in bar seating.

We'll also show you some of the tools and equipment you'll need in your bar, and give you tips on preparing and serving memorable nonalcoholic beverages as well.

In This Chapter

- Making the bar an effective marketing tool
- Current trends in bar seating
- Creating an eat-in friendly bar
- Tools of the bartending trade
- Service of nonalcoholic beverages

The Bar as Marketing Tool

The bar is an important gathering place for your guests. For a restaurateur, it's a major profit center if you manage your inventory and your bartender. The bar is a strong marketing tool when it's planned properly. Merchandising and staging is an art form. The back bar display—bottles of liquid sparkling in the light—is the focal point of your bar. If you stack a random collection of liquor bottles together, it doesn't convey a message. In creating your bar staging, you want to evoke a particular emotional reaction.

The strongest emotion you want to evoke is to make the customer want to have a drink (or two) in your restaurant's bar. Remember alcohol, soft drinks, coffee, and tea are all high-profit items.

For a high-end Italian steakhouse, Jody used the back bar to create a real feeling of "Wow! Let's have a drink here!" He took a supermarket shelf approach, rather than placing single bottles of each brand next to one another. He created a powerful graphic by selecting a case of each bottle by color. Bands of blue bottles, clear, amber, white, and green also gave a feeling of abundance that worked with the expensive, indulgent food menu.

You should give the bar a clean and uncluttered look that puts the focus on the bottles. This is not the place to tuck or tack up photos, slogans, or lotto cards.

Bottle Placement

Bottles should not be set up randomly every day. Your design should be blueprinted so you can spot bottles that need replacing, and so the bartenders' access is standard from shift to shift. You've got to make sure your bartenders understand that they're not allowed to alter your system. As you analyze your bar sales, you might end up adjusting your display later on, but that change should be blueprinted, too.

The traditional way of setting up the back bar takes into consideration that we read from left to right. On your speed rail, the shelf containing the well or rail bottles—the brands the house uses when a customer doesn't request a brand—are kept at the ready, along with the bottles you use most often for making drinks. For instance, a Mexican restaurant will include two brands of tequila and a bottle of triple sec on the speed rail. A Cuban restaurant will include extra brands of rum on the speed rail. This is your working shelf. As much as possible, the back bar should be a display.

SMART MOVE

With creative lighting, your bar can look like a temple. There are many ways to use lighting to draw guests to your bar, and many options for lighting from long-lasting LED lights to colored and string lights. Creative lighting can evoke any mood your concept calls for.

Place the distilled spirits you sell the most at the left end of the most accessible shelf. That's usually vodka, though brown spirits such as bourbon and scotch are catching up. Place all your brands of vodka in a row. Follow them with your tequila brands (if that's what you sell the most of), then with rum, gin, scotch, bourbon, brandies, and finally after-dinner drinks. Make sure all the labels face forward and can be seen. Lesser-used bottles go on the higher shelves.

Wines can be displayed much the same way, with your most popular sellers running from left to right. If your restaurant specializes in wine, there are many shelving options to provide a bountiful display.

With the growth of the American craft beer movement, many restaurants and bars have expanded the number of brews on tap, and many offer locally produced brews. Some beer-centric restaurants keep their supplies of beer behind the bar in tall, refrigerated display cases. The creative labels on craft beer bottles add to the visual energy.

You should mount the POS at the front bar. It's a great way to minimize skimming by the bartender. The display is close to the guests and they can see if the bartender has rung up their drinks at the correct price. This was a ground-breaking change in controlling the bartender.

Eat-In Bars

Eating at the bar is more popular than ever, and many savvy diners prefer it. It's perfect for dining alone because it takes away the loneliness of sitting at a table by oneself, as the waiter removes all the other place settings.

You can offer your full menu or a bar menu. Late-night menus are also popular. Think about how and where the servers will deliver the food to the bar, and who will deliver it to the customer. Bartenders usually offer menus to guests and place napkins on the bar as tablecloths, a simple yet hospitable touch. The bartender will need storage for napkins, cutlery, and condiments.

Barstools with backs are more comfortable than those without. A trend in bar seating is upholstered seats and backs. Backless metal stools, though appealing to a contemporary aesthetic, are hard and uncomfortable and your guests will not linger long.

Hooks beneath the bar, for customers to hang purses or bags, are definitely necessary. Customers can then stash their bags out of the way, which is good for the restaurant, and they're comfortable having their stuff close by.

Couture Cocktails

The trend of bartenders becoming beverage chefs or mixologists is a bit overplayed. Jody feels the same way about bartenders as he does about chefs. Any cocktails they create must express the restaurant's concept and be profitable. The recipes are blueprinted and made to measure. No tweaking is allowed.

Recently, there's been a renaissance of craft distilling, and many contemporary bartenders are using whiskey from Colorado, brandy from California, and gin from Long Island. These small-batch spirits are expensive to make, so they cost more. If it ties into your concept to use craft spirits and your market will bear higher prices, then go to it. Otherwise, stick to the tried-and-true commercial brands.

Along with a movement toward major liquor companies selling flavored vodkas, contemporary bartenders are infusing liquors with flavorings such as hot peppers, fruits, and spices. House-infused liquor can make your drinks stand out and are lower cost, since you're using standard brands of liquor.

> **POTENTIAL PITFALL**
>
> Some state alcohol control boards, such as Tennessee's, are beginning to crack down on house-infused liquors. Infusing distilled spirits without having a distillery permit is against federal law. With the strong trend toward artisan products, there's a pushback against the crackdown. Stay on top of your local food news for developments.

Remember the popularity, preparation, and profitability (PPP) test we talked about in Chapter 5? After the first month, you should run the PPP test on the cocktails and make adjustments accordingly.

Garnishes such as orange slices, limes, olives, pickled onions, house-brandied cherries, jalapeños, mint, and cilantro provide a fresh and colorful working display at the bar, and can entice customers into ordering your restaurant's signature cocktail. Note that the balance of cool cocktails and great garnishes needs to be filtered against how much time it takes to execute.

Bar Seating

Lounge or residential seating in a bar is popular and comfortable. Also, if you place it right, it won't limit your flexibility. A large cluster of seats like a mini living room can lose its sense of invitation if two people sit in it. No one else will want to invade their space.

To counter this, don't create tight areas. Try to keep the room more open. If the chairs can be pulled together or moved, it makes people feel at home. Couches also have an intimacy. If you want to commit a large space to a sofa and one person sits on it and no one else feels comfortable sitting there, too, it's a waste of space. A smaller loveseat is a better way to go.

A cocktail table is good for resting drinks, but as more people like to order and share food in lounge areas an intermediate-height table, which is between a café and a cocktail table height of around 36 inches, is a better solution. There are also tables with adjustable legs that can be raised if guests order food.

Small side tables for drinks and trays prevent guests from trying to balance a drink or plate on the arm of a sofa. Large, upholstered, amorphous-shaped seating pieces are useful, as they can be placed back to back. Floor lamps and accent lights warm these areas.

A fireplace is a home run, but during summer you'll need to stage it with candles or a goldfish bowl. Don't leave it clean and empty. The same is true of outdoor patios. Be thoughtful of what they look like out of season. They should always be staged.

Bar Tools

The cost of bar equipment can really add up, so the beginning restaurateur on a limited budget should look at used equipment and bartender hacks. Here are the tools of the bartending trade:

- A professional stainless steel (18/8) shaker
- Long spoons or implements for stirring
- Strainer spoons
- A sharp paring knife
- Cutting boards
- Zesters
- Peelers
- *Muddlers*
- Jiggers and measurers
- Corkscrews
- A blender
- Specialized ice cube trays or ice machine
- A recipe book with house versions of classic and house special cocktails

DEFINITION

A **muddler** is a baton-like instrument bartenders use to mash ingredients such as lemons and mint to extract juices and flavors for cocktails.

Having the recipe book available is useful to the entire staff. Servers might need to reference it to describe certain drink ingredients. Many professional bartenders keep notebooks in which they note flavors of brands, and keep records of drinks they create and their equipment hacks.

A great hack for a muddler was shared online by bartender Jeffrey Morgenthaler of Portland, Oregon. He saves money and creates a customized muddler by sawing a 10-inch French rolling pin (the kind with tapered ends) in half. He sands both ends and rubs them with food-grade mineral oil. The two different-sized tapered ends make the muddler more versatile.

Ice Cubes

Ice cubes have become part of the repertoire of the contemporary mixologist, no matter whether they're big spheres, 2 × 2-inch cubes, little cubes, or pebbles of clear ice. Bartenders are also freezing cubes of frozen blood orange, ginger beer spheres, square cubes filled with intricate patterns of cucumber, and clear cubes filled with house-made brandied cherries.

Bartenders do amazing things with ice. Bartender "Boston Mike" at Max's Downtown in Hartford developed a drink based on a cube of smoked ice. He smoked the water and froze it in 2 × 2-inch molds. Water can be smoked by placing a container of water in a wood-fired smoker, or by adding a liquid smoke product to the water. He then infused bourbon with Tahitian vanilla beans and citrus zest. To make his signature Vanilla on a Rock, he shook the infused bourbon with *dry curacao* and *bitters*. Every mixologist worth his Himalayan salt swears by his favorite bottle of bitters.

DEFINITION

> **Dry curacao** is a clear brandy flavored with orange skins, then mixed with cognac and spiced with anise and sweetened. **Bitters** are concentrated botanical extracts made from various herbs, flowers, roots, or seeds. Originally created as a cure for ailments, today bitters are a trendy ingredient in cocktails. Added in small doses or dashes, they add depth and balance to drinks.

The Vanilla on the Rock's smoked ice slowly melts, and the smoke flavor enhances the vanilla flavors of the infused bourbon. The play of strong brown spirits and sweet and deep flavors made this drink an experience for which the high-end business clientele were willing to pay top dollar.

When it comes to ice, you've got to figure out if the wow factor—do you need six different types of ice?—is worth it. If you're selling glasses of rare bourbons at $30 to $50 a glass, waking them up with a 3-inch sphere of ice (which won't water down the drink) makes it more special.

Kold Draft ice machines filter the water and make clear, pure, condensed cubes that many bartenders love. The machines are expensive, ranging up to around $4,000. If special ice cubes are intrinsic to your concept, save money by picking up a secondhand ice machine.

Your Coffee, Tea, and Soft Drinks Setup

Serving espresso at the bar gives a restaurant a European style. But only a few highly trained staff should operate the espresso maker. Having every waiter making cappuccinos for their customers is risky, especially because they often forsake finesse for speed. Espresso makers are complicated machines, and they're expensive. A brand-new commercial four-dispenser machine runs in the $16,000 range. You can get a decent two- to three-handle machine for around $5,000. Think about how much espresso you'll be serving before you make such an investment.

Coffee and Specialty Drinks

Coffee and specialty drinks should be made at the bar if you don't have convenient room in the kitchen. Having the waiters or crew going back to the bowels of the restaurant to make coffee isn't a good idea. They like to get out of sight and will stay lost if you let them.

The kitchen, however, can be a staging area for coffee drinks if there's room. You can brew it in the back kitchen and hold it in airpots—thermal vessels that will maintain quality and heat for long periods without creating a burnt or sour flavor. However, it's best to brew coffee fresh in the service area. Don't co-mingle a coffee station with a clean, dry POS station.

> **SMART MOVE**
>
> Sugar comes in many forms, and bringing your guest a choice of sugars—white, raw, artificial, or plant-based stevia—tells the guest about your restaurant's attention to detail. Don't ask a customer who orders coffee if they want sugar; just bring it.

Cold Beverages

Cold beverages are usually kept in the waiter station, if space allows. The beverage station can be staged to look part of the design aesthetic. It could be a farm table with bowls of lemons and limes, sugar cane, and pitchers of iced tea and lemonade lined up.

The bar is also a great staging area for cold beverages. The rule is to arrange for efficiency and to gather all pre-service–style drinks (water, iced tea, etc.) in one location, and use that same location to gather the after-service drinks.

The dining room has several service needs. The days of a bussing station are over, thank you! Stacking dirty dishes in a greasy bus bin in a holding area in the dining room until the busboy, often with an ill-fitting, dirty apron, totes them back to the kitchen seems unsanitary these days.

Today, tables are cleared by hand or on trays and brought straight back to the dish drop-off area.

Water requires storage. You can install an in-house water bottling station where you can fill bottles with filtered clear or bubbling water. If you don't have room for this at the bar, it can be placed in the kitchen.

The dining room service station for resetting tables can be a great piece of furniture or a hutch. Place linens in the two lower drawers, silverware in the top drawer, and glasses on the shelves. The POS and resetting stations should be separate, as they have different uses.

You can distinguish your restaurant with great cold beverages, such as iced tea, if you take the time to select an attractive glass and layer it with fresh mint and clementine slices. Simple syrup for sweetening iced tea is a given nowadays, as opposed to trying to dissolve a sugar cube. Free refills are another choice that needs to be considered in light of the average check and the quality of service. Free refills generate goodwill.

Standard juices, lemonade, and drinks that come from a soda gun in a post-mix fashion are losing popularity, as they are low quality. Bottling your own organic soda can be a cool touch sure to be noticed by your patrons. Fresh-squeezed limeade or lemonade can be a great refreshing beverage, but the amount of production will determine the price.

Many bars opt for club service, in which they sell individual bottles of cola. There's a big price difference, so you need to gauge your selling price before you go this route.

The Least You Need to Know

- Alcohol and nonalcoholic drinks are high-profit items, so staging your bar correctly is important to your business.
- Use your back bar display to merchandize your beverage offerings.
- Eating while seated at the bar has become more popular than ever, and there are many creative ways to accommodate this.
- Lounge and residential seating in a bar requires 36-inch cocktail tables so that guests can order and share food.

CHAPTER 12

Laying Out the Back of the House

In this chapter, we're going to talk about the design and layout of the back of the house. We'll look at the work that needs to be done there, the timing of that work, making the most of the space available, and how to set up the stations for the cooks and the all-important dishwasher. We'll also look at the equipment you'll need to run a restaurant kitchen.

The back of the house is used for other functions besides cooking. Goods and products are delivered here, and must be stored and organized. We'll discuss the best places to safely store products, prep ingredients, and have them ready for the chef to cook.

The back of the house also contains your office. This office should be small, but organized and functional.

Working Space

Functionality is key in the back of the house. Understanding what you do in each space is essential for planning the space. What tasks need to be performed? How many people need to work in the space? How will they move through the space? The basic rule is, keep what's needed close at hand—the fewer the steps, the better. Reach-in freezer drawers could be placed right next to the fryer, so the cook has easy access to frozen fries, wings, or dumplings—whatever the most popular dishes are. During service, you don't want a cook to have to leave the line to run to the walk-in freezer to locate more fries. That breaks down the system.

The back of the house takes up one fourth to one third of your total restaurant space. Along with the kitchen, the back of the house also has receiving and storage areas for dry, refrigerated, and frozen food; locked storage for valuable inventory; staff lockers, cubbies, changing areas, and a staff bathroom; and your office.

The Kitchen

Restaurant kitchens are divided into stations. Within each station, there are fixed equipment pieces necessary to execute the restaurant's core menu items. The equipment you need varies according to your restaurant's concept.

The basic stations are sauté, grill, fry, salads, appetizers, and desserts. There may also be an assembly station or two for garnish and pickup. The *expeditor* station, arguably the most important station, is located near where the servers set up their trays.

> 📖 **DEFINITION**
>
> The **expeditor** is the connection between the front of the house and the back of the house during service. Usually it's the executive chef or the chef-owner. The expeditor inspects the plated dishes to make sure they're what the diner ordered and that they've been cooked to order. He or she adds a final garnish and tells the server to pick up and deliver. Managers should give the expeditor a heads-up when a large party or VIP is in the dining room.

As we discussed in Chapter 9, your kitchen will operate more efficiently if you spread your menu over a number of stations, so that no one station gets backed up. (If your restaurant's concept puts additional work on a particular station, have two line cooks work it.)

You'll find that some kitchen equipment is essential and other equipment might not be needed in your kitchen.

Necessary equipment:

- Stove(s)
- Grill
- Deep fryer(s)
- Exhaust hoods
- Salamander (a mini broiler used for melting cheese and browning surfaces)
- Walk-in refrigerators
- Walk-in freezer
- Reach-in refrigerators
- Reach-in freezers
- Food processor
- Blender
- Standing mixers
- Sinks
- Dishwasher

Optional equipment:

- Pizza oven
- Hardwood grill
- Meat slicer
- Heating lamps
- Heat trays
- Rice cooker
- Pasta makers
- Ice machine
- Ice cream maker
- Juicers
- Dehydrators
- Vacuum packager and *sous-vide* cooker

> **DEFINITION**
>
> **Sous-vide** is a cooking technique in which food is cooked super low and slow (temperatures vary according to thickness and cut) in a bath of circulating water. Meats or proteins are vacuum-packed with flavorings and placed in the water. The result is exceptionally tender proteins. Chefs also experiment with cooking desserts, such as cheesecakes, sous-vide in mason jars.

Jody doesn't use microwave ovens in his restaurants. However, some restaurateurs find microwaves can be handy to heat cooked tapas or appetizers that are served hot to lukewarm. Microwaving in the serving dish saves the dishwasher from washing a pan. However, the downside of the microwave is that unless you really blast it, the food doesn't stay hot long. Making it worse, when you get slammed and orders are flying off the printer, you're cramming the microwave full to keep up with the rush, and the food's not getting hot enough. Your appetizers or tapas are tepid by the time they reach your guests' table. Use a sauté pan to reheat cold dishes thoroughly and efficiently during rushes.

Exhaust hoods and ventilation systems are required over all your cooktops. They remove smoke, grease, and steam, and replace the tainted air with tempered air. Specialty equipment, such as pizza ovens or hardwood grills, requires special ventilation and the ventilated air needs to be balanced for a smoke-free environment. Discuss your equipment plans with your health and fire departments first, and find out exactly what type of ventilation and hoods they require before installing them.

Cold Prep

Cold prep can be isolated from the kitchen, or set off from the main action on the line. Salads, cold dishes, and often desserts are prepped, assembled, and plated here. This station has reach-in fridges and freezer (optional, but handy if frozen items will be prepped here), and could include a deli slicer for cured meat dishes such as dry sausages and aged hams.

Microwave ovens are sometimes used (but not in Jody's restaurants) to take the chill off desserts like carrot cake or chocolate cake, or to heat cold-prepped items like meatballs, sausages, and figs. Sometimes there's a small deep fryer in the pantry area to fry goat cheese balls for the beet salad, for instance, or to fry the empanada appetizer.

Pastry

Desserts, if they're made in-house, are made in a separate area in the bowels of the restaurant. Pastry chefs start early in the morning, and aren't around during service. Whether your concept calls for special desserts, the added labor cost of a pastry chef is something you'll need to consider. Markups on desserts can run about 35 percent, but it's rare that an entire table will order them unless it's a special occasion.

Portions today are large, and by the time dessert rolls around, fewer people have room. If dessert is tempting enough, for instance, two couples will share two desserts. There are a couple options for serving desserts without having a pastry chef. You can add dessert-making to the sous chef's duties, and keep it simple. You can also supplement with purchased desserts; however, they won't meet the quality of house-made, you have less portion control over them, and the profit margin will be lower. Garnish, a swirl of caramel sauce, a dollop of whipped cream, or a piping of raspberry sauce can make them seem more special.

But even if you're taking the easiest way out and purchasing ice cream for dessert (that's where the reach-in freezer in the cold-prep station comes in handy), let that ice cream speak to your concept. If your restaurant is Southwestern, offer ice cream that will get your customers talking. How about sweet corn ice cream with spicy chocolate dessert sauce mole?

The traditional French brigade had both a pastry chef and a baker. Over time, the two jobs were consolidated. Today, few pastry chefs bake their own bread because it's time-consuming. Fine homemade desserts can make your restaurant stand out. Whether you have the space to dedicate to desserts, the resources to devote to labor and the ability to project a profit from desserts will take some consideration.

Prep

When you plan your BOH layout, you'll need to think about production. Will prep be done in the kitchen, or is there a basement or separate prep room? Timing is key. Prep work needs to be done before cooks are cranking out dishes during meal service. Have your prep cooks come in during the day when a manager is there receiving orders, checking stock, and so on. Now your prep work can be an uninterrupted assembly line process of efficiency.

When your doors open for dinner and your cooks are on the line, they need to be able to complete each dish for service by being able to reach the prepared ingredients—known as the mise en place—tools, and equipment without walking. Steps should be kept at a minimum.

There are four steps to completing a dish:

1. Prepare the mise en place; have all your raw and cooked ingredients prepared—cleaned, peeled, chopped, portioned, and measured—and ready in containers at the cook or chef's station.

2. Assemble, combine, and cook the ingredients of your mise en place.

3. Plate the dish and garnish. The expeditor, usually the executive chef, checks the dish, touches up, and adds the final garnish.

4. Serve the dish. The server or a runner and a server promptly deliver the dishes to the table.

Economies of Scale

When prepping, think economies of scale. Plan to make several days' worth of menu items that keep well. Doing so will reduce your cost of production because it saves on labor costs. It spreads out the cost of the long set-up time over more products, and reduces your production cost per unit of the dish.

When planning your prep space, think about your menu, how many items you'll be making ahead of time, and how much space is needed. Plan your prep work to take advantage of economies of scale whenever possible.

A cook's mise en place can include chopped raw and pre-cooked ingredients. Depending on the complexity of your dishes, certain components might require multiple steps. The mise might include sliced garlic, roasted garlic cloves, chocolate sauce or whipped cream in piping bags, partially cooked risotto, crepes, braised duck, short ribs, slow-roasted pork, fresh-cut green beans, chopped parsley, fresh lemon juice, partially cooked lobster tails, or cut filets of fish. When you plan your kitchen, think about what the cooks will be making and how much room they'll need to prep, cook, and store their mise.

Storage Space

Bulk storage should be limited to lower-value real estate. If possible, shelving near the receiving entrance is a good place. Health departments don't want bags of food and ingredients stored on the floor. Make sure your storage area is dry and has adequate ventilation to prevent mold. It also must be free of rodents and insects.

SMART MOVE

Use coated metro shelving to prevent tarnish in your walk-ins. Lockable and organized storage is important—you're dealing with perishable inventory worth thousands of dollars. Clearly label food products with dates. Rotate your stock, so you use the oldest products first.

The kitchen refrigeration should hold enough mise en place to get through an entire meal service without needing to be replenished. Decide if you want your line cooks to be responsible for their own mise at their stations, or if the prep cooks are responsible for all the mise for all stations, or a combination of the two.

If you get unexpectedly slammed during dinner service and start running low on items, have your sous chef ready to run to the walk-ins and restock before you run out. When you run out of items, when a line cook is searching in the back walk-in for more thawed squid, you're pulling a cook off the line and the orders become backlogged. As a result, the line cooks, expeditors, servers, and managers get stressed. Now you're *in the weeds*. Plan ahead and don't let your mise get too low.

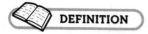 **DEFINITION**

In the weeds is kitchen slang for getting slammed, being swamped, and falling behind during service. It happens on busy nights, and it can create a downward spiral. You must train your sous chef to be ready to jump in to help the line cooks at a moment's notice to prevent getting in the weeds.

Having refrigerated drawers located by cooking tops is the modern way to execute â la minute. Steam tables are a bit of a dinosaur, as holding cooked food at temperature for service dilutes quality and taste (not to mention it comes under more regulation by the health department). Keep your drawers stocked with your mise. Keep cooked meat and raw vegetable mise in a top drawer, and raw meats and seafood in the bottom drawer.

Locking storage will be essential for linen, liquor, and other expensive items. If you don't have a dedicated storage room, use your office. A tall lockable storage unit can be built of inexpensive chicken wire and 2 × 4 lumber.

Dishwashing

The dishwashing area needs to be strategically placed. It must be near the table where servers drop off dirty plates. This is an important spot because this is where breakage can cut into profit for years. First of all, waiters have to be trained to *place* dirty plates and glasses in the bins, not to *toss* them. Jody was very upset when he discovered how many glasses were being broken in his restaurant because of this.

Delicate glasses and stemware should be hand-washed or washed under counter at the bar to avoid breaking. Your glassware's quality elevates the experience of your restaurant and can be reflected in the prices. But for the beginning restaurateur, we recommend purchasing sturdy glasses that are less likely to break and are dishwasher-safe.

Staff Area

Many states require that staff have a dedicated area with lockers. They can bring their own locks, and lock up their personal items during their shifts. Don't permit staff to bring backpacks and packages into the restaurant. That rule will help prevent theft.

These lockers are daily cubbyhole storage. The staff area also needs a big laundry basket for dirty uniforms. You don't want the staff leaving uniforms in their lockers overnight, because it causes odors and cleanliness issues. Should you have a washing machine and dryer to wash uniforms and linens? We recommend using a professional linen service for a clean professional look. You can't wash out food stains and grease using a normal civilian machine; you need industrial strength. (Be sure the service charges only for dirty pick-up and not a static inventory.)

We knew a restaurant owner who wanted to save money on uniforms by having his own washer and dryer. Those were some sad gray, dull, tired uniforms his vibrant staff put on each day. It was bad for morale; it showed the owner didn't care about his staff. And it was bad for business. The staff didn't look crisp and clean, and the business floundered.

The Office

Make your office space tiny. A restaurant requires people to be on the battlefield, not sitting in an office on the phone during dinner service.

When you consider we clean, chop, slice, primp, and stage all day for an hour and a half at lunch and three hours at dinner (the peak business times), we really should be in the middle of the action and focused on work for those few hours.

The restaurant's office has just a few purposes:

- Counting money
- Storing limited files
- Disciplining staff

All other business should take place in the dining room or kitchen. Many chefs share office space with the general manager (GM).

> **POTENTIAL PITFALL**
>
> A staff bathroom is essential in all good dining establishments. Staff should not share the customers' restroom. But be warned: don't make the staff bathroom too remote from work areas. Don't let it become a place for staff to hide.

The office door needs a deadbolt lock so it can be locked inside as well as from outside. Restaurants can be large and have basements, corridors, and plenty of places for an intruder to hide. At the end of the evening, it's a good practice to do a walk-through of the entire space with another staff member to make sure the restaurant is empty. After that staff member leaves, lock yourself in to count the money.

Jody has been robbed twice in his restaurants. Once with a gun, which turned out to be plastic, but he grew up in Greenwich so he had no clue until the police found it and smirked at him for thinking it was real.

Equip your restaurant with alarms; they need to be direct to the police to be effective. If they just buzz, beep, or wail, they're about as effective as a car alarm. It's simply a nuisance. Motion sensors and door-window contacts are the best alarm systems. Shop for reasonable monthly monitoring fees combined with free or inexpensive installation from the same firm. Restaurant association discounts are available with many services.

Today's technology allows owners to monitor the BOH from offsite. There's an app that will let you know if the temperature has gone off in the freezer and fridge. Anaren Cellular Machines sells a Temperature Monitoring Kit for about $500. Camera systems can be activated and monitored from a smart phone. Alarms can also be armed from a smart phone.

Advisors

If you're new to the restaurant business and/or have never cooked in a restaurant kitchen, seek advice from a seasoned professional. You can hire a consultant or chef to review your menu and the back of the house design. You don't want the consultant to come up with plans to move the plumbing and gas lines. Hire them to analyze your needs and retrofit your kitchen for optimum use.

The Least You Need to Know

- The layout of the back of the house is determined by how it will be used.
- Preparation and execution of your menu should be spread out among kitchen stations to prevent service backing up.
- Each kitchen station should be outfitted with the necessary equipment and enough space to make execution efficient.
- Keep the office tiny to prevent your managers from hanging out there during service, when all staff should be working and taking care of customers.

CHAPTER 13

Restaurant Maintenance

Cleaning is one of the most important daily tasks in a restaurant, and it doesn't stop there. In this chapter, we'll show you how to involve your staff and professional commercial cleaning services. We'll talk about the best practices to follow to keep a sanitary restaurant.

Maintaining equipment, such as heating and cooling systems, ovens, refrigerators, and freezers, requires a good relationship with servicing companies, handymen, and plumbers. Being handy is an advantage for a restaurant owner, but there are definitely jobs you should never try on your own.

In This Chapter

- Why you need professional cleaners as well as help from staff
- How to manage regular cleaning tasks using checklists
- Good practices to follow to keep a clean kitchen
- How to maintain your equipment and appliances
- What *not* to try to fix yourself

Cleaning

Have you ever noticed how cluttered, dusty spaces make you feel? Clear the surfaces, dust, vacuum, and polish, and your spirits lift. Cleanliness creates energy. Maybe it's something about the light reflecting off clean surfaces? People subliminally register this and it enhances their mood.

Cleaning must be a daily routine. In a restaurant, a combination of daily cleaning incorporated into the FOH's daily side work keeps a handle on the dining room. In the kitchen, the BOH cleans every evening. A professional service is needed for heavy kitchen cleaning and bathrooms.

The truth is, your FOH staff is going to try to do the minimum, wiping up crumbs and getting rid of clutter. Everybody likes a shortcut. Plus, your staff is tired at the end of a busy night; they don't have the energy or motivation.

So add a professional service, either daily or weekly. They'll arrive wearing gloves and will bring the right products, equipment, and energy to make the dining room sparkle. In the BOH, a hood service company will really deep-clean and get out the grease. The heavy, greasy work in a restaurant is best left to professionals.

Training Staff in Cleaning 101

Use color-coded mops and sponges for the bathroom, dining room, and kitchen. Make sure your staff knows that a bathroom sponge is never used in the kitchen or the dining room because it spreads germs. There's a basic sensibility to working in a restaurant, and if any your staff don't understand that, they shouldn't be working there.

> **SMART MOVE**
>
> An opening and closing checklist, kept on a clipboard, is the best tool for the daily work of the team. It allocates duties, reminds them of their responsibilities, and they check off each task when they've completed it.

Using the kitchen mop in the dining room is another offense. If you get grease in a mop, no matter how hard you try, you won't be able to get it out. People have different degrees of cleanliness standards. When they use a wet, dirty rag instead of a clean one, a dirty restaurant follows. That's how you end up with the disgusting kitchens you see on those television shows about failing restaurants.

Using Your Waiters

Waiters might scatter and hide, but they're your most affordable army. Put them to work in 15 minute bursts instead of big Saturday projects. In 15 minutes, the waiters can wipe down all the bases of the tables and legs of chairs. Assign all staff pre- and post-service duties.

The list of side work for the FOH may include the following:

- Cleaning and resetting all candles.

- Rolling 50 napkins with silverware.

- Cleaning all menus and sorting out torn or soiled ones.

- Filling 50 containers of hot sauce.

Daily cleaning and pre- and post-service tasks include:

- Wiping down table bases and legs.

- Washing banisters and baseboards.

- Dusting picture frames.

- Dusting ceiling corners and upper walls to remove cobwebs.

In some cases, the FOH staff clean the windows. The most important glass in your restaurant is in the front door and front windows. Nothing makes a worse first impression than a grimy front door. It should be cleaned outside and in from top to bottom once a week, and spot-checked every morning and before dinner service.

If you're a family-friendly restaurant where children's grubby hands leave a snail-like trail of smears on doors and windows, you'll have to clean more frequently, perhaps a couple times a day. Anything made of glass should gleam. If you have a glass window separating the kitchen from the dining room, it needs special attention.

 **POTENTIAL PITFALL**

A cleaning professional once said that door handles are the most overlooked dirty places. In a restaurant, many hands touch them. Cleaning and sanitizing door handles, from front door to bathrooms, should be on your list of daily post-service cleaning tasks.

If it's a rainy night and sales are slow, you could send everyone home, but that means they'll make less money. Or you can order a pizza, open a bottle of wine, and reorganize the supply closet. (Of course, you should avoid staff drinking as a practice but use it as a special treat. It can be a useful reward when dispensed with care.) There's a constant need to stay on top of cleaning and organizing, and you've got to find ways to reinforce teamwork while doing it.

Votives and Vases

Dirty votive candle holders and flower vases also make an awful impression. Be careful to not spend too much on flowers, and make sure they're fresh. They need to last at least four to five days—anything else isn't practical.

Each night, remove vases and store them in the walk-in if there's room. The cool air helps preserve the flowers, just as it does in the cooler at the florist's shop. In the morning, a pre-service FOH task is to wash the vases, change the water, and clip the stem slightly on an angle to let it absorb more water and last longer.

Putting water in the bottom of the glass votive will make it easy to pop out the used hardened wax with a table knife. Glass votive holders can be cleaned by filling them with hot water, which will melt any wax residue. Make sure your staff doesn't throw the waxy water down the bar drain, because the wax will harden and clog it. Pour it through a strainer to catch the wax.

Working Neat

Any cleaning expert will tell you the best way to keep things clean is to not make a mess. You can establish your protocols and train the staff to follow them, but in the heat of the moment, stuff starts flying. Make each person on your staff responsible for cleaning their workstation.

The biggest mess staff makes is the trash bags. We've seen staff perplexed by having to remove a lemon wedge from a glass of ice. What do they do? Dump it, ice and all, in the garbage. The same goes for celery in Bloody Marys—they dump the melted tomato water and ice into the garbage. At the end of the evening, the busboy drags this leaking bag across the room, leaving another mess to clean up.

Filter baskets in all sink drains are one of the most important small items you can have on hand. They prevent stirrers, straws, and other items from going down the drains and causing clogs, inevitably on a busy Saturday night. Have extra filter baskets on hand, as they are always getting lost.

SMART MOVE

Train your staff not to spray cleaners or disinfectants on dining room tables when guests are in the room. The spray and smell are carried through the air, and will ruin a guest's dining experience. A rag sprayed with disinfectant can be used more discreetly, without bothering other guests.

Checklists

The key to managing cleaning is to use checklists. You should have checklists for daily, weekly, monthly, and seasonal tasks. In addition, keep checklists for the professional cleaners, too. Review the checklist when you hire them, and show how you want them to check off the tasks when completed.

In the bathroom, for instance, you don't want a trace of grime around the bottom of the faucets, handles, or the edges of sinks. Scrubbing them with a clean toothbrush is the only way to thoroughly clean them. Extra effort has to go into keeping it that way.

Weekly BOH cleaning includes tasks such as cleaning out the shelves in the bar coolers. Monthly tasks include taking all the shelves out of the walk-in for a good scrubbing.

BOH Cleaning

The kitchen needs professional cleaners with heavy equipment to keep it in top shape for passing inspections. Staff cannot get the floors and hoods really clean without weekly help from an industrial-strength service.

Every night, each station is cleaned, and mats are removed and cleaned. The floors are swept, the drain filter is cleared, and the floors are washed and hosed down. Then bleach is poured down the floor drain.

The floor drain also requires special attention. Plumbing is one thing that will make you tear your hair out. Make sure the floor drain filter is in place. Have a supply of extras on hand to replace disappearing drain filters. When the drain is open, all sorts of stuff, such as lemon wedges, garlic, and grape stems, gets into the pipes and causes clogs. When drains back up, it can really mess with your business. Once a week, pour pipe drain solution down the floor drain.

Exterminators

The best exterminator Jody ever worked with was in California. He guaranteed his customers wouldn't have bugs as long as his guys came in and looked over the place and discovered any deficiencies. They put red flags in every area that was drawing pests or vermin, and the staff had to clean up those areas or the guarantee would be invalid.

But you can't be lax just because you have an exterminator. You need a coordinated effort to fight pests. Cockroaches eat the glue found in cardboard boxes, so every time you open a box you likely bring in cockroaches. You have to constantly try to keep them from breeding.

An obsessive owner cleans in every corner, using degreasers and disinfectants where needed. No dirty wet things, such as a used rag, can be left overnight. Used towels, uniforms, aprons, and napkins must be collected and placed in laundry bags, ready for pick-up the next day.

Maintenance

Scheduling maintenance, and following those schedules, is the key to keeping your equipment running. You must keep daily, weekly, monthly, and seasonal to-do lists. If you don't, you run the risk of breakdowns. What can be worse on a freakishly hot early spring day than to discover your air conditioner isn't working? Or when you realize on a cold November day that you forgot to have the furnace serviced, and you've got a dining room full of freezing guests and dirty workmen are walking in and out?

Heating, Ventilating, and Air Conditioning

Heating, ventilating, and air conditioning (HVAC) systems are the biggest maintenance items. Many restaurants are located in old buildings with outdated, poorly functioning HVAC systems. Restaurants in newly constructed or renovated buildings often have HVAC systems with enough horsepower to recover temperature well. You need to learn your system's limitations so you can regulate the temperature.

POTENTIAL PITFALL

If every staff member has the ability to adjust the restaurant's heat at whim, your electric, gas, or oil bills will be exorbitant, and your customers might complain about being too hot or too cold. You need to control the temperature. Invest in locking thermostat covers to prevent people from turning the heat up and down. Only you and your manager should be able to unlock the thermostat.

Controlling the heat is an important part of creating the right environment in a restaurant. We suggest you keep it at 68°. But if you know it will be a busy winter night, drop it to 65° so it doesn't get too warm when the room is full of people. On a hot summer day, set the temperature at 60°. When the place fills up, it won't get too hot.

New or old, HVAC filters need to be checked regularly, the systems cleaned, and filters replaced. Put these maintenance items and service calls on your yearly calendar.

Plumbers

Treat your plumbers well. There are always plumbing issues in restaurants because people stuff things down the toilet, or the bar sink backs up. Be prepared to tackle emergency clogs yourself. Keep a professional plunger and a snake on hand. If you're not handy, make sure someone on your staff is, and pay them extra if they step outside their usual role (dishwashing, for example) to get things working. Having a handyman in the neighborhood with a range of fix-it skills is also a good idea.

Handyman

Having a guy with a toolbox around is great. There's always something coming apart in a restaurant. In most restaurants, the stove handles get loose. If you screw them in every week, you can prevent a bigger job when they fall off and roll away into an inaccessible corner. Forming a relationship with a handyman is important, because things always break at 8 o'clock on a busy Friday night, not at 10 o'clock Tuesday morning. A plumber who will leave his own dinner table on a rainy night to come to your restaurant to fix an emergency is invaluable.

> **SMART MOVE**
>
> There's no end to the work that needs to be done to keep a restaurant running. The fuel jets on the stove get clogged. You take a bamboo skewer to clean out each hole. Those are the tasks that, if left unattended, slow down the entire system during service.

Knives

Most chefs nowadays own a set of knives and sharpen them themselves. In the old days, the kitchen supplied the knives and there was a service to send the knives out to be sharpened. But those services are losing their market grip.

Chefs tote their knife collection with great pride, unfurling leather pouches with carbon blades and Japanese composite blades. They sharpen their knives in-house with a steel and whetstone. No one else touches their knives. They don't even let the dishwasher wash them. The kitchen provides a couple of house knives for the prep cooks. The chefs teach the cooks to sharpen those knives.

Appliance Repair

Establish a relationship with a local commercial appliance maintenance and repair firm and their technicians. Make sure you have their cell phone numbers for emergencies.

> **SMART MOVE**
>
> Temperatures in ovens, refrigerators, and freezers should be calibrated twice a year. Many people only do this once a year. Check temperatures with a thermometer every month. Health inspectors will cite you if your refrigerators and freezers are at an improper temperature.

Some of these firms have service contracts, and you'll have to weigh whether it's worth paying more for the yearly checkup and free 24-hour emergency service. It also depends on how old your equipment is, and whether you are handy. One theory is that when the company knows it's on the hook for 24-hour emergency service, they'll make an annual service call to make sure the system will be working all year. Schedule a yearly October date for having the furnace system checked.

Do Not Attempt!

Unless you're a licensed and insured appliance technician, don't attempt to fix any major gas-fired appliances. And don't mess with your electrical circuit breaker wires, either.

We know a chef-owner who was desperate to save money, so he tried to fix a broken gas oven himself. He thought it might be a clog in the gas line, so he took the air compressor, and while the oven was on, started to blow air into the line.

BOOOOM! The oven door flung open with force, hit him on the head, and threw him across the room. The front doors swung open from the pressure. The restaurant was closed, but the staff felt their ears pop. Luckily, he was the only person in that part of the kitchen.

The chef-owner was a stoic guy, but as he lay on the floor, singed and smoking, he said, "I think I have to go to the hospital." The fire department came. The ambulance arrived and carried him out on a stretcher. His face and hair were burned, and his eyebrows were gone. He could have been killed; instead, he was back at work the next day. Hurting, yes, but back on the job, having learned a very scary yet valuable lesson: leave certain dangerous repairs to a professional.

Finding Good Tradespeople

How do you find good tradespeople? Get references—someone always knows somebody they can recommend. A waiter has an uncle, a hostess has a brother-in-law; your restaurant is a collection of people who know people in the trades. However, you don't want a plumber or electrician whose clients are all residential. Other environments don't always translate to a commercial restaurant space. You want tradespeople with skills within your domain, the restaurant business.

We all want to help our friends, but a beginning restaurateur who hires a friend who is a residential electrician may have to have the work redone to bring it to commercial levels.

It's sad there isn't more sharing of this kind of information within the restaurant community these days. It could be a useful resource in many ways. Restaurants used to be more social. Nowadays, it's not the fraternity it could be. Many restaurateurs are too competitive and secretive to help others.

Grease Traps

There's a lot of grease and fat in the restaurant business. To keep it out of sewer pipes and septic systems, grease filter systems are required by departments of health. These systems need to be serviced regularly by a commercial grease trap cleaner who will vacuum out the disgusting stuff and haul it away.

If grease traps are not serviced, the most vile odor in the world will infiltrate your restaurant. If they're not regularly serviced they can overflow, and a disgusting rancid smell will permeate the place. We suggest you use electric systems that constantly skim the grease from the surface. Be extremely diligent about having your grease trap serviced.

Fire Prevention

Fire is a major safety concern in a restaurant. Fire extinguishers have an expiration date, and by law you need a service person to refuel and charge them. Then this person will give the extinguishers stickers showing they've been serviced. The fire department will check for that during inspections.

Smoke alarms, emergency lights, and carbon monoxide alarms need to have their batteries tested every week. Batteries need to be replaced every couple of months.

Sidewalks/Entrances/Parking Lots

Keep your sidewalks clean. Check for trash each morning, sweep the sidewalks, and wash them if necessary. Shake out the front mat, water and freshen plants, and pull off yellowed leaves and spent blossoms. These tasks are usually assigned to the bus staff. They'll pick up trash and cigarette butts in the parking lot, too. Parking lot maintenance is usually managed by the landlord and shared by tenants who pay a common area charge. We discussed this in detail in Chapter 7.

Décor and Furnishings

Keep an eye on how your soft furnishings are holding up. Clean stains daily as needed, and check weekly for wear, tears, or frays. Fixing small things holds off having to buy expensive replacement furnishings. Keep decorative elements dust-free and polished.

Here's a thought on vintage pieces. Jody has worked with vintage in some of his restaurants, and really loves it. An old leather suitcase can be beautiful if it's been kept in good condition. But battered, scratched, and worn beyond repair? That's junk. A vintage upholstered chair is cool, but a vintage upholstered chair with broken springs and worn, faded, dirty-looking fabric? That's junk. Keep your soft furnishings looking fresh and attractive.

Maintaining a restaurant is an ongoing campaign. But if you mobilize your troops, maintain your equipment, and stay vigilant, you can indeed win the war.

The Least You Need to Know

- Hire professionals for heavy cleaning and grease removal.
- Keep daily, weekly, monthly, and seasonal cleaning task checklists for your FOH and BOH staff, and for professional cleaners.
- Use recommended tradespeople who are experienced in working in restaurants.
- Make friends with your appliance repairmen, plumbers, and handymen.
- Don't attempt repairs on gas-fired appliances or gas lines, or on your electrical circuit box; leave those tasks to licensed professionals.

PART 4

An Owner's Role in Management

Restaurant folk are their own special breed. Understanding their motivation is the key to creating and managing an effective team. In this part, we'll tell you where to find employees, and how to ground them in the basics of service.

We'll delve further into money, as we set up the restaurant's office and cash control systems. We'll discuss many techniques to keep your staff productive by addressing systemic weaknesses in the business.

In addition, we'll talk about ways to have effective relationships with your vendors and delivery people.

All of this leads up to your grand opening party! This is the party that will start the buzz about your restaurant and lead into your successful opening weekend.

CHAPTER 14

Hiring Your Staff

As a restaurant owner, you need to hire the right staff to work together to run a tight, profitable ship. Finding the best employees, those hardy warriors of food service, reveals another facet of the same right-brain/left-brain quality that pervades the restaurant business.

In this chapter, we'll guide you through the positions you'll need to fill and the kinds of personalities you need to fill them. We'll also show you various ways to find your staff.

In This Chapter

- Qualities to look for in restaurant staff
- What roles to fill in the kitchen and the dining room
- How to find the best candidates for your staff
- Preparing job duty lists for new employees

Looking for the Right Qualities

That right-brain/left-brain thing comes up again when you're building a talented staff. Think about the qualities you want in a manager. On one hand, you want someone who has aesthetic sensibilities, the kind of person who will lower the dining lights to the right level at the right time. You want someone who is good with flowers and décor. On the other hand, you also want a manager who can deal with the mechanics of the restaurant, such as keeping track of when the grease trap needs to be cleaned. You want someone who is good with scheduling and budgets.

It's not easy to find a person who has the right combination of creativity and organization. And the person who has them both is likely to be the sort who'll go on to start a restaurant. Jody is the kind of guy who can balance the two sides. And one of the keys to his success is he's always relied on and managed his team members to bolster his weaknesses.

Looking for a perfect manager? He or she doesn't exist. So Jody hires two managers: one is oriented to service and guests and the other to operations and finances. Together, they cover all the restaurant's needs. Keep this balance in mind when you hire staff, and hire a mix of people whose skills and sensibilities overlap but aren't identical.

Don't assume a good manager is also the best host. Sometimes a great host can take a lot of pressure off the manager, who focuses on the operating aspects. Guests love a warm welcome and recognition, and when they depart, a gentle hand on the shoulder with a sincere thank you.

You need managers the staff knows they can lean on, people they can come to when something goes wrong. That communication between managers and staff keeps the restaurant running smoothly, and keeps customers flowing in the door. But if the staff doesn't feel their manager will calmly provide a solution or reassurance, it knocks the business off kilter.

For example, Jody's friendly hostess, taking in a flood of guests on a Saturday night, was yelled at by a man who, fueled by a cocktail at the bar, shouted that she'd told him the waiting time would only be a half hour. Rattled, she led his party to a table that had not been cleared. She was so upset she started telling *walk-ins* there was an hour and a half wait because she didn't want anyone else to yell at her.

> **DEFINITION**
>
> **Walk-ins** are customers who walk into the restaurant without a reservation.

The walk-ins walked back out, even though the dinner rush was actually waning. If the hostess had felt she could rely on her manager, she could have alerted him to the situation with the impatient guest at the bar, and he could have addressed it before it became a problem. The manager could have sent the grumbling guy's party an appetizer. Nothing changes a mood faster than a freebie, especially if it's food.

Jody hires more people than he needs. Turnover can be a challenge in the industry. That's why Jody tries to run restaurants where people *want* to work. We'll look at ways to create a positive work environment in Chapter 21.

Restaurant People

Compared to civilians, restaurant people can be a rough bunch. It's the nature of the business— it's a physical job, they're on their feet for hours, they lift and carry a lot of heavy weight, and they work in intense heat. In the front of the house they smile under pressure, they get sweaty, they work hard. Often they work in a nightlife environment. Many restaurant workers also drink more and party more than other people.

But the great thing about restaurant people is they create a family. Long friendships develop in the restaurant business, and that's one of the things you should foster and encourage in your restaurant. The bond the staff feels working together makes them want to come to work. It's one of the ways to motivate your staff. Another is cash, which we'll talk more about in Chapter 21.

Restaurant staff is divided into front of the house (FOH) and back of the house (BOH) staff. The most important members of your staff are your chef and your manager. Each has his or her own domain. The chef is in charge of the kitchen, the back of the house, and the manager is in charge of the dining room, the front of the house.

The Chef

It's a Top Chef world on television, but you won't see Jody opening chef-centric restaurants. He learned this lesson at his first successful restaurant. Things were going great—it was the hot spot in town, busy every night, the chef was getting great press, and customers raved. Then the chef quit. The kitchen lost its mooring. Jody's successful restaurant went down fast, in just nine months. He vowed to never again allow a restaurant's success to be based on the chef.

We suggest you don't look for the hot-shot chefs, people who want to be stars. Too many people expect the chef to be a wizard and create magic. You want your chef to follow the blueprinted menu you've created. Too many culinary school graduates come into kitchens and try to reinvent the wheel every day. That creates imbalance in the kitchen, and hurts efficiency and profits.

There are a lot of Latin Americans cooking in many restaurants in America. One of the reasons that works so well is they come from a tradition in which there's a cultural pride in a routine performed well—for example, creating the perfect risotto every time. That's what you need in your kitchen: people who will execute the carefully developed, yield-tested recipes that express your restaurant's concept and keep your food costs on budget.

The chef is the leader and manager of the kitchen. You need a chef who is organized, who can order food, manage a schedule, make the sauce, and get the plates out to the tables on time. It's better to have a person who can put out a decent product and also manage the rest of the job than it is to have a culinary genius. If a chef can't run food costs, that chef is no good to the restaurant. Of course, it can go the other way, too. Some corporate restaurants get so caught up in efficiencies that the food product suffers.

Sous Chef and Line Cooks

Contemporary restaurant kitchens are run under a streamlined version of the hierarchical French brigade system. Created by Auguste Escoffier (1846-1935), this system brought a unified military order and structure to the kitchen. When we think of Escoffier, author of *Le Guide Culinaire,* which codified French cuisine and committed the repertoire of recipes to paper, we often forget that his contribution to the profession was to refine and simplify it. Under the influence of Marie-Antoine Carême (1783-1833), father of La Grande Cuisine, food had become elaborate and ostentatious.

Under the classic brigade system, the chef de cuisine and sous chef oversee the work of the chefs de parties. Traditionally, these chefs devote themselves to one of 10 stations where they create sauces, cook fish, roast and braise meats, grill, fry, prepare vegetables and soups, compose salads and cold appetizers, and bake pastries and desserts.

The following table shows a breakdown of the terms, which you'll encounter in many American restaurant kitchens. Note that you're unlikely to find a staff of this size, unless it's in a fine-dining French restaurant. Today's restaurant kitchens are staffed by an executive chef, sous chef, and line cooks.

The Classic French Brigade Terms and Contemporary Counterparts

French Term	English Term	Duties
Chef de cuisine	Executive chef	Leads and manages the kitchen
Sous chef	Assistant chef	Prepares food under the direction of the executive chef
Saucier	Sauté chef	Sautés and prepares sauces
Poissonier (Often combined with the position of saucier)	Fish chef	Butchers and prepares fish
Rôtisseur	Roast and rotisserie chef	Roasts meats

French Term	English Term	Duties
Grillardin (Often combined with the rôtisseur)	Grill chef	Grills meats
Friturier	Fry chef	Fries food
Chef de tournant	A chef who jumps into any station where needed	Does it all
Entremetier (Traditionally broken down into the legumier and potager)	Vegetable and soup chef	Prepares vegetables and soups
Garde-manger	Cook in charge of salad and cold dishes	Prepares salads and cold appetizers and dishes
Patissier	Pastry chef	Makes desserts and pastries
Boucher	Butcher	Today, some farm-to-table chefs are bringing in whole animals and butchering them onsite.
Apprentice	Apprentice	Today, culinary students intern for free in the kitchens of famous chefs.

The traditional form of training was apprenticeship. Young boys age 12 or 13 went to work in restaurant kitchens, learning from the ground up, doing the lowliest jobs as they trained at each station. Today, chefs are mostly taught in culinary schools, which turn out graduates in two years or less. Many of these chefs are fueled by visions of fame inspired by cooking shows on television. Unfortunately, many of them will not be able to sustain the daily grind of restaurant life.

Your restaurant's concept dictates what staffing you'll need and how to allocate your labor resources. In a busy contemporary Spanish tapas restaurant you might find the executive chef expediting, while the sous chef oversees the line cooks and jumps in to help at any station where he's needed.

SMART MOVE

Expediting is usually the role of the executive chef, who manages the timing of the preparation of each order by telling the chefs when to cook each component of each plate. The expeditor also inspects and adds the final garnish on each plate before it's sent to the dining room.

The line cooks in a busy contemporary tapas restaurant might include a chef each on the sauté station, grill, and fryer, with another person preparing salads and desserts and heating appetizers.

Expediting

The key to expediting is communication. The expediting chef communicates with the waiters and the chefs. He yells *"Fire"* to tell chefs to begin cooking various components of the dish. Chefs don't (always) yell because they're angry. They do so because they need to be heard over the noise of a busy kitchen. "Yes, chef!" the line cooks respond, letting the chef know they've heard the order.

 **DEFINITION**

To **fire** a dish means to start cooking it. The command "Fire" is kitchen shorthand, used by the executive chef or expeditor to tell his sous chef and/or line cooks to start cooking a dish.

This clear, concise communication between members of the FOH and BOH orchestrates the moving of dishes out of the kitchen.

The expeditor is also in charge of quality control. The executive chef examines the dish to make sure the sous chef and line cooks have properly executed and plated the dish according to the standards of the restaurant, and the way the guest ordered it. He'll check to see that the proteins are cooked to the right temperature, and that special requests were followed, such as leaving pecans out of the salad. (You don't want the guest going into anaphylactic shock!). The expeditor also garnishes the dish. Chefs like to do this because they get to place their imprint on the dish.

In addition, the expeditor wipes the rim of the dish of dribs and drabs and greasy smears. When the dish is finished, the expeditor makes sure the server gets it to the table promptly, while it's still hot. He keeps an eye on how the server holds the plate. Holding it at an angle could mess up that ring of sauce. When delivering plates to guests, servers should not place their thumbs on plate rims.

This is another reason why simple plating is your friend. A precious tower of ingredients, with each micro herb placed just so, takes time to create—and in the rush of delivering it, it's likely it could be a mess when it reaches the table.

The expeditor is in charge of quality control, and prevents dishes from being returned. "Refiring," or recooking a dish, costs time and money. Refires disrupt the kitchen's timing and efficiency.

Some restaurants whose location and clientele create intense, brief rushes of guests use several expeditors to keep things under control. A good example is a bistro in the theatre district that serves busloads of pre-theatre crowds.

The timing of preparation and service of dishes is specific to each restaurant. Some tapas restaurants can send out each dish as it's finished, starting with what's quickest to prepare. At a French bistro serving a half-roasted chicken, the chicken will need to be seasoned and fired right away in order for it to be ready when the guest has finished his or her appetizers or salad. After the chicken is taken from the oven, the chef uses the pan drippings to make a wine sauce to go with it, and finishes cooking pre-blanched vegetables. Many dishes that take a long time to cook, such as braises or stews, are cooked ahead of time, and only need to be heated for service.

How to Find Your Staff

How does Jody find his restaurant staff? He shamelessly poaches the best people from other restaurants in town. His rule is to hire people who already have jobs, which is another reason why knowing your local restaurant scene will give you a leg up. Is everyone digging a certain bartender in town? Is he the right guy to execute your drinks program? Is he friendly? Does he make people feel at home, and like he'll take good care of them?

If you know people in your local restaurant business, you'll know management people and chefs. It's wiser to hire a known entity than an unknown off the street with several references.

Your chef and manager are critical people in your business. They'll make important decisions with you in meetings, and they'll be in charge of budgets. Your ability to communicate, interact, understand, and motivate them will determine how much stress you'll have in your job as a restaurant owner. Remember, you're putting your business in their hands.

Experience is great, but there's also a drawback. Old habits die hard for restaurant veterans. They have a tendency to complain, "We used to do it *this way* at my last job." You don't want that. You don't want a manager who's always sighing and getting exasperated about the ways things are done in your restaurant. Jody tells his staff, "For the first 30 days, don't even think about making a suggestion. Do it my way. Then, after you've experienced the way our restaurant works for 30 days, if you still think something is not working well, offer me a solution. Don't tell me something *could* be better, tell me how you would *make* it better."

You don't want a contrarian trying to teach you a new way to do something. There are 10 different ways you can serve wine, but the most important thing in a restaurant is that it's done the same way every time. Fighting a stubborn person who wants to upset carefully thought-out systems just because they did it differently at some other place makes you want to hire a young person who has no experience, but is willing to learn. You can train that person.

SMART MOVE

Hire enthusiastic young people as well as experienced industry veterans. They'll bring different attitudes, approaches, and skill sets that can make your staff a stronger team.

Depending on the type of restaurant you own, you'll need various levels of knowledge in your staff. If you've created a serious foodie place, you'll need to be more selective in hiring your staff. You'll want servers who will relay their enthusiasm for contemporary cooking techniques, or the special baby lettuce leaves grown on a farm down the road. You'll want staff with a greater level of food knowledge, interest, and commitment.

Another one of Jody's recruiting tricks is to hire one or two really good workers and ask them if their friends are looking for jobs. Some owners might not encourage hiring friends of existing staff, but in Jody's experience having their friends there makes work a place they want to be.

POTENTIAL PITFALL

Should you let the staff date one another? Try to stop them. Sure, sometimes it can add an element of drama to an already volatile work environment. But often it works out just fine. Jody married a woman who worked with him and they have two great kids. Who is he to tell the staff they can't date?

The basic way to recruit an entire staff for a new restaurant is to run a mini job fair, consisting of a session or two where candidates come in with their résumés and have an interview. You can run ads announcing the job interviews at online sites such as Craigslist and Goodfoodjobs.com.

Job Advertising

Ads are a great way to get the flavor of your restaurant across. Try to reflect the spirit of your restaurant's concept in your ad. What you say in your ad determines who will respond to it. One time Jody wrote an ad in code. "Five tables, $45 per seat, two and a half turns." It was targeted to professional waiters. Waiters read that and immediately starting calculating their take-home pay. That's the way waiters are. Write the right ad, and the right people will respond.

We've also seen ads that go too far in an attempt to be clever. Here's an example: "Al avvv won moh befaw ah go ome," read an ad for an experienced bartender "who can decipher this babble" for a big international hotel bar. Though the intention is humorous, we wouldn't joke around with a potentially litigious situation.

During walk-in interviews, usually held in the afternoons between lunch and dinner service, give applicants a short multiple-choice test to make sure they know the basics and the steps of service, and that they're familiar with the POS system.

Chef Tests

We suggest you give a cooking test to final chef candidates. Ask them to give you a written menu of dishes that fit your restaurant's concept. Then ask them to cook. You want to see two things: how they'll execute a recipe that you've already created for your restaurant, and what they'll do with a mystery basket filled with ingredients that you chose. (Kind of like the television show *Chopped*, but without the bizarre ingredients.) Both dishes must express the restaurant's concept. Midway through, you might throw in an imaginary allergy they'll have to make a substitution for. Observe how they handle this, in addition to how they work with the kitchen staff.

What you want to see in the dishes the chef creates is not an ode to the culinary gods. You want to see speed, finesse, attention to detail, leadership, and an eye on the bottom line. You want your chef candidate to sublimate his creativity to your concept and business model. In addition, you want him to know the cost per plate.

Manager Tests

When Jody was starting a high-end restaurant in Greenwich, he devised a program for final manager candidates. He gave them $500 and told them to throw a dinner party. Jody didn't tell them how to do it, but he watched what they did. Did they send an invitation? What kind of invitation was it? Did they let people know where to park? Were the dining room lights turned down? Food was less important than service and presentation. It didn't matter if they'd brought the food in or if someone else had cooked it. He wanted to see how they served it.

Doing this helps you see where a manager's sensibilities lie. You want to know if they can manage the experience of hosting guests. Can they create the right energy? Can they make their guests happy?

An exercise like this can be difficult and expensive to execute for a super busy first-time restaurateur. It can, however, be a useful "virtual" assignment to give to manager candidates.

You also want to know that managers are experienced in working with the POS system and know how to run financial reports.

Job Descriptions

Every employee you hire should be presented with a job description that clearly and concisely lists the following:

- Restaurant name
- Job description
- Who the employee reports to

- Daily job duties

- Standard core requirements

- The employee's name, signature, and the date

The manager should walk the employee through this form. The form lays out the chain of command, lists the employee's daily responsibilities, and explains the restaurant's standards. Keep the number of job duty bullets to a manageable number—no more than seven, for example. You want to make sure it's easy for the employee to read whenever he or she needs a refresher.

You should also create lists of daily job duties that underscore that the staff must have a high level of hospitality and customer service, along with full knowledge of the menu, cocktails, wine lists, and offerings. You'll find examples of job descriptions in Appendix D.

An employee job description is a useful place to state your restaurant's standards. Here's an example of what Jody created for the restaurants in a resort hotel:

Sample Standard Core Requirements

- Give each customer exceptional customer service. Provide a friendly environment. Greet and acknowledge every customer.

- Maintain a professional appearance and demeanor.

- Attend to all of the customer's needs quickly and efficiently.

- Be proactive.

- Clock in/out daily at your scheduled shift.

- Report to your assigned work area on time.

- Ensure all health and food safety practices adhere to standards.

These core requirements have a secondary purpose: they establish a legal basis for terminating employees who do not live up to them. We'll talk more about the process of terminating an employee in Chapter 21.

The Least You Need to Know

- Hire a mix of people whose skills and sensibilities create a staff of right-brain and left-brain people.
- Your chef and managers make up your leadership team. They're the most important staff you will hire.
- It's a good practice to hire people who already are successfully employed in the restaurant business.
- Give each employee a written job description detailing all of their daily duties.
- Recruit an entire new staff by holding a job fair during the afternoon. Let your ad for the job fair reflect the spirit of your restaurant, so you draw potential staff who are a good fit for your place.

CHAPTER 15

Purchasing Supplies

You've got to be strong to work in the restaurant business. You have to be strong enough not to care when everyone thinks you're acting like a jerk. (You're not really acting like a jerk, of course; you're doing your job by keeping an eye on the bottom line.) When it comes to the hustle businesses—salespeople, vendors, delivery guys—you've got to establish your policies from day one. That's the way to keep everyone honest and your restaurant profitable.

In this chapter, we'll show you how to train your vendors to live up to your standards. We'll talk about salespeople and how you can help prevent them from wrapping their tentacles around your staff. You'll also learn how to work with delivery people.

In This Chapter

- Finding good restaurant suppliers
- Managing relationships with salespeople
- Managing the deliveries
- Watching your cash flow

Finding Your Suppliers

Many restaurateurs cherry-pick their suppliers weekly for the best price. The better way is to work with a smaller number of vendors. To keep everyone honest, be open that you're always seeking quality service and value.

What kind of vendors will you need? You'll need specialty foods, beer, wine, liquor, restaurant supplies, glasses, dishes, and so on, depending on your type of restaurant.

Although most supplies can be ordered online, salespeople feel that face time induces a sale. Salespeople bombard owners with lowball prices. But in the end you need to balance service, quality, and price. During the introductory gesture of lowball prices, the company's level of service and quality are unknown.

Vendors maintain tier pricing classifications based on how much you buy and whether you pay on time. This information isn't something they share.

Vendors' Tier Pricing Classifications

Volume/Payment	Class
High purchase/timely payment	Class 1/best prices
High purchase/late payment	Class 2/pricing
Low volume/late payment	Class 3/high prices based upon risk

Paying your vendors on time is good for business. You'll quickly gain a reputation for your good payment practice, and that can set your vendor class among all suppliers.

As we'll discuss more in Chapter 17, vendors are paid one month after delivery. If you're new to the business and don't have a history, you might need to earn credit in the beginning. However, don't personally guarantee payment.

You can establish credit with vendors by paying in full for the previous week's deliveries. After a time, try to stretch it to 14 days, and then eventually, you can establish the standard 30-day cycle with them.

Specialty Products

The vendors that supply your specialty products, such as organic produce, ethnic foods, or limited-selection items, know their importance to your business. These businesses are often smaller in scale, and personal connections can and should be managed by owners and chefs in a closer manner than when you're dealing with conglomerate providers to whom you're just an account number. The big suppliers are all about the money. For the smaller suppliers, it's often about the passion.

Prepare to have beekeepers, bakers, and cheese-makers knocking on your door. Local is a hot trend, and owners and chefs often build relationships with local artisans. Farmers are often willing to negotiate better prices based on the volume bought and the exposure of being featured locally on a hot chef's menu.

POTENTIAL PITFALL

Most local, small-scale farmers don't have the time or manpower to deliver to restaurants, and many chefs don't have the time to travel to a farm. Distribution is a problem. Sometimes like-minded chefs form a collective to purchase and pick up produce from a farm. The produce is fresher and the quality is higher, but the prices may be higher, too.

Beware the Salesman

Vendor salespeople will try to cajole your purchasing staff with tickets to events and wine-tasting invitations to sweeten the business relationship. Salespeople have quotas, and to make their quota they'll work the weakest buyers.

Jody has walked into his bar many times and spotted a bottle of an absurd infused vodka such as peanut butter vodka. Then he'd peek in the liquor storage, and find 23 more bottles of the same vile concoction. He'd question his staff, and hear, "Yup, gotta great deal … gonna make a cool signature cocktail."

This type of dynamic has been played out many times. An attractive female sales rep flirts with a restaurant's manager and bartender. She bears gifts of cheap mirrors with beer and liquor logos. The bartender wants to show her he has the power to make decisions. That's how you end up with a case of bubble-gum vodka and ugly mirrors that don't go with your restaurant's design.

Sales reps try to become buddies with the staff. They offer tickets to major sporting events and concerts. Beware of them forming an alliance. Your staff is on your team, not the liquor reps'. Salespeople aren't devious, but they do have quotas, and they prey on the new and vulnerable.

To combat the hustle, you've got to set purchasing standards and practices. You must drill them into your purchasing staff (chefs generally purchase the food; managers the supplies; and bartenders the wine, beer, and distilled spirits) that they're not to buy anything that's not on the approved purchase list. Tell them, "This is our product line and it has to be sacred."

For instance, if you want to carry bourbon, then educate yourself and get a great selection of bourbons. Don't clutter your back bar with a gold-flecked dessert liqueur you've never heard of. Your back bar isn't a curio shelf.

> **SMART MOVE**
>
> Take a picture of your bar setup. Create a picture that's a silhouette, and caption it like a photo in a magazine. "From left, front row, 1. Absolut, 2. Grey Goose, 3. Stoli" ... and so on. That's the way a bar should be: uniform with no room for new bottles. If something's missing, you can tell at a glance.

Sample inventory forms to help with ordering and delivery can be found in Appendix D.

Liquor Discounts

Salespeople will also try to get you excited about discounts. Liquor prices are set and regulated by state alcohol control boards. Every bar and restaurant gets the same price when they buy booze. It's illegal for a distributor to lower the price. The state gives one distributor exclusive rights to represent certain brands. In Connecticut, if you want to offer Budweiser at your restaurant, there's only one distributor to go to.

Alcohol control boards also allocate discounts. In Connecticut, it's called a *post-off*. It's a sale. For example, during November, Grey Goose will be posted off at $20 a case. Say you go through 10 bottles a week. That's about 40 bottles a month. An extra case and your discount is $80 for the next month.

> **DEFINITION**
>
> A post-off is a reduction in the wholesale price set by state liquor authorities.

But there's a problem with the post-off. A first-time restaurant owner needs to always remember that cash is king. You must always, in everything you do, be mindful of your cash flow. That $80 you saved by buying the Grey Goose you don't need right now? It's probably more important to keep it in your cash register. Right now, you aren't in a position to take advantage of deals.

This all ties back to the liquor salespeople. When prices are all the same, all they have to offer is being friendly. Being friendly, pushing you to buy more, and offering treats. Salespeople work it and try to form a bond with your purchasing people, which can leave the owner as the odd man out.

How should you deal with it? Be upfront with the salespeople from the very start. Say, "Our drinks program is set. The staff's not allowed to buy anything that's not on our purchasing list, without permission from me." It's simply being professional.

> **POTENTIAL PITFALL**
>
> Never ask a wine salesman to help you create your wine list. People say, "But they'll help me for free." However, around 80 percent of your list will end up being their wines. It's better to be in a position to tell them what you're looking for than to let them tell you what they want to sell you. A new restaurant owner shouldn't limit their wine list to one distributor.

If you don't have skills in choosing wine to match your concept and menu, start by doing a little research to help allocate the popular wine categories so you can be contemporary and relevant in your choices. Don't bring to market a wine list you can't marry to your menu's concept.

Visit a local wine store and ask what brands are popular sellers. Discover the lesser-known varietals in the same price range. You can also turn to a friend or associate for help in building your wine list. If you have a strong menu, you can ask a wine rep for some input, but you do need to manage the process and be mindful that there's a potential conflict of interest.

Budget

Bartenders must get a monthly budget that's based on how much alcohol was used the previous month. If they run out of the obligatory liquors, everyone knows. Make it very clear that they have to stay within their budget. Don't give them spending latitude. When a bartender blows the budget, he'll try to rationalize by saying a regular customer drinks whatever he just bought. You've got to call them on it.

Delivery

Delivery is a hustle business. From day one, meet the delivery guys at the back-door receiving area, where you have a big, intimidating scale and a clipboard in your hand. You need to check what you ordered, the price, and amount, against what has been delivered. You also need to check the quality. Make sure that produce is at a cool temperature. Smell the fish. If they're whole (and that's how you'll get fresher fish), check for clear eyes and bright-red gills. Check harvest dates on bags of oysters and clams.

Weigh produce and proteins. Open each box and count the contents. Open up wine boxes and check vintages. Start off tough with the delivery guys. Be anal-retentive about your process and even over the top. They'll all tell you you're being a jerk, asking, "Don't you trust me?" Tell them yes, but you can't run a business on that.

The receiving area is where most staffs drop the ball. For example, your chef goes to the trouble of calling three vendors and finds salmon at $4.95 a pound, so he orders 30 pounds of it. However, he's not there when the delivery guy arrives, and your prep chef receives the delivery of 40 pounds at $6.50 a pound, and he signs for it, thus accepting an incorrect order.

However, if you, the owner, are at the door with your clipboard, matching the delivery to the order form, you can catch this little oversight. You can pick up the phone and call the vendor to tell him about the discrepancy. He'll say, "You're right," and they'll change the price. You then won't accept the extra fish.

In addition, if something's not right, send it back. By the third delivery, the driver will return and tell his boss what a pain you are to work with. As a result, they'll start ensuring your order is right. You become the one stop where the weight must be accurate and they can't deliver before 2 p.m. It's a battle you can win.

However, it takes fortitude. The driver will see you checking each vintage. He'll get surly, and say, "I don't have time to wait for that, I've got to go." Reply with, "I've got to call your boss and ask him about my weekly $3,000 account."

Beware of drivers who want to "help out" by packing your shelves. They can just as easily help themselves to your stock or short you on delivery, which you'll assume is safely tucked away. They can bring in five cases and leave with one. When someone leaves stuff down in your base-ment, unattended, such as bottles of booze sitting unlocked for even a short time, it's an invitation or temptation, depending on who comes across it.

Delivery Schedules

A good driver is a blessing. A bad driver is a nightmare. A good driver will double back if you aren't there, or adjust his lunch break so that he doesn't invade your restaurant during your lunch service. He will make sure his dolly wheels are clean before he tracks it into your restaurant.

A bad driver is the guy who shows up late and complains a lot. Bad drivers can and do lose busi-ness accounts for smaller vendors.

SMART MOVE

You want the driver on your side. Have the cook make him a meatball sandwich while he waits for the delivery to be checked. Give him a soda. You can even play the game the salespeople play on you. Find out who your delivery guy's favorite sports team is and buy some tickets to a game.

You need to establish delivery times up front. Take a hard line. If you're open for lunch, no deliveries will be taken between 11 A.M. and 2 P.M.

A driver wheeling cases of beer through the dining room via the front door is an obvious problem. The less obvious but equally disturbing problem is that, while in service, a staff member must abandon his or her post to check in delivery Another issue is that, during the lunch service, no one has time to properly receive and pack away deliveries and secure them, leaving you open to theft.

You've got to let vendors know they have to treat your business with respect. One afternoon, Jody's restaurant was open for lunch, the customers were still lunching, and a liquor salesman opened the front door, saw Jody behind the bar and yelled out, "Hey Jody, how's it going? You need anything?" Jody waved him over and quietly said, "If you really want to know, come back when I can talk."

However, if your delivery guy shows up at 5:30 instead of 3:00, tell him he must take the order back and bring it tomorrow. It takes some courage to do that. But if you don't, you've shown you'll put up with bad service. The other customers who've shown backbone are the ones who'll be getting deliveries on time.

If you have a large receiving area that affords a steward, you can hire a full-time person to accept deliveries and unpack them. Sometimes the cleaning guy plays that role.

Contracts and Negotiations

Don't enter into contracts, if possible. You need to be in control. The only time it's justified is if the vendor needs to make an investment in what you need and you have no obligation to purchase, for example, custom linen that only you use.

When you deal with the big companies, don't let field managers negotiate. They have more of a social exchange with you and your managers. Owners should set policy. They must be the only ones who can approve orders.

Hidden Inventory Costs

Always avoid par stock charges that are automatically billed regardless of consumption. We'll talk more in Chapter 17 about how par stock, the minimum amount of each product you need on hand, is an important tool in managing inventory.

It's all about cash flow. A new restaurateur can't afford to have empty stockrooms and no cash to manage the business. The economic cycle of a restaurant is based on a simple scenario. You get an apple on credit and sell it, and from that sale you pay the vendor and keep the profit. So let the vendors warehouse your profits. Buy only what you need now.

> **SMART MOVE**
>
> Until you're well established, order only what you need. Don't try to forecast purchases based on the coffee bean freeze or overfarming of tomatillos. That's for larger operations. A salesperson who will call a competitor to borrow an out-of-stock product you need is a valuable service.

Stealing

There's so much stealing on a petty level in a restaurant. Staff will steal toilet paper. Sometimes staff boldly goes for the expensive stuff. For example, Jody's restaurant had three bottles of Dom Perignon, and a customer wanted to buy two. One was in the bar fridge, and when Jody went into the liquor closet to put the other on ice, there were no bottles left.

A few days afterward, a staff member was showing Jody a picture online of a party a junior manager had. He was pointing out something someone was wearing. But Jody noticed something else. There on the back shelf were two bottles of Dom Perignon. "There are the missing bottles," Jody said.

People get touchy and defensive when you bring up stealing. "Oh, no, he'd never do that," the staff member said, and he meant it. "I know how much he makes," Jody said, "and those bottles are the most expensive thing in his apartment." Jody now lets his staff know up front that if they steal, he's probably going to find out they did it.

When people think about how difficult the restaurant business is, they always think it's about the big things. Yet it's not the big monsters that will get you, it's death by a hundred paper cuts. The profit margin is lost in all the little things, the waste, skimming, and scamming.

The discipline you establish in the first 90 days is your blueprint for the future. Establish a protocol in the beginning, and people will be more accepting of it. But try to change a pattern or routine, and people have an emotional reaction and resist. It will put you at odds with vendors, salespeople, delivery drivers, and your staff. You have to have a strong constitution to be in the restaurant business.

The Least You Need to Know

- Establish and enforce your purchasing and delivery policies from day one.
- Personally check your deliveries' weight and count against purchasing forms.
- Don't accept deliveries during service hours.
- Store and secure deliveries immediately after they arrive.
- Keep an eye on salespeople befriending your staff to try to make more sales.
- Don't tie up your cash purchasing unnecessary supplies just to get bulk discounts.

CHAPTER 16

Running Your Office

In this chapter, we'll teach you how to control your cash by setting up smart systems. We'll show you how to use systems such as surprise audits to keep employees honest.

The POS system is vital, and we'll show you how to get the most out of it. You'll use the data from your POS system to create reports that will give you snapshots of how your business is progressing—especially at the all-important first three quarterly milestones. We'll discuss the components of a financial statement and how you can compare your costs and profits over time.

In This Chapter

- How to set up cash control systems
- How cash control systems thwart theft
- Your first three accounting milestones
- Running profit and loss and balance statements
- Making the most of your POS system

Cash Control Systems

To understand financial statement information, you should have an understanding of generally accepted accounting principles (GAAP). Although your accountant will help you through this, we recommend getting an accounting textbook to reference and educate yourself. After all, accounting is the language of business, and this is your business; you need to know the language.

Jody uses an internal control system for dealing with cash. It provides good protection for cash receipts and cash disbursements. There are three basic principles:

- **Separate the duties.** Staff that handles cash should not be in charge of the register/cash draw. Payments are made at the bar or the payment desk. Separating the duties makes it more difficult for your staff to steal cash from you. Two or more people would have to be in on the embezzlement and the cover-up or void the transaction. That's not very likely.

- **Daily Deposit.** You should deposit all cash receipts intact and daily. This keeps your staff from taking a loan on the cash before making the deposit.

- **Pay by Check.** Embezzlement doesn't always involve cash, but can be payments for fake invoices. If a manager has the authority to sign checks, don't let him or her have access to accounting records or have the authority or ability to generate an invoice.

Your bank statements will give you another view of your cash disbursements.

> **SMART MOVE**
>
> Use an accounting software package, such as Quickbooks, to track payments to vendors, payroll, and receipts. Whether you meet your vendor at the door with a clipboard in your hand or an iPad, your inventory template spreadsheet is the key to keeping food costs within budget. And that begins the moment they come through the back door.

How to Make the POS System Your Best Friend

The POS system is the heartbeat of the restaurant. Take the time to learn its many functions. If your staff knows the system better than you, it could be trouble.

Most people underutilize their POS systems. It can be used as a time clock; it tracks every transaction from order to check; and it can be used to manage your cash control systems. Your credit card sales are deposited daily through the POS system.

It's not, however, good at doing inventory. It requires too much input and advanced features, and you're better off working in Excel spreadsheets. Examples of the spreadsheets you'll need can be found in Appendix D.

If you don't know Excel, learn. If you need to hire someone to show you how to use it, it's well worth the cost.

Adapting Your POS to Your Business

First off, remove all the void functions that don't require a specific key or card swipe, and control the card.

Every single transaction must be entered into the POS and come from a printer. If a drink or food item is ever produced that didn't come through the POS, you need to take immediate extreme measures. Even the owner's meal must come through the system.

Explain to kitchen staff that if the printer doesn't produce the order, *no matter what*, they are forbidden to prepare the dish. An excited waiter who didn't remember to ring in a table will often rush to the expeditor and say what they need. The staff should wait until the order is rung in.

If everything gets rung, you have a revenue total and now you just need to track how it was resolved.

Handling Voids

The POS will look to close out the transaction. A void would mean the item was prepared and then taken off the check. You need to know about this.

Jody has a strong void control system in place to control costs and theft. Only the manager on duty has the authority and ability to void. The manager is accountable for the total voids, which are detailed in the end-of-the-day report.

Never use server or manager codes. They always get compromised and borrowed. Use hardcopy swipe cards and keep them in the restaurant; they should never go home with the staff.

If a guest ordered a steak and it came out well done and she didn't eat it, and the server asked the manager to remove it from the check, you should require the server, manager, and chef to sign the back of the ticket with an explanation. This gets placed in the nightly log. Yes, this is cumbersome—but it's very important.

POTENTIAL PITFALL

Since when should giving refunds be made easier? The goal is to avoid mistakes and refunds, not facilitate an efficient processing method for the staff.

When the staff arrives for work, and are in uniform and ready to start, they should come to the manager, who issues their card to sign in to the POS. The POS is a time clock that can also track productivity and measure sales patterns against hourly labor. In addition, it can warn you about a potential overtime scenario.

Make sure the staff has to see the manager to sign in, because if an employee has the ability to punch in without seeing the manager, they could sign in their friends and/or sign in way before their shift begins.

At the end of the night, the same thing must occur for staff to sign out. The staff must bring their cards back to the manager when they've finished with side work. They're then tipped out while they reconcile the daily report.

Self Banking

These days, most full-service restaurants have only one active cash drawer—the bartender's. The cash drawer is delivered to the bartender by the manager at the beginning of the shift and is verified and signed for by the bartender.

No one else can get into the cash drawer once it's issued to the bartender. That includes any other bartenders who may be on duty. Even the manager has no right to touch the drawer. Only one cash attendant to a drawer is a critical rule. The POS can have multiple cash drawers that staff can sign into, but no one goes into another drawer.

Each time the bartender opens the drawer without a transaction, a receipt pops out of the printer and he needs to sign it and explain why the drawer was opened, and then place the receipt in the cash drawer. If a guest needs change and his server doesn't have any, he may get it from the bar.

At the end of the shift, the POS prints out a chit that tells the manager how much the server owes in cash and credit cards and house charges. They need to provide the exact amount to the manager.

Keeping Your Bartender Honest

Hiring honest people isn't always a reality—you just can't know that they're honest. And even honest people will do dishonest things in extreme circumstances. You have to battle theft by removing opportunity, and watching the cash.

Question everything, and don't let people say you don't trust them. It's your manager's job to verify the controls you've set in place. No one should take it personally.

Bartenders often need to stuff the drawer with the extra cash they're trying to steal (which they've accumulated by under-charging or other nefarious means), and they need a method to extract their ill-gotten gains at some point during the evening. Permitting them to cash out their own tips is too risky. Allowing them to take their tips and cash them in is also a bad idea.

If the cash builds up during a shift, a "drop" should be made. The bartender counts a pre-determined amount, and the manager verifies the amount and signs a receipt, which is left in the drawer by the bartender. The manager then places the cash in the safe.

When the shift is over, the manager immediately escorts the bartender and his drawer to the office or counting room. With the manager standing as witness, the bartender counts the original bank and returns it. Then the manager counts up cash and credit card charges. You don't have to give a total and have the bartender prove that number. Keep the goal line in darkness. If they're over, it's just as bad as being under because it means they're not keeping track of how much they've charged.

> **POTENTIAL PITFALL**
>
> If you suspect someone of stealing, don't accuse them; there's too much potential liability. Remember you can terminate someone who can't perform the function of selling items and collecting the correct amount of tender. (Be sure that's stated in your employee manual.)

During the shift, take hourly readings of your POS system and be visible about this so your staff knows you're doing so. Ask the bartender to perform a quick cash count, and then look at the tape, and perhaps even scratch your head. Then take the tape and walk away. This act will blow their confidence if they are scamming, and it will likely prevent the evening's larceny. Fifty percent of controlling the cash is psychological. Controlling the cash is a chess game, and you have to be on your toes.

Cameras Can Be a Theft Deterrent

Video cameras can be very helpful in deterring theft. We suggest you set them up over the bar, in the kitchen, in the office, and by the primary staff's work area. Video is a record, and you should hang on to it for a couple of weeks so you can view it if you suspect problems. It can be sent to your laptop, iPad, or iPhone. Be careful to not let watching video become an obsession.

As for theft, you should be tipped off when a staff member makes a request or performs an action that takes you off the floor or out of the restaurant. Scheming staff usually try to get you out of sight so they can make their move. If they're loading the register with cash they're accumulating by undercharging, for instance, they'll need to remove it before you do your count.

We suggest you utilize a couple of techniques with people you suspect of stealing. They often keep track of the cash they're collecting, so interrupting their program throws them off. Random cash audits mid-shift are a great way to curb theft. You should require two cash audits per shift on bar registers to be documented.

POTENTIAL PITFALL

How can a bartender rip you off? The techniques are endless. However, don't focus on how they do it, but on your methods and systems of interrupting and stopping them from stealing your profits.

You can throw a bartender off guard when she least expects it by performing a second audit shortly after the first. She'll think it's smooth sailing ahead, but you've now discovered too much money in her drawer.

Keep your eyes peeled for accomplices. Sometimes a bartender will have an accomplice show up, sit at the bar, and buy a drink. When the bartender gives his accomplice change for the drink, it will include the night's grab.

Another control is to have each transaction printed and placed in front of the guest in a shot glass. The manager can meander by at any time and slip the ticket out and glance at the amount. If you saw the bartender just make a batch of margaritas and the ticket in front of the guest says one shot, the bartender is busted.

Require your bartender to return to the register after every single transaction and ring up the sale. Don't allow him to wait and ring up several at the same time. He's not allowed to make any drinks for the service bar without a printed ticket. You should not have a printer at the service bar—it undermines the program if staff calls out an order. The order should be rung to avoid any verbal commands.

A bottle-for-bottle perpetual inventory also helps minimize stealing. We'll talk about this more in Chapter 17, when we discuss how food and beverage inventories keep costs within budget.

Remember, a bartender can sneak his own few bottles into your bar. By giving away the drinks off those bottles, your pouring cost percentage won't show up with a change. But you'll be bringing in less revenue, so watch for any unexpected dips in beverage sales, especially during busy times like holidays.

Furthermore, to prevent a bartender from sneaking in his own bottles, secure all deliveries in a locked area and have a template of the back bar with specific placement of all bottles. When the bottles are delivered, you can mark the labels with a special black-light signature stamp. A sweep of the bar with a black light will reveal any unauthorized bottles.

These controls should be used when owners deem appropriate. The good news for would-be restaurant owners is that most cash transactions are limited in this age of credit cards.

Financial Statements

Keeping good daily and weekly records creates the foundation of your financial statements. Remember, financial statements exist to give you snapshots of your business over time. To be useful, these statements need to be timely and accurate reports. These are stop-the-clock moments, when the restaurant comes to a standstill to generate these reports—because items in the kitchen are constantly being transformed. A bag of onions has a different value on Monday than it does on Tuesday after it's been turned into onion soup.

Restaurants are a cash business, and that always must be paramount in your mind before you spend any money. Your financial statements give you great insight into what's changing in your business.

When you look at financial statements, you should look at them comparatively. You should examine two or more accounting periods in side-by-side columns on one statement.

The most important accounting milestones for a new restaurant are three, six, and nine months. Three-month success is almost assured by virtue of curiosity in the market. But don't mistake this wave of business as any measure of sustained success. You're in the introductory stage, the getting-to-know-you phase. There's an opportunity percolating. In your financial statements, you'll want to look at your actual expenses and profits compared to your pro formas. You'll want to look at whether certain dishes are profitable and selling well.

The six-month financial statement will tell you if the folks who came in earlier are coming back and bringing their friends. When the friends come back with their friends, you're off to a good start. When you run your financials, look to see if your sales are increasing. Are you doing more covers? Are your revenues up? Are your food and beverage costs on budget and a blend of 25 to 30 percent?

The nine-month financial statement is when the first economic reality takes hold for many restaurateurs. There are all sorts of ways a new business can pace through its first three quarters, making excuses and anticipating things will settle to where you want them.

The nine-month window is usually the first face-to-face meeting with economic reality. Your financial statement will reveal the trajectory of your business. Your accountant might be able to help you make some adjustments to your profit and loss statements. In addition, you might be able to make some adjustments in the kitchen. But once again, sticking to your concept and your plan is key.

Re-examining your menu mix, pure food cost vs. actual food cost, inventory analysis, and *shrinkage* will help you determine which fire to put out first and which solutions to implement.

DEFINITION

Shrinkage is the amount of inventory lost through waste, spoiling, stealing, mistakes, or sloppiness.

The important thing is to take financial matters in hand from the beginning and never let go. As your restaurant continues to operate, you'll be able to compare profits and losses of various aspects of your business weekly, monthly, quarterly, and yearly. You can use these comparisons to highlight changes in any financial statement. Look for dollar value changes or percentage changes from one period when compared to another or over a certain period of time.

An important formula to understand is the percentage change formula, discussed next.

Calculating Percentage Change

The percentage change formula calculates the percent change from one accounting period to the next:

$$\frac{P_2 - P_1}{P_1} = \Delta\%$$

P = accounting period

Δ = change

P_2 = recent data, P_1 = previous data

Say your sales for the first quarter were $178,323 and sales for the second quarter were $154,247.

$$\frac{(\$178,323 - \$154,247)}{\$154,247} = 15.6\%$$

What this shows is that your second quarter sales are down 15.6 percent. You'll want to make this calculation in your spreadsheet so you can quickly see where large percentage changes have occurred. You'll also want to address this immediately by looking further and making adjustments where necessary.

The Income Statement

The income statement will be your most used financial statement. It shows your revenues and expenses and the resulting profit:

Sales - Expenses = Profit

Get used to looking at this statement on a daily, weekly, monthly, quarterly, and annual basis. To make the data as meaningful and actionable as possible, always compare similar accounting periods and use your percentage change formula, which we discussed above.

Balance Sheet

A balance sheet shows your restaurant's financial position on a specific date. It's a snapshot of your financial bearing. Your accountant can help prepare a balance sheet for you. Liabilities are subtracted from the assets to get a value of the company on a specific date:

Assets = Liabilities + Owners Equity or Assets – Liabilities = Owner Equity

If you plan to use the balance sheet to entice investors, realize that investors are looking for trends or financial strength. They want to see if the restaurant's net worth has been increasing over time, or if growth of the restaurant's net worth has been slowing.

Cash Flow Statement

A cash flow statement details how a business gets and spends money, borrows and repays, sells and repurchases ownership, pays dividends and distributions, and other factors that affect liquidity.

A cash flow statement breaks down where the business revenue comes from. Business revenue can come from operating, investing, or financing. For restaurants, revenue is based on sales. If your business can show that it brings in more money than it spends, potential investors obviously will view that more favorably than a business that has to sell assets to operate.

Paying Taxes

It's almost unfair to give restaurants a fiduciary role in holding on to taxes. For a cash business, doing so is a trap. Use a payroll service for taking care of payroll and holding taxes. Set up a bank account for accruals—those expenses you know are coming, such as rent, taxes, and insurance. You don't want to know how many restaurant owners find themselves over their head in expenses and behind in paying taxes. Proactive financial planning in a restaurant is sorely needed. Be sure to meet with your accountant every quarter.

When you stay on top of your daily, weekly, and monthly financials and meet with your accountant regularly, paying taxes doesn't become a nightmare. Always use a good accountant who's experienced in doing taxes for businesses, and restaurants in particular.

The Least You Need to Know

- Know how to use your POS system and adapt it to your restaurant's needs.
- Cash control is a system to keep your staff and vendors honest. Keep a good system in place from the start.
- Running weekly, monthly, and quarterly financial statements will keep you on budget.
- Meet with your accountant every three months, especially the first year you're open.

CHAPTER 17

Understanding Costs

Success in the restaurant business depends on managing food and beverage costs. To keep their blended costs within 25 percent of sales, you need to take several steps before and after your restaurant opens.

In this chapter, we'll show you how to run yield tests to cost out each dish on the menu. You'll learn about building up data in spreadsheets on product costs. We'll also discuss how to keep food costs on budget by monitoring vendor deliveries and doing weekly inventories.

This is your money; you have to be involved. You need to run the inventories. It also shows the staff and vendors that you're in control and you run a business with an eye on the bottom line.

In This Chapter

- How to determine the cost and profit of each dish
- Why you need to do a weekly food and liquor inventory
- Why spreadsheets are a vital tool in controlling costs
- How to run the numbers to make sure your costs are on budget
- How much should you pay your staff?

Food and Beverage Costs

You begin managing food costs during pre-opening. You'll start by running the *yield* tests of your recipes on your menu, and then determining the exact cost per plate.

> **DEFINITION**
>
> **Yield** is the difference between how much a food item weighed when it came in the door versus its edible weight. It's the net weight of food after it has been processed.

The goal is to build up a database of tested standardized recipes that will express your restaurant concept, while staying within budget.

Liquor is even more of a profit center, and you'll run your drink recipes through the same series of tests, as well as use several inventory methods to monitor use, cost, and profit, and prevent waste and theft.

Inventory Template

Your food costs will be determined by your yield tests. Menu item costs are built from spreadsheets listing each ingredient amount and the cost per unit. From that listing, we determine the cost per dish.

You'll add this data to your inventory template—a spreadsheet that will calculate your yields and costs. You can purchase spreadsheet programs for offices or build your own if you're well-versed in creating software. Be sure you understand your software well or have someone tutor you in working with it.

The components of your inventory spreadsheet are listed in the following table. Examples of these spreadsheets can be found in Appendix D.

The Inventory Template

Spreadsheet Name	What It Does	What You Learn
Converter	Convert measurements	A gallon = 3.79 liters
List	Defines: Type of dish Inventory categories Recipe units Inventory location	 Entrée Dairy, seafood Ounces, grams, each Cold box, freezer, or pantry

Spreadsheet Name	What It Does	What You Learn
Portion Yield	Measures the percent of sales of each portion	
Yield Test	Measures the product before and after production	Yield percentage = edible portion (EP) weight ÷ As Purchased (AP) weight × 100.
Inventory	Lists location, position, count, prices, order units, vendors, daily counts, and inventory extension amounts	Inventory extension is the number of units × price. Add all of the items to get total daily and weekly inventories.
Recipe Index	Lists recipes by name and calculates the recipe cost and unit cost	
Plate Costing Index	Lists plate name, menu price, plate cost, food cost, items sold, total sales, and total cost per plate	The roast chicken entrée is on the menu for $15.99. It's a high-profit plate and you're selling lots of them.
Recipe Template	Measures ingredients, quantity, measurement, prep, and cost	Recipe cost: in $ Unit cost: $ Food cost %
Plate Template	Measures ingredients, quantity, measurement, prep, and cost	Plate cost: $ Menu price: $ Food cost: %
Plate, 1, 2, 3, etc.	Measures ingredients, quantity, measurement, prep, and cost	

The spreadsheets for the plate costing index, recipe template, plate template, and plate 1, 2, 3, etc., contain a category titled Method, which refers to the steps to create each dish, recipe, and plate. This comes in particularly useful when evaluating dishes according to the profitability, production, and popularity (PPP) test we talked about in Chapter 5. How much time is it taking to make? Can you streamline production to make it more profitable?

Determining the cost mix of menu items and the profitability of each dish will give you an overall average of food profitability. Each item must lose value in order to create value. A bell pepper might weigh 8 ounces and cost $0.50 or $0.0625 per ounce. After you take out the core, stem, and ribs, you might be left with 5 ounces of bell pepper. Now you see that you paid $0.50 for 5 ounces of bell pepper or $0.10 per ounce. When you transform the bell pepper into your Mediterranean ratatouille—a medley of eggplant, peppers, tomatoes, and onions—it contributes to the cost of the dish. It adds value.

Waste Not

Get yourself a pair of long, thick rubber gloves and look through your garbage for waste. This is how you ensure your staff is maximizing the yield of all of your food products. The fortunes of many a famous successful chef have been built on braving the black plastic bag to find food waste. Cutting off and tossing out too much of an onion, tomato, asparagus, or bell pepper decreases the amount of useable product you can sell. It increases your cost per plate. Yes, you *want* your staff to fear you going through the garbage.

Another way many restaurants prevent waste is to buy larger cuts of meat and cut their own steaks and chops. Pre-cut steaks and chops are more expensive to purchase than the larger piece of meat you cut yourself, but the weight of each piece is verified.

The trimmings and bones can also be used in many ways. Trimmings can become meatballs. Bones are the basis for deep-flavored stocks.

Portion control is essential, especially with your most expensive ingredients, proteins, and liquor. If each steak or chop is supposed to weigh 12 ounces, but if the chef cuts the steaks a bit thicker, you might end up with a 14-ounce steak. You're giving away your profits. Likewise, if the steak gets cut to 10 ounces, you can't sell that steak; it has to be used for a different purpose, most likely at a lower profit margin.

Food Costs to Sales Percentage

We talk a lot about percentages in the restaurant business. Food costs should be 30 to 35 percent of sales (the lower the better). One aspect to keep in mind is that some food items might not have a large profit margin, but that doesn't mean you're not making good money on it. Steak is a good example. Your cost per steak is $25 and you're selling it for $48, so your food cost is 52 percent. However, you get a higher revenue on that steak than you would have with a hamburger, which at 25 percent has better food percentage (cost is $1 and it sells for $4). If you sell just one steak, you make $23. You'll have to sell eight hamburgers to make $24. The point is that some items will not only have a higher revenue, but also a higher cost percentage.

Steak vs. Burger Cost to Sales Ratio vs. Profits

	Steak	Burger
Cost	$25.00	$1.00
Sale	$48.00	$4.00
Cost to Sales Ratio (Cost ÷ Sale)	52%	25%
Profit	$23.00	$3.00

This table shows that even though the steak has a much higher food ratio of cost to sales than you'd like to see, you make $23. Compare that to the burger, which has a low ratio of cost to sales (which you like to see) where you only make $3.

If you sell 2 steaks and 10 burgers, you profit $46 from the steaks compared to $30 from the burgers.

	Steaks	**Burgers**
Number sold	2 steaks	10 burgers
Profit	$46.00	$30.00

Another thing to take into consideration is the blended cost of each plate. If you're adding a baked potato to the steak dish, for example, it's a low-cost item at around 8 percent. Steakhouses often charge extra for sides, and they make a good profit on the creamed spinach, the iceberg wedge, and the tomato salad. A steakhouse has higher food costs, but the revenues are also higher.

It's the same with wine. You can multiply a bottle of $10 wine four times to sell it at $40. But if you paid $30 for a bottle of wine, you can't really sell it for $120—especially if the bottle is one the customer can purchase at the liquor store for $40. (Liquor stores and restaurants buy liquor at the exact same state-regulated price.) If you sell a $30 bottle for $75, your margins are less but you just put $45 into the bank. That's like two steaks and a whole lot of hamburgers.

When costing out a plate, don't forget to add wrap-around costs—the freebies you give away, such as steak sauce, hot sauce, lemons, and candies at the end of the meal.

Some restaurants just bring an obligatory basket of bread and foil-wrapped butter, but others serve artisan breads and pour expensive olive oil. Depending on the gesture, the cost can range from low to high but it's important to recognize the incremental effect on food costs. Imagine if a burger joint didn't take into consideration the cost of ketchup.

The same applies to beverages—while a mojito might have a fixed cost, the expense of fresh mint is potentially significant in the actual cost. Wrap-around costs include take-home "doggie-bag" packaging. However, if takeout is a significant part of your business, packaging would be listed as a line item in your P&L, rather than being included in wrap-around costs.

The best way to calculate wrap-around costs is to track the overall category of this expense and divide by total covers for the month. In a spreadsheet, plug in this number per guest, and then repeat the exercise for two more months. The three-month average can be used, until there's a material change in the cost of an item or two. This exercise might make you reconsider your menu price or the level of generosity your concept can afford. Warning: if you let your chef be in charge of welcoming freebies, it can get expensive.

Market factors affect food costs, and thus your food cost percentages. Your actual food cost percentage of your food sales will vary based on market factors such as weather, drought, crop infection, import restrictions, seasonality, etc.

> **POTENTIAL PITFALL**
>
> Don't tie your food specifically to a special imported item or brand. When imported brands grow popular, U.S. producers of that product can bring unfair trade cases against the company. This means your special imported pasta could soar in price because the International Trade Commission placed a tariff on it.

As menu items become less profitable due to these market factors, either your prices will have to increase so your profitability stays the same, or your menu items might need to change to keep your profits.

Back in 2014, the price of limes tripled in a few short weeks. Restaurants sucked up the additional cost, raised their prices, switched to another citrus, or changed the menu item. However, some menu items like guacamole and margaritas can't be made without limes. Most restaurants that couldn't substitute for limes simply ate the additional cost. Luckily, the lime shortage was short-lived. The USDA publishes a market news report for fruits and vegetables. Use this report to keep a pulse on prices. Talk to your suppliers regularly to stay on top of any price shocks or anticipated shortages.

When Jody was buying for 12 restaurants, he paid attention to how an unexpected freeze in Brazil was affecting coffee prices. Yet he was mindful of his competitors, and before raising prices, he thought about what it would cost his restaurants in pricing and posture, and what the market would bear. Be mindful about what other restaurants charge, which is how the guest is going to judge your restaurant.

Don't raise prices in response to a food shortage when you're establishing a new restaurant, because that's what customers will remember. Once you're established, you can get away with it. In response to the increase in the price of limes, you could bump up prices a little, but try to misdirect the customer by serving the margarita in a different glass, and dip the rim in fancy red sugar. You should work a little harder for that extra money.

Inventory

Your inventory is the cost of your food and beverages you haven't sold yet. Although food and beverage items in your inventory are considered an asset on your balance sheet, they're expensive and they can spoil, be damaged, or get stolen.

We recommend you perform a weekly inventory. Your staff will try to convince you that you can do it monthly, but managing your food costs is such an important part of your business that you really need to do it weekly. In the future when your food and beverage costs are completely steady, you might be able to perform it monthly. For now, do it weekly.

Inventory has to be done at a time when business comes to a close. It's a freeze-frame moment. Restaurants are like a moving body, so you have to find the rare moments when it's at a standstill. It can be at the end of a Sunday night or at 7 A.M. on Monday. Note, the restaurant must be closed. You must be disciplined and should allot time for this process. We suggest you block out from 10 P.M. to midnight on Sunday. You'll need one staff member to help. Make it more fun by ordering a pizza, making some coffee, and turning up the music.

Your inventory lists should be arranged to correspond exactly with how the food is stored in the walk-ins and freezers, and the way your bar is set up. (A noticeable vacant spot in your bar setup lets you know what's needed at a glance.)

Keep a clipboard on the door of your walk-in with an inventory list of your premium products, so your chef can mark down every time he uses a protein. At the end of the night, he should do an inventory count of his proteins to ensure a lobster, for example, doesn't end up in someone's bag and become the entrée for a staff member's romantic dinner at home, rather than a customer's meal in the restaurant. The chef will check his proteins again at the beginning of the day and mark the inventory. As a result, he knows that when he has only six lobsters left, it's time to order more. You have to establish a *par stock*, which is the amount at which you need to order more.

DEFINITION

Par stock is the minimum amount of any food or beverage item you should have on hand before ordering more. Defining your par stock will keep you from running out of food or ordering too much. It varies vastly according to food category, and your inventory will reveal your restaurant's usage patterns.

Running a careful weekly inventory system prevents theft and spoilage, and it makes ordering orderly and organized.

Your par stock should be equal to three to four days of usage. That means if you're doing $40,000 in food sales weekly, it comes out to about $10,000 to $11,000 of food usage. If orders come in Monday, the lowest point of food in your kitchen will be Sunday. At that point, if you're doing $40,000 in food sales weekly, you should have only $4,000 to $5,000 in food inventory. Those figures will help you keep a meaningful inventory.

If you've bought two and a half weeks' worth of food, you can label everything all you want but it's likely that when a cook rushes to the walk-in during service on a busy night, he'll grab newer inventory instead of inventory that should be used first. These days, you can get deliveries two to three times a week, so there's no need to load up on supplies.

There's a fine line between keeping inventories low and running out of ingredients. A sous chef, who was filling in for the vacationing head chef, was so intent on showing the owners how good he was at keeping costs down, he focused on keeping the inventory down. He did such a great job keeping inventory low that the restaurant was running out of vegetables, meats, and cheeses. Then he started substituting ingredients without telling the customers. He was making himself look good to the owners at the expense of their business. It was a bad situation.

A restaurant running a weekly inventory soon gets into a rhythm, with deliveries coming every week, and that keeps you from running out of food.

> **SMART MOVE**
>
> Running out of food isn't something that should be happening in a well-run restaurant. But sometimes it does happen. Make sure you know the locations of your closest grocery stores, and use them for emergency purposes only.

You shouldn't be running out of chicken, for example. But if you're prepping and discover you don't have enough, send someone out to a store to buy it. If there's a shortage, one of those "Oh, man!" moments, discover it during the afternoon, not during service. It's disappointing for guests to look at a menu and imagine eating a dish, and then be told it's not available. That's the sort of disappointment that can put your guests out of sorts, especially if they came there craving your oven-roasted chicken.

Now, if you run out of a special, that's okay. It was a special, after all, with the purpose of moving something you bought too much of or need to use by today. But your staple inventory items shouldn't be so volatile.

Inventories also help you keep your chef on top of what food needs to be used before it expires. Making soup on a Monday is a good way to keep the food in the walk-in moving on out. Specials are also good ways to move product. At Baang, a restaurant Jody opened in Greenwich, duck was on the menu. Leftover duck was featured in spring rolls, pancakes, curries, and staff meals.

Liquor Inventory

Your inventory sheets should be set up exactly like a template of how your bottles are used, displayed, and stored at the bar, at every station, and in storage. For example, you'll have a bottle of a popular vodka at the bar, at the service bar, in the cabinet below the bar, and in the liquor storeroom. So what you want at all times is four bottles of that same popular vodka.

Remember that it's illegal to marry liquor by pouring the contents of one bottle into another. Everyone tries to do it, but it's a bad idea. Even though it seems to make sense to fill up a bottle that's only 25 percent full, you shouldn't because it's not legal.

Think about it from the perspective of someone who's less honorable than you. If the law allowed you to fill a bottle of quality vodka from another bottle of the same vodka, what would prevent you (or some devious member of your staff) from filling it up with *well* vodka—or water?

> **DEFINITION**
>
> **Well** liquor, also called "rail," is a generic or lower-end brand of distilled spirits, such as gin, vodka, whisky, or tequila. There's been a resurgence of interest in distilled spirits, with status brands, flavored spirits, and craft spirits capturing more of the market.

Perpetual Bottle-for-Bottle Inventory

This inventory accounts for every bottle of liquor used daily. Every day, every single empty liquor and wine bottle is saved in a dedicated trash can in the back of or under the bar. At the end of the shift, they're all placed on top of the bar and counted and logged into an inventory sheet.

Then you run the POS mix—the printout that shows how many of each product has been sold during a shift—and verify that all the empty wine and liquor bottles have been rung up. Once the empties have been verified, they're removed, destroyed (broken), or recycled (marked with an X across the label to make sure it will not be refilled).

Another function of the perpetual liquor inventory is that you're giving a visual message to the entire staff that you check every bottle against the POS system's reports.

The inventory sheet is then given to the manager for requisitioning from the stockroom the next morning. When the bottles are delivered from the stockroom the next morning, you can mark the labels with a special black light signature stamp. A sweep of the bar with a black light will show you if any foreign bottles have been brought in.

You set a par stock for liquor just as you do for food. You've got the same bottle in the same place every day. You keep your back-up in the cabinet. And in the middle of a busy Friday night, when you run out of the bottle on your speed rail, you won't have to leave the floor to retrieve a back-up bottle from the locked basement storage, because you've already got a bottle in the cabinet beneath the bar.

You should never have to go to a liquor store during the middle of a shift. You need to stay in the restaurant, so send a staff member to the liquor store in an emergency.

POTENTIAL PITFALL

Liquor distributors are going to offer you deals. Resist all offers in the beginning until you realize what's moving and selling at your restaurant. If you're not careful, you could end up with a case of peppermint vodka you can't sell.

Don't tie up or deplete your cash flow on anything you can't move. This is a cash-flow business, so be sure to always keep that in mind. Don't commit to bulk purchases, even if they're being offered to you as a "deal." Wait until you know the flow of what products you're using the most of and when you need to reorder. Once you know that further on down the road, you can then take advantage of those discounted deals.

Having enough is part of the system of running a successful restaurant. Think about glassware, for example. You need enough to set the tables and enough to fill your waiter stations, while one set is with the dishwasher and another is in storage. If and when the manager decides to pull another case from storage and move it into the working inventory, he must put a note on his clipboard to order another set of glasses to ensure you never run out. Remember, your storeroom is your back-up, not your working inventory.

For accounting and tax purposes, inventories may be calculated differently. You'll need to speak with your accountant about how to cost your inventory. There are three methods to cost inventory:

1. First-in, first-out (FIFO)

2. Last-in, first-out (LIFO)

3. Weighted average

Whichever accounting method you decide on with your accountant, that method will be applied from year to year.

Note: none of the methods of costing inventory has any bearing on the actual flow of how your items are used from inventory. You'll probably finish the tomatoes from yesterday before you open the box that was delivered today. Of course, you want to minimize your inventory to reduce the costs associated with it.

Incoming: Watching Your Purchases

When orders come in, it's very important to match the purchase orders to your invoices. The weight, the cost per ounce or unit price per case, and the charge should be found on the purchase order. If the person who's ordering is not the person receiving, it's especially important to match the purchase order to the appropriate invoice.

SMART MOVE

Consider putting a big, intimidating scale by the inside receiving area. Vendor drivers need to know that you check weights. Be a stickler up front and check weights right from your first delivery. You want the driver to pass the word to the warehouse that your restaurant checks weights.

Count bottles and check the vintage on wine. If it's incorrect, send it back. Drivers hate having to return stuff. They get paid for deliveries, not for returns. Send things back right then and there, and they'll put more effort into making sure your order is correct from then on.

Once again, it's a chess game of strategy. Don't worry about being liked by suppliers. Be respected as an honest business person, with a smile and a handshake for all.

Food and Beverage Sales Mix

The typical sales mix in a full-service restaurant is that beverages make up 35 percent of sales, while food makes up 65 percent. Another scenario is 40/60. But the smaller beverage segment of sales is the most profitable. Liquor and nonalcoholic drinks have high profit margins.

There are many tricks of the trade for increasing your beverage sales, from training your staff to make suggestions to offering drinks at the right moment in points of service. These days, people enjoy pairing drinks and food. What started with wine, matching the qualities and flavors with the flavor and texture palette, has now moved on to beer and distilled spirits.

Depending on your restaurant concept, your servers could suggest starting the meal with a glass of (high-profit) cava, the Spanish bubbling wine, and tapas. After the table has finished the appetizers and before the entrées are to be served, a server might suggest to the customer that a bottle of a light red wine will work with the fish and meat dishes ordered by the table. After dinner, your servers could recommend pairing a scotch with your chef's special chocolate truffles made with estate-grown cocoa beans.

Aligning your food and beverage programs will help you increase your profitability.

All the information that you gather and enter into your spreadsheets, along with the information generated from your POS system, will help you begin to understand the flow of your business throughout the day, week, month, season, and year. It also helps you run your restaurant every day. These spreadsheets tie into your ordering, inventory, scheduling your labor, and adjusting your menu.

Operating Costs

Your operating costs are the same as your selling, general, and administrative (SG&A) expenses. These are the costs that are not directly related to making food. They include management salaries, benefits for nonproduction employees, accounting expenses, legal fees, office supplies, property taxes, rent, advertising, and more. Of your operating costs, only your rent is fixed. All the other operating costs are variable. Keep a close eye on the variable components to see how they're affecting your profits and cash flow.

Many of these costs are paid once a month. We highly recommend that you set up an accrual account into which you put the balance of income, after you subtract your weekly expenses for labor. Then at the end of the month you will have enough money to cover your rent, property taxes, insurance, and the estimated cost of your utilities.

Remember, restaurants are a business where you bring in $20 at a time and you receive bills for $10,000. Be prepared to cover your monthly expenses, while putting away money for maintenance and so on. Cash flow is the tipping point for success or failure. Having an accrual account set up so you're ready to write really big checks is a good idea. Not having an accrual account is what gets most of the restaurant guys. Their restaurants become a pervasive climate of chasing their tails. And then all the special things, the details that made the restaurant such a hospitable experience, start to disappear. They start cutting back on the special cardamom-spiced soap in the men's room and the roses are replaced with mums in the dining room.

Linen is also an area to watch closely. Most linen companies try to get you to agree to pay a stocking fee, which means that regardless of how many dirty aprons and napkins they pick up to launder, they charge your restaurant for a set amount. Try to hire a usage-type linen service where you pay for what you actually use. Linen companies also send a phantom invoice for damage every now and then. You should always ask for the damaged ones to be presented before you pay.

The relationship between the linen driver and the restaurant can be good. If you offer him and his wife a free meal once in a while, he might bring back the ton of forks and knives that end up in the linen bin each week. (Dishwashers have magnetic rims to reduce silverware being tossed. But usually, silverware ends up entangled in the linens.)

Paying Your Employees

Restaurant employee pay is determined by the market rate. It varies according to the cost of living in your part of the country. The Labor Board of Statistics is a good resource for information on pay rates for restaurant jobs (see Appendix D). You should also have enough contacts and experience in your local market to learn what the going rates are. If not, start talking to people about the different pay rates according to the employee's role.

The Manager. Jody's approach is to spend money on key roles, such as the manager, who is salaried and rarely gets overtime. For managers, hours aren't measured as much as results. Owners should focus on making managers effective, rather than having them just hanging around the restaurant.

The Host or Hostess. You might want to spend more money on your host or hostess. They're the first person to greet the customer, and that first impression is very important. A host can be the face or identity of a restaurant. You want to ensure you pick the right personality and style that goes with your restaurant's concept. Of course, having a host with too strong an identity for hospitality can have its downsides. When he's off-duty, guests will have a very different experience in your restaurant.

> **POTENTIAL PITFALL**
>
> Your investors might say, "I've got an idea that'll save you money. My daughter will be home from college this summer. She'll work as the hostess for minimum wage." The answer is always no. You need a professional who will be around for months to come.

In Jody's neck of the woods in Fairfield County, Connecticut, the going rate for a host/hostess ranges between $10 and $12 an hour. But Jody will pay $100 a night for a good hostess who smiles at the guests and makes them feel genuinely cared for.

Servers. Servers get what is called a "special" rate, which means the base salary is lower. They also receive a meal allowance and tips. So what they earn relates to how many tables they have, what nights they work, how many times the tables turn, and whether or not they have to pool their tips with others.

We don't recommend pooling tips in the beginning, when you open a new restaurant. Pooling the tips kills the motivation of the talent. It's smarter to let all the servers keep the tips they earn individually (paying back a percentage to runners and bussers), and hope the less-experienced servers will pick up the experience and skills that will make them more valuable team members who can work the best tables on the best nights.

The meal allowance is more of a technicality, so restaurants can pay below the minimum hourly wage to servers who make tips. It's a payroll factor mechanism. Staff doesn't pay for the chef's family meal, which is not from the menu, but almost always a different style of food from what the restaurant serves, to break up the routine. Most restaurants offer an option where staff can order off the menu for a considerable discount (50 percent).

The chef's family meal, which is offered to the entire staff, is a quick moment when the staff breaks bread together, thus reinforcing the team spirit while discussing particular details of the night ahead.

At the end of a successful shift, some restaurants let the staff toast with a cocktail. However, it's a bad idea to do so because it can create many compromised situations. If your staff worked extra hard and you want to reward them, find an affordable nearby tavern and meet there to unwind while you buy them a round. It's better to move the situation of staff sharing an after-shift drink offsite.

Another reason you don't want staff drinking onsite is because you don't want that image seen by the customers. Say a staff member gets off early and goes to the bar for his drink. Now he's standing there, drinking next to customers he might have waited on earlier. It's a confusing message to all concerned. Require staff to change their uniforms and leave the restaurant when their shift ends.

The Bartender. The bartender gets an hourly salary and he or she keeps tips. (The numbers of female bar staff are strong and growing, and women make great bartenders.)

Back of the House. In the BOH, most of the salary goes to the main talent—the executive chef and the sous chef. Cooks are paid market rate.

One of the most important roles in the kitchen is the dishwasher. A good dishwasher is key. Without him, the whole system bogs down. He works for a low salary and shows up every day. This guy's watching your back. Jody buys the guy's loyalty by finding something to do for him. Is he walking to work? Buy him a secondhand bike or a pair of headphones to listen to music on his way there. One time Jody rewarded a dishwasher with a metro pass for the train he was taking to work.

Jody also highly recommends that an owner spend one evening working the dishwasher station. We don't know how many owners will be up to the challenge. However, that's where Jody learned that the reason he had to keep replacing wine glasses—was the waiters were throwing them in the bins and breaking them. He also learned how soon the dishwasher ran out of hot water. The dishwasher had just accepted it, instead of letting the manager know.

Employees don't get rich working in a restaurant kitchen. What you can offer them is a great place to work and a stimulating environment. Jody hires the kind of people who'd love to come to his restaurant as a guest. You'll get more out of your employees by inspiring them, since you can't pay them more because their actual pay rates are locked into the business P&L and market rate average. They love being part of the ensemble and the vibe. They love being respected and working in a well-respected restaurant.

The Least You Need to Know

- Your inventory is your cash. Keep a daily inventory on your proteins and liquor, and do weekly Sunday inventories on all food and beverages.

- Deliveries represent cash. Check your invoices and make sure you get what you pay for.

- Food percentages don't always tell the whole story; food revenues can wildly vary your food profits.

- Know the market rate for restaurant staff and be prepared to pay extra for key positions such as manager, hostess, executive chef, and sous chef. Reward your loyal lower-paid employees with perks.

CHAPTER 18

Beginning Your Marketing Blitz

In this chapter, we'll discuss how to throw an opening party that will be the first stage in your marketing blitz. You'll learn everything Jody has figured out from years of hosting opening parties. You'll learn exactly how to invite the right people, who will spread the word so quickly your phone will be ringing for reservations your first weekend.

We'll also discuss dealing with the press and online reviews. The field has shifted dramatically with the decline of newspapers. Online reviews by uncredentialed, anonymous people can be devastating. We'll teach you ways to deal with negative reviews.

In This Chapter

- How to throw a great opening party
- Why your party rockets your restaurant to success
- Inviting the right people to your opening
- How to start the buzz about your restaurant
- Getting people to call for reservations for opening weekend

The Opening Party

The opening party is vital to launching your restaurant. It's not just a party—it's a party with a message about your new restaurant and its concept. Your party should relate to your core concept and send a message to your target audience. You're letting them know they've got a great new place to go to eat.

Invitations

Your grand opening party begins with an invitation, and it must be thoughtful. It's the first real branded piece of information you're sending out. This party is the first time your target audience is coming into contact with your restaurant. Think about the story you want to tell. Remember, sometimes it's not so much what you say as how you say it. This relates to your concept. You can be playful, racy, elegant, organic, and imaginative. Don't be flat and functional.

Send real invitations. In this day and age, email invitations, eblasts, and evites just seem lazy. Not to mention they simply clutter inboxes. An actual physical invitation, designed especially in keeping with your restaurant's brand, excites people about the restaurant and makes them want to come.

Establish a tone, a style, and a point of view with your invitation. Make it consistent with your identity. If you're a homespun organic Berkeley bistro, for example, you'll want to use recycled paper and make sure your messaging isn't too slick or cryptic.

Your invitation should tell the guests something about the style of the event, such as it's a cocktail party. Noting the style of the event lets guests decide if they need to go home first and put on a jacket or change into a cocktail dress. Few restaurant openings are black tie; but it does make people feel more special when they must dress up for an occasion.

What words should you use to tell them what to wear? You see a lot of people trying to be creative, but a lot of times these descriptions—"Black tie fun" and "Creative casual"—raise more questions than they answer. And answering questions about what your guests should wear is the last thing on your list.

> **SMART MOVE**
>
> If your invitation specifies "cocktails" at your opening party, it lets your guests assume a certain level of spiffing themselves up is needed, while letting them interpret that in whatever elegant, artsy, or understated manner they choose.

For Jody's opening party for Bleu in Greenwich, his team hand-delivered invitations with blue bottles of champagne. It let people know, "You are special. And we are creative and fun." Driving around hand-delivering those bottles was a lot of work, but it was an effective tool for getting buzz started.

Asking people to RSVP is important, too. It lets guests know that this is not an anonymous event. It tells them they were specially chosen to come to this event.

Picking the Grand Opening Date

Stick with your opening date. As the opening date approaches, many owners panic and chicken out, thinking they need another week. But it's like having a baby—it's coming, and you can't put it off.

The truth is, you'll never be ready. At your opening party, something inevitably will go wrong. There may be a little piece of cardboard floating in someone's glass of red wine. There's wet paint somewhere, it's just a matter of whether somebody touches it or not. You might run out of a favorite dish.

We almost always pick Thursday for the grand opening party. People love the notion of going out on a Thursday. It spices up their life, and it's close enough to the weekend to garner you more attention. It starts the buzz that's going to make your first weekend hot.

Check the local social calendar. You'll want to make sure that your opening party will not be colliding with any major social or weekend events. You want the opening of your new restaurant to be the major social event of the weekend!

What Time?

Parties should be from 7 to 10 P.M. or 6 to 9 P.M., depending on the kind of place it is. If it's a clubby place or a cool experience-driven place, hold the party from 7 to 10 P.M. It's likely that the people who stop by for the later party will already have eaten something and taken the edge off their appetite. With a 6 to 9 P.M. party, people will arrive hungry. You're not doing a sit-down dinner, but you'll have to serve enough food to satisfy people. For many guests, this will be dinner.

> **POTENTIAL PITFALL**
>
> There's no reason to send out a save the date notice for your opening party 30 days in advance. It's not a trip to China. It's a party, and you don't want to raise expectations so high that people are disappointed. You can send out the invitations two weeks before the party.

Guest List

The opening party isn't a party for your old friends or your investor's old friends. The most important people you invite to this party are people who will spread the word about your restaurant. They're ambassadors who meet and come into contact with people every day. They can be the guy who does hair color at the hottest salon in town. Or car dealers, real estate agents, health coaches, Pilates teachers, masseuses, and people who work in busy retail shops. They're people who will tell others about this hot new place.

You also want to invite popular people to your party. Invite people everyone wants to see, talk to, and hang out with where they hang out. Do some research and find out who your local celebrities are, and invite them.

Jody once saw his opening of a restaurant in a chic hotel derail before his eyes. As the party began, a family wandered in, exhausted from a day of sightseeing. There they were—a middle-aged couple with three kids off the leash, and the detached parents collapsed onto the couch in the restaurant's lounge. They were the first thing people entering the restaurant saw—and it confused them. Was this an upscale restaurant, a place for business people of the city? Or was this a family restaurant?

SMART MOVE

To help set the tone of the opening party, invite friends who you think represent the spirit of the restaurant and who will dress the way your ideal guests will dress. Have them stand near the entrance to provide newcomers with the right message.

It's important to show who you built this restaurant for, and that it speaks to this particular audience. If you don't give them any clues, they won't know.

Party Rules

The party's schedule must be tight. It needs a beginning, a middle, and an end. It needs a climax. Live entertainment is a great way to control the rhythm. The band then can give a gentle notice that it's over.

The party must end for many important reasons. First, the party is meant to be a teaser. It's meant to show your ambassadors your concept and get them excited enough to talk to others about it.

Instead of waiting for the party to take a turn for the worse, end the evening nicely and professionally, shaking hands and wrapping it up. Thank your guests for coming. Help them into their coats and hand them a gift bag on their way to the door. The ones still wanting a nightcap will exit onto the street, all dressed up. People will ask, "Where were you?" and they'll be happy to tell them. This starts the buzz about your restaurant.

On Friday morning, when all your guests are back at work, they'll love telling their office mates about being at your grand opening, how wonderful the appetizers were and the special cocktail they had. They'll fuel interest in your restaurant, and people will start calling to make reservations that weekend.

Your guests become advocates for your restaurant. People love to share their discoveries, turning a friend on to a great new place to dine. This word-of-mouth approach keeps an insider buzz going around your restaurant.

This insider buzz is the best form of advertising today. Ads in newspapers aren't very effective anymore. You can get some more buzz by inviting local luminaries and the press. But keep the mayor and his giant scissors away from your restaurant. That's been done a million times. At the opening of Jody's Red Lulu, the mayor posed with the go-go dancers. That's a picture people notice and won't forget.

Preparing for the Opening

Never decorate your restaurant for the party. That's like saying, "I'm going to introduce you to someone, but she'll be wearing a mask." You want people to experience your restaurant's concept and décor.

To prepare for the party, move some of the tables and chairs out of the way. You want people to understand that, for the most part, this is a cocktail party where people will stand, rather than a sit-down dinner.

This is the one night of your restaurant's existence when you really get to control everything about what is served. This is your night to show off your food exactly the way you want it. The food and service will reflect that. In addition, passed appetizers keep some control on food consumption and behavior.

One thing you really don't want to do is solicit opinions about the food. You already know it's great. Sure, you might notice a tweak is needed here or there, and your well-trained team is on it with a word from you. However, you don't want to show any sign of weakness to your guests.

Don't give guests too much food—leave them wanting more. You want people making reservations for the weekend right then and there. Have your hostess ready to take those reservations. This party needs to build into the weekend, the following week, and beyond.

Parting Gifts

We suggest you give guests a gift bag when they leave to make them reflect and remember your restaurant. You could create custom-mixed CDs for the restaurant, and put one of these on a USB stick for the gift bag. You can reproduce the menu in miniature on velum, rolled and tied with jute. You should also include something savory or sweet, such as a nut mix served at the bar or a mini bottle of an exotic liquor. Don't forget to include a business card/contact information for your restaurant. Give guests just enough to make them wake up the next day and remember the evening. You've piqued their interest, and provoked the first follow-up visit.

The "Dusty Shoe"

In the week between the friends and family dinner and the grand opening, we suggest you hold a "dusty shoe," which is a dinner where you invite 8 to 12 influential food people. They can range from the local media, to representatives from influential publications, to the most-followed bloggers.

The purpose of this dinner is to give your invitees from the media a behind-the-scenes look at the restaurant and a chance to talk to the chef. It's a way to open the minds of those who pride themselves on their opinions. Giving them a preview is a great way to show them respect. Have the chef visit the table and talk about how he or she has been trying to cook the dish a couple different ways. You and your chef should prepare yourself to be charming and humble to your guests.

The media and bloggers will want to impart their opinions and feel important. Just listen to them and smile. The point of this evening is to put your restaurant on their radar. They'll do previews and profiles, and they'll return to do reviews. The bloggers will post pictures and live tweets.

The Soft Opening

At the end of the grand opening party, you and your staff will feel a sense of euphoria. Everyone will be buzzed and excited. However, that all changes the following day. The party guests have made the restaurant come to life, and now they're gone.

By now, you've been working on this restaurant for six months or more. When you open, open with confidence. Don't open your restaurant with the mindset that it's a work in progress.

We recommend opening with dinner service only. When your restaurant is new, there are still too many possible variables that could make your opening weeks rocky. If your FOH staff quits or your chef disappears, at least you have all day to regroup and create solutions.

If you start serving lunch, you'll have to have your staff back in the restaurant prepping at 9 A.M., and they may not have finished cleaning up from the night before.

Go into lunch service with open eyes. Realize that for many restaurants, it's not a moneymaker. Lunch is based on traffic. Serve lunch if you're located downtown where there's lots of business, shopping, and pedestrian traffic. Unless you're doing serious volume at lunch, the only reason for opening for lunch is to drive awareness of your restaurant.

> **POTENTIAL PITFALL**
>
> Serving lunch is good for the customer but not so good for the restaurateur. It requires the same effort and expense as dinner but is sold at a much lower rate, sometimes half the price. Furthermore, wine and cocktails—both high-profit items—are rarely ordered at lunch. Customers come in and order a chicken Caesar salad and an iced tea. They want to eat in an hour because they have to get back to work.

It can be difficult to get people to walk a block off the main avenue during the week. People have to leave work, get in their car, and drive to have this lunch experience. Your restaurant has to really have a draw. However, you can sometimes secure a lunch crowd on a specific afternoon. For example, Jody worked with an upscale steakhouse that, after much debate, instituted a special Friday lunch—the day the hedge fund guys cut out early and went to spend their money on expensive wines, raw oysters, and dry-aged porterhouse steaks.

The restaurant became a destination, like a club. It even had brown leather chairs around a big stone fireplace and a great copper-topped bar.

Saturday lunch and brunches, which are now popping up, sound better than they are. On Saturdays, people have busy schedules with their kids. If they do go out, it's going to be to a family-friendly place that likely serves pizza or burgers.

Next, you'll add Sunday brunch. Brunch can be a moneymaker. The biggest mistake restaurants make with brunch is they schedule the Saturday night staff on it. This crew is dragging, tired, and resentful, and that affects the energy of the restaurant. Always try to put a fresh crew on your Sunday brunch.

Depending on your restaurant concept and the market, you'll need to evaluate whether or not to open for lunch.

Service and Marketing

The early days of a restaurant can be bumpy in terms of the staff. They haven't had enough time to find the rhythm and routine to give guests a smooth experience. It's like learning to dance. It takes a little time and practice to stop counting and looking down at your feet.

Since staffing is integral to hospitality, we suggest you hire six shifts, so the same people work the same times on the same days. They'll know the restaurant's rhythm, tricks, and saves—how to rescue a moment from disaster. You want that, because one morning soon, you're going to wake up and find yourself short-staffed.

Say you trained eight solid servers and four fringe servers, who are less experienced and will gain experience working for you. Your opening was delayed, the restaurant has gotten a slow start, and your manager turned out to be toxic. You've lost four of your best servers.

Now you have only four good servers and four fringe servers. In this situation, switch to zone serving (one waiter per 3 to 4 tables) rather than man-on-man. Split the dining room in half and have your best waiters as the only point of contact with the tables. Even though you've lost four of your best people, your guests haven't been thrown into the abyss. Instead, each table is getting professional tableside service, and the four fringe servers are the runners.

You must have a back-up game plan to handle the unexpected situations that occur. Jody once had an entire kitchen crew, driving from Queens to Connecticut, have their van break down on the interstate. Luckily, he had other restaurants he could pull people from. That was the only reason he'd hired an entire kitchen of nonlocals. You should never hire a staff of people who live an hour away.

The point is that even when you have a brand-new staff and high hopes, you've got to be prepared for some not to show up. Restaurant people can be unreliable, so you need to have on-call staff who commit to being available if needed on a given day. They have to be available until 4:30 or 5 P.M., until you know everyone has shown up. They don't get paid for being on call. It's simply part of the job, but it always evens out. Someone will be on call for that staff member next time, and if he or she can't make their shift, they'll be covered.

Getting the Word Out

Should you hire a marketing firm to help you get the word out, and will a local or more prominent firm be more useful? Restaurant marketers are connected with and keep media lists of writers and bloggers who cover food and entertainment. When you hire a marketing company, think about what market you're trying to reach. Really put some thought into who you hire.

Don't hire a fancy big-name New York City marketing firm, hoping your little restaurant can compete with a big account such as an international hotel chain. They'll put a young new hire on the job with little to no experience, who'll end up targeting a wider market instead of your local one.

We suggest that new restaurateurs work with local marketing firms who'll know all the players—the writers, editors, bloggers, and other restaurateurs. Local press drives your sales, while national press simply brings awareness.

When you hire your local restaurant marketer, you're trading on her relationships. She arranges complimentary dinners at your restaurant, invites the press and bloggers, and acts as a liaison for you.

Handling Reviews

Don't pay attention to reviews. Jody doesn't read them; he has his staff read them and tell him if there's something that really needs to be brought to his attention. Otherwise, he doesn't want to hear about it.

Reviews can be painful. It's like someone's criticizing your kid. New restaurateurs can be victimized by bloggers and online sites like Yelp. It's not just your customers who are leaving comments. Every restaurant owner knows if you fire a server, her boyfriend will launch a toxic internet campaign. Commenters don't realize that people's livelihoods are at stake.

Seasoned professional reviewers bring experience and knowledge to their role. Reviewers typically are educated and objective; however, they can get too hung up on the nuance of the food.

A new restaurateur needs conviction. Don't respond to your online critics. Online comments have become a detriment to the industry. The reviewers have no credentials and their comments are anonymous. Everyone's a critic. It often gets too personal, and the restaurant loses when it attempts to defend itself.

Understanding Online Reviews

Linguistics professor Dan Jurafsky and colleagues conducted a revealing study of online restaurant reviews. They studied 900,000 Yelp reviews and discovered that people who write negative reviews often tell a story of trauma, one of being victimized at the hands of the restaurant and its employees.

When people write reviews of expensive places, they tend to use big words to show how well educated they are. People writing positive reviews about expensive restaurants tend to describe the sensory pleasures of dining, using words like "lust" and "orgasmic." They found that desserts are especially sexy, and that women wrote more positive remarks about desserts.

When people write reviews of less-expensive places, they're more likely to use vague language. Positive reviews are often framed as cravings or addictions, with drug references. Reviews of less-expensive places tended to mention cravings for fat, carbs, and chocolate rather than Brussels sprouts.

The study also found that online reviews are a vehicle for self-expression, whether as a victim, a sexy gourmand, or a chocolate addict.

Managing Online Reviews

You should coach your staff to be cognizant of the fact it's just dinner, and to keep things in perspective. You aren't changing your guests' lives; you're simply adding a moment to their lives. Ask your staff to consider this: did you really cause that much grief to this person's life that they rushed home and instead of walking the dog, they're banging out their negative emotions in an Urban Spoon review? What went so wrong as to bring this wrath? Usually, it's a pretty small thing such as the candle being unlit at their table or the owner said hello to the people at the next table but not to them.

If something goes wrong during an evening, your staff should be trained to correct it before the guest hits the parking lot—even if that means walking them to a taxi.

There are hundreds of things that can go wrong in a single night from the car valet being slow to the restroom paper towels running low. Now add whatever personal social dynamic exists among the diners, plus 8 ounces of alcohol, and shake.

There are so many moving parts in an organic experience. It leaves many opportunities for disappointment. But as long as your staff are genuine, honest, and make an effort to correct an issue then and there, there shouldn't be a toxic review. However, today anything goes.

Here's how your staff should deal with difficult customers:

- Most people want to be heard, so be patient, listen, and empathize with them.
- Permit guests to express themselves.
- Don't challenge guests or defend yourself to them.
- Recognize and give acknowledgment to their grievances.
- Explain to the guests that you understand their issue.
- Tell them how you will correct this issue.

Repeating the complainers' words back to them can help make them feel listened to: "I understand the foie gras was frozen in the center."

Offer to fix it: "May I bring you another?" It's understandable that after a taste of raw foie gras, the guest might not want another. Offer another appetizer in lieu at no charge.

Notice what's not on that list: apologizing. Apologizing weakens the restaurant, and it empowers the poison pen.

Sometimes your restaurant's concept won't set well with patrons because it's outside the box. Here are a couple of examples of how to handle such a complaint:

Scenario One:

Customer: "The music's too loud."

Manager: "Yes, it's—"

Customer: "What?"

Manager: (leans in, smiles, and speaks clearly) "Yes, this table is near a speaker. Let me see if I can relocate you to a quieter spot …"

or

Manager: "Yes, the place gets jumping about this hour … I know it can be a bit much, but permit me to give you my card. Next time, call me first and I'll arrange a table out of the fray. The dining room stays rather quiet until around 9:00 each night, so if you're looking for a great spot before the movie, you'll find it less noisy."

Scenario Two:

Guest: "It's too dark."

Server (smiling): "Ah yes, sometimes I go to dinner with my husband and we can't read the menu because the mood lighting can be too low .I'll be right back."

(Server returns with several candles on a tray and places them on the table in front of the customer.)

Server: "That should work better, or perhaps if you prefer, I can move you to a brighter spot, although you're sitting in our most requested cozy booth."

Remember, don't apologize and don't relent. If you lower the music or raise the lights at the request of a single guest, you've weakened your position and credibility. You think you've given the guest what they wanted, but you really just showed them how weak you are.

Online Presence

Your webpage, Facebook, Twitter, Instagram, and Pinterest are all good mediums for getting out the news about your restaurant. Remember to make use of visuals. A picture of a luscious-looking dish will be more enticing than a thousand descriptive words. But posting to these sites in a consistent and meaningful manner is often more than one restaurant owner can fit into a day, along with everything else. You must remember that social media contributes to word of mouth about your restaurant, so it's worth investing the time.

Adding to your operating costs by hiring someone to update these regularly isn't in the budget for many beginners. Your youthful staff, however, is a great resource for utilizing the latest technology and posting luscious promotional food pictures on social media.

The Least You Need to Know

- Your opening party is very important—it's the beginning of your marketing blitz.
- The opening party should send a message about your concept and your target audience.
- Invite some press and bloggers to a dinner to get some positive buzz out about your restaurant.
- Be prepared for glitches in the opening days so unexpected incidents don't affect your hospitality and service.

Running Your Restaurant

Now that your restaurant is open, you need to put the focus on keeping your guests comfortable and happy. In this part, we'll talk about how to build upon initial staff training to create a culture of hospitality. This culture must be extended to every guest from the minute they walk through the door to the moment they leave. That's what will keep people coming back to your restaurant.

You'll love the familial aspect of the restaurant business, and you'll learn fun ways to motivate your team, reward success, and discourage bad behavior. We'll also talk about running a safe restaurant—making sure your employees follow food safety protocols that prevent the spread of foodborne illnesses. Finally, we'll talk about how to grow your business. At this point, we come full circle. Your strong restaurant concept, executed by your team, under your watchful eye, following your systems … this is the formula for success.

CHAPTER 19

Fostering a Culture of Hospitality

The opening days and months of your restaurant are the most important. You're new in town and you want to make new friends. Just as in life, people will like your restaurant more if you treat them well. The restaurant business is actually as much about hospitality as it is about food.

In this chapter, we'll talk about contemporary standards of hospitality. We'll show you how you can easily adapt the steps of service to your restaurant. Managing a friendly and efficient staff takes a lot of practice.

In This Chapter

- Why making friends in the first 60 days is important
- Understanding the contemporary culture of hospitality
- Tailoring the steps of service to your restaurant
- Dealing with unexpected difficulties

Making New Friends

Making new friends is more important than making money during the first two months your restaurant is open. You can always go back and refine the efficiencies and yield a stronger profit, but you can't go back and change someone's opinion.

No one writes off a new restaurant because it has a high food cost. But if the service is indifferent or the food comes out of the kitchen too slowly, they might decide to pass on it. It's hard to win someone back after they've formed a negative opinion. Refining the economics can be addressed over the first several months to arrive at optimum performance if they aren't outrageously off the mark.

Getting your early guests to become advocates of your restaurant requires making them feel good about being there. Ultimately, you're cultivating a relationship with your guests, with the meal experience as the centerpiece.

The Basics of Hospitality

Restaurants aren't just in the food business; they're in the hospitality business. Chef-owners and foodies sometimes forget this. People go out to restaurants at night for a range of reasons. A patron could be an out-of-town visitor on business, who needs a quiet dinner by himself or who simply wants to chat about the city with the bartender. Guests could be a group of women getting together for a girls' night out away from husbands, or a family celebrating a birthday. Perhaps they're a discreet couple looking to have a romantic dinner to celebrate something special. Each of these groups has different needs.

Read Your Guests

You should ask your staff to read the guests and treat them accordingly. A business lunch will have a different, more formal tone, and the people at the table may not know each other well. It's especially important that the server determine and connect with the diner who is hosting the meal. It's he or she who will let the table know what to expect, whether wine will be ordered, and if they will order appetizers and entrées.

SMART MOVE

Many of your customers come to your restaurant to enjoy the hospitality engendered by the design. At home, they might live in clutter and chaos, but your restaurant—whether your concept dictates that it be cushy, cool, serene, or bustling—makes them step outside their ordinary lives and feel like they're living well.

Contemporary Culture of Hospitality

Restaurant culture has changed a lot over the last 25 years. Those old and stuffy days of being looked down upon by the staff are long gone. No award-winning meal is worth eating if you have to put up with arrogance. At the same time, our super-friendly, relaxed culture has led to a decline in standards of service. The well-intentioned "Hi, my name is Joni and I'll be your server" is cheesy in an independent restaurant.

The goal of your restaurant should be friendly and efficient service that exceeds customer expectations. Choose your FOH staff for their friendliness, skills, and experience. Good FOH people also have poise. You want them to build confidence in the guest from the moment the guest steps in the door. Your staff should recognize that they are brand ambassadors.

Hospitality Begins with the Host

Your host or hostess must make eye contact with customers and smile at them as they enter the door. That welcoming eye contact and smile, that initial connection, builds confidence. Your guests immediately know they'll be taken care of.

The second step in hospitality is efficiency. The hostess's quick communication with the manager enables her to lead the party to their table, or if there is a wait, to suggest they wait at the bar. The hostess should never apologize for the lack of tables. She must always present it in a positive way: "We're having a busy night. I could seat you at the bar right now, or you could have a drink at the bar and a table in the dining room will be ready in about 15 minutes or so."

The hostess should always offer choices to guests. It gives them the illusion of power. Making the guest *feel* in charge is the goal, but don't ever let the guest actually *be* in charge

Listening and being observant is the basis of hospitality. For example, is the candle on the guests' table lit? You'll get a lot of points for lighting it.

Size up your guests; who is the host of their group? You need to align your forces with them to make their night a success. Learn about your customers by watching and listening like a keen salesperson, anticipating their needs and quickly bringing anything they need.

Hospitality is the little things. It's helping a guest with an umbrella, hailing a cab, taking an interest in their children as they're leaving—these are the touches your guests will remember long after the memory of truffle risotto has faded. Making your guests realize you care and you're glad they're in your house is key to your success.

Teamwork and Hospitality

Many events need to connect in order to give the guest a great experience. Your staff needs to practice its moves during afternoon training. The goal is a seamless ensemble performance. The staff needs to interact in shorthand—a look, a gesture, a nod of the head—that lets one another know which guests need what now.

> **POTENTIAL PITFALL**
>
> Don't forget that training is ongoing. It's not something you do before you open your restaurant and then forget about. New staff will need to be integrated. Continue to practice mock service with the team to help build upon their knowledge.

Some high-end restaurants have taught their staff posture, bearing, and acting techniques. For the beginning restaurateur, the best you can do is to remind everyone to stand up straight and practice a calm demeanor. The calmness of a server and the assuredness of a manager are key in maintaining confidence in the guests. Have your staff role-play difficult guest situations during training. They should practice listening to the complaining customer and coordinate all of their forces to fix the problem.

Tailoring the Steps of Service

The steps of service should be genuine. Sure, you've rehearsed them many times—but now the curtain has risen. When it comes to the actual performance, there shouldn't be a sense of a rehearsed script imposed with a patient smile. An impatient server provokes nervousness and/or hostility in a guest. Here's a list of things waiters should never do with or in front of your guests:

- Talk about themselves.

- Mention their personal dietary restrictions.

- Sit down at the table with a guest, even if tired or invited to do so. When your customers know your staff is tired, it's hard for them to relax.

- Lean on an empty chair, a wall, a doorway, or any other person or structure while on duty or especially when speaking to the guest. They should always stand up straight.

- Text or talk on a cellphone on the floor. Staff should refrain from using cellphones in the kitchen unless it's an emergency.

- Turn the lights on when a guest is finishing dining.

- Ask a guest about a low tip.

- Follow a guest out onto the street.

Dealing with Difficulties

A difficult moment is just one single moment in one day. It's dinner ... it's not life. It's a good idea to remind your staff to put that moment in perspective. They must realize that they're entertaining and illuminating a moment in their customer's day. When customers leave your restaurant, you want them to feel satisfied and uplifted.

But you can't change your guests' lives, fix their marriages, or make them taller. Your staff is creating a moment, so they should make it count. When your customer craves that moment again, it transcends the food and becomes about the way you made them feel *being* in your restaurant, which is what matters most.

The same goes for your staff. This is just one day in their lives. They've got to keep a calm demeanor despite the irritations. Most of all, they've got to keep personal issues parked until after work. People can be unpleasant. Customers and waiters can behave inappropriately, but the good outweighs the bad. Encourage your team to defer to the customer, and blow off steam with the team later. Try to find the humor and the humanity in each situation.

It's the same with your staff; sometimes you hire a bad employee. It might be a manager with lots of experience but a negative attitude or a bad temper. It could be a waiter who argues with a customer, turns on the lights on guests in the dining room, or makes a guest cry. That person is a detriment to your business.

You need to know about the bad behavior, which means you need good communication with your entire staff. In addition, you need to get rid of that toxic staff member. Your employee manual and the job description he signed when hired both state that he must uphold the restaurant's high standards of hospitality and respect for guests and staff. Document his failure to meet those standards, and get him out of your restaurant.

Tracking Comps

Comps are part of the restaurant business. They must be tracked carefully to ensure they are not abused.

> **DEFINITION**
>
> The term **comps** is restaurant-speak for complimentary items, which can be free drinks, appetizers, and meals given to customers.

Too often comps are wasted gestures. They're best used as recognition, such as if you want to acknowledge a good regular customer. If a guest just spent a lot at dinner, you might send an after-dinner gesture to acknowledge your appreciation. You can acknowledge a regular by sending the chef's new appetizer to the table, or by delivering an after-dinner drink. Sending over a little bottle of Moscato d'Asti at the end of an Italian meal is so much more impressive and less expensive than, say, having the waiter ask the table what they would like as a free drink. That seems so cold and obligatory.

Dessert is too expensive to comp, yet many people do because it's at the end of the meal. Give guests an after-dinner digestive, such as a limoncello, instead.

Giving a buyback allowance to the bartenders allows them to be generous to regulars, and help create new ones, but it's all rung up and allocated in the budget. Buying their spouse a drink is allowed, as long as it's rung as well. Fellow industry chefs and managers expect to be comped, and it's reciprocal. None of them get out much, so they're unlikely to become regulars.

Points of Service

These are the points of service Jody developed and adapted to his restaurants, depending on the concept. He's known for having high wrap-around costs. Jody likes to give things to his guests. At Lolita Cocina and Tequila Bar, he served guests complimentary smoking grapefruit granitas with a splash of tequila. It started the evening off with the message that this isn't your ordinary Mexican restaurant. Bringing your customers a gift relaxes them. That act of hospitality is also a marketing device—it gets people talking.

Jody's points of service have 38 steps and lots of notes. Depending on your concept, your *steps of service* could be simpler or more detailed. Your concept is the prism.

> **DEFINITION**
>
> The **steps of service** are the blueprint for how your FOH staff will treat guests, from initial eye contact to final goodbye. You can adapt the steps of service according to your restaurant's concept.

The Steps of Service

1. The guests arrive and are greeted warmly and enthusiastically by the host/hostess.

2. The host/hostess confirms the seating arrangements.

3. The host/hostess leads the guests at a pace that is comfortable for them and *never rushes ahead*.

4. The host/hostess shows the guests to their table and pulls out chairs for the guests. (At least one chair should be pulled out to indicate the party should be seated.)

5. The host/hostess places menus *in the hands of* the seated guests.

6. The host/hostess completes the process of placing the table by leaning in and making eye contact with the guests and saying in a sincere tone, "It's nice to have you with us."

7. A copy of any special requests is given to the server, who follows up immediately.

8. The server greets guests, carrying warm bread. The server makes eye contact with the guests with a "Good evening. May I bring you a craft beer or cocktail from our bar?" The customers should use this opportunity to familiarize themselves with the menu.

   Note: Servers should never touch customers or squat by the table.

   Note: Anytime a table has more than eight guests, a server is required to get a helper to take the drink and food order from opposite sides to avoid painful waiting by the guests.

9. The server should try hard to figure out who is the host/hostess of the table and align himself or herself with that person.

10. The server repeats the drink order back as long as it doesn't seem too cumbersome.

11. After repeating the order, the server asks, "May I bring a bottle of water for the table?" followed by "Sparkling or still?"

    Note: Mineral water is to be replenished without asking up until the entrées have been served. At that point, the server should ask the table's host, "May I bring another bottle of water for the table?" Never refer to tap water as anything other than iced water.

    Iced water: no garnish

    Still water: lemon

    Sparkling water: lime

12. The server uses one of three predetermined signals to command the busboy to bring the water of choice to the table. The busboy is the person assigned to bring water to the table.

13. The server immediately brings the order to the POS. He should never stop at another table to take another order. However, he may pass by to clear and assess his station en route to the POS terminal. (Every pass through the restaurant should be meaningful.)

    Note: Orders must be *written down* and *repeated* back to the table in your menu terms. Servers should look for acknowledgment and eye contact from the guests before the order is placed in the POS. Once the complete order is entered into the POS, the server must audit the screen before they fire any food to ensure everything is entered correctly.

14. The busboy immediately approaches the table and pours water. He only asks which guest gets what if more than one type of water has been chosen.

Note: If six or more people are at the table, the server should suggest a shared appetizer to help shift the table as a group into the order process.

If they order too much food, feel free to mention this to them as it will be viewed as gracious. If they order too little, servers should try selling side dishes to round out the table.

Every waiter should be able to sell a second round of drinks to all the customers.

Servers should never refer to a quantity of anything consumed. Don't say, "May I bring you another/second/third glass of wine?" Simply say, "May I bring you a glass of merlot?" (or whatever they're drinking) or "May I refresh your drink?" This is a hard habit to break.

Remember servers should never sound as if they aren't sure the food is good or cooked correctly. They should only ask, "Is there anything else I may bring you?"

Servers should only recommend items they sincerely believe in, yet never say anything negative about a menu item when asked. Always find something good to say about every item. Don't say, "I'm not sure, I don't eat pork." Instead say, "My guests who have ordered it have really enjoyed it."

15. Servers fire the dishes as they want them to appear. They need to be aware of the kitchen flow and ticket times. For example, if there are no tickets in the window and the server fires food, he will get it very quickly. If the window is backed up, he should fire your dishes a bit earlier.

16. The server marks the table with appropriate service pieces, such as silverware, steak knives, lobster crackers, etc. and notes the time. Position numbers that indicate the placement of each guest at each specific table number will be used, unless it's an order "for the table" (seat 0).

17. The server/runner delivers the first courses, announcing the dishes in your menu terms, setting them in front of the guests by their position numbers.

Note: Announcing the dish is a proud statement. Don't mumble the name of the dish to patrons.

Note: if the menu is served family-style, the runner shouldn't announce the dish until it's set on the table. Otherwise, the person who ordered the dish thinks they are supposed to claim it and the rest of the table will feel awkward about digging in to have a try. All the guests will be waiting while one person has a large plate of food sitting in front of them.

18. The server must check back with the table within 3 to 5 minutes to check on appetizers, if any additional items are required, to refresh beverages, and to pre-bus the table. Afterwards, servers should cross off items at table on a dupe pad (order pads are called dupe pads in reference to the pre-POS days when order pads had carbon sheets to create copies) to check for any missing items.

19. Bus staff then clear and restock the tables.

20. It's the server's responsibility to reconcile what has been delivered to their table with what was ordered. He should know at all times what appetizers or entrées still need to be delivered.

21. When a table is enjoying a bottle of wine, the server should attempt to pour off the balance of the first bottle prior to the entrée being served. Or sell another cocktail, beer, etc., as the case may be. The gap between the course break of the appetizer and entrée is the best time to sell a second bottle of wine or round of drinks to the host of table.

22. The table is cleared and marked with clean silverware. Servers should also clear the plate "landing area," creating room for when the entrées are delivered to the table.

23. The server notes the time. Should a gap of more than 7 to 10 minutes occur between the clearing of the first course and the service of the second course, the server should notify the dining room manager.

24. The server or runner delivers the second courses, announcing each dish by the menu terms, and sets them in front of the guest according to position numbers.

25. Whenever possible, the server should be present when entrées are being delivered. If not, the server should check back with the table within 3 to 5 minutes to ensure that service is correct and ask if there is anything else he or she can bring to the table.

26. Once all guests have finished eating, the table can be cleared. It's only acceptable to remove one or more guest dishes before everyone is finished if the guest has pushed the plates aside, stacked them, or specifically requested they be removed.

27. The table should be reset with the coffee service set up and a teaspoon in front of each guest by the server. The goal is to remove everything after the entrées are finished.

28. The server presents the dessert menu to each guest and suggests a dessert and after-dinner coffee by name: "Lia's desserts are not to be missed." They should act proud when delivering the dessert menu.

29. When dessert is ordered, the server must write down and ring the order in the computer immediately.

30. The server delivers the coffee/drink order.

31. The server delivers the dessert order.

32. If no dessert is requested, the server collects the teaspoons and coffee service, and asks the table's host if there's anything else she can get for them. She then prints up the check and waits for a cue from the host to present it to table. Upon placing the check, the server is to make eye contact and give a sincere thank-you while telling them she will

be back for the check when the guests are ready. The server should present the check holder in such a manner (squared off in the corner of square tables) so that she can detect when it has been picked up and avoid checking back before anyone has had a chance to review it.

33. The server then processes the check.

34. The server presents the check back to the table, formally thanking the host by name if a credit card was used. (Guests should be thanked using Mr. or Ms. and their last name, unless they've introduced themselves by their first name.).

35. Unless a server is specifically told to keep the change, all cash transactions must be paid and cash returned in the check holder to the table. (Customers don't like feeling uncertain about whether they're receiving change.)

36. The server must retrieve the credit card voucher, if a credit card was used, before guests leave the building.

37. Guests are again thanked as they leave and *invited to return*: "Please come back and see us again."

38. The server makes sure the chairs are pushed in before anything else takes place. The team then resets the table.

Here are some additional ideas to remember:

- Always say, "Thank you, good night" to departing guests as they pass you, even if they were not your guests. Every employee of the restaurant should say goodbye, "Have a great night" or "Enjoy the rest of your evening," to guests as they pass by.

- The only phrase to use at the table when checking to see if plates, glasses, etc. can be cleared is "May I?" There is nothing offensive, rushed, or presumptuous about that sentence. It can be utilized for pouring more wine, water, etc.

- The goal isn't formality, but efficiency and friendliness. Think of yourself as hosts at a dinner party. Speak to your guests as if you're happy they are there, just as you would your friends.

- Read your guests! Four men having a business dinner will need different attention/ service than a couple on their first date, a 'meet the parents' table, and so on.

Always Meet and Exceed Expectations

The goal in your restaurant is to meet and exceed customer expectations. This begins with the owner. A restaurateur must have an instinct for taking care of and pleasing people. Your ability to care for and manage your staff and employees will create an environment in which staff will want to work and customers will want to dine.

The Least You Need to Know

- Your restaurant's hospitality is just as important as the food.
- Your host or hostess should make eye contact with your customers and welcome them with a smile.
- All staff members are responsible for the quality of your guests' experience.
- Adapt and practice the points of service to fit with your restaurant's concept.

CHAPTER 20

Running a Safe Restaurant

Food poisoning should not be on your restaurant's menu. Most foodborne illnesses are linked to restaurants, because many restaurant workers don't follow safe food handling practices. In this chapter, you'll learn how to run a clean and safe restaurant, with systems to prevent the spread and growth of dangerous bacteria that could make your guests ill. We'll also talk about steps you can take to prevent accidents and injuries in your restaurant.

Finally, we'll take a look at cleanliness and the open kitchen. Your BOH staff is on stage in an open kitchen; they must behave professionally, and they must look neat and clean and follow all health and safety codes.

In This Chapter

- How to avoid the most common health code infractions
- How to prevent accidents and injuries
- Safely storing, handling, and preparing food
- Keeping all your restaurant areas clean
- Considerations for an open kitchen

Health and Safety Codes

Safety in the restaurant means two things: taking care of your customers and taking care of your employees. If you take care of your employees, they can take better care of your customers. It comes full circle. Learning to spot risks and prevent accidents also reduces your risk of a business lawsuit.

As we discussed in Chapter 4, health and safety codes are administered locally. The U.S. Food and Drug Administration (FDA) has a Model Food Code, which is adapted by states, counties, and municipalities. (It's often stricter on the local level.)

The U.S. Occupational Safety and Health Administration (OSHA) state offices provide restaurants resources on safety. Contact your local health department and OSHA offices for all up-to-date information, available in English and Spanish.

Your local health department will inspect your restaurant a couple times per year, and cite any code violations. Fines, bad press, or worse—making people ill—are not what you want your restaurant to be known for. Bacteria that cause illness such as salmonellosis can be passed from raw chicken to the chopping block to cilantro to customer. To prevent bad things from happening, you must have systems in place for running a clean restaurant.

Training Staff in Health and Safety

Restaurant workers, especially managers, need better training, according to a recent study published by the School of Public Health at the University of Minnesota. In fact, 80 percent of the foodborne illnesses in the United States are caused by salmonella, E. coli, and norovirus. Furthermore, infected food workers caused 70 percent of the 20 million outbreaks of norovirus, according to a 2014 report by the Centers for Disease Control and Prevention (CDCP).

The study reported that many restaurant managers don't use basic methods of preventing the spread of food poisoning. Forty percent of the respondents said they didn't designate separate cutting boards for raw meat. Many reported that they pool raw eggs (one salmonella-infected egg can infect the whole bowl), and held them at temperatures above 40°F for four hours or more. That's a potential petri bowl of bacteria.

> **SMART MOVE**
>
> Raw eggs should be stored below 41°F and cooked to 160°F, according the Centers for Disease Control (CDC). Any utensil used to prepare the eggs—a whisk, fork, spoon, spatula—should be properly washed before being used in any other food.

In addition, the study noted how infrequently managers used thermometers to check the delivery temperature of leafy greens to make sure they were cool enough, and used a thermometer to ensure meats had been cooked to temperatures recommended by the FDA.

Daily discipline in following health and safety procedures is the key to running a clean and safe restaurant. Working clean and safe is a culture, and you've got to practice what you preach to promote this culture in your restaurant.

Personal Hygiene

Poor personal cleanliness is a common violation health department inspectors cite restaurants for, including such things as staff wearing dirty uniforms and having unrestrained hair.

Your employees' work contract should stipulate that they maintain a professional appearance and demeanor, practice good hygiene, and ensure all health and food safety practices are followed.

Staff must come to work clean, change into their clean uniforms, and see a manager to sign in. There are a couple ways to handle the uniforms. You can sometimes charge staff for the uniform and cleaning by deducting the cost from their paychecks. However, be sure to check your local labor laws. Often it's legal to charge an employee for a uniform only if it doesn't drop their salary below minimum wage.

Some restaurants let BOH employees wear their own uniforms, and provide aprons for wearing over the jackets. In this case, it must be strongly stipulated that the staff agree to wear only clean jackets. If they start their shift in a jacket with dirty sleeves, you should require them to put on a clean jacket, and designate them to the worst restaurant job status.

Traditional chef uniforms—white, long-sleeved, double-buttoned jackets—protect arms from burns and chests from heat. The jackets also absorb sweat, as it can get roaring hot in the kitchen. Sweat will be rolling down the faces and necks of your employees. Think of the traditional French chef wearing his front-knotted neckerchief to absorb sweat. Some chefs wear towels beneath their jackets.

Today, chefs' uniforms can be ordered in a range of colors or they can be customized. For a beginning restaurateur, we recommend going with the traditional white jacket and checked pants. It's the most practical and cost-effective. If you have an open kitchen, the choice of uniforms for the BOH is more important. You'll want to choose uniforms that underscore your concept, as they are visible to the public.

There are lots of choices in FOH uniforms these days. Uniforms strengthen the visual presentation of your concept, and add style. Remember, staff members wear a uniform to let the guests know they're staff. If it's a family-friendly breakfast and lunch restaurant, it fits to have all the FOH wearing blue gingham shirts. But if it's a high-end steakhouse, you don't want your bartenders looking like they work on Wall Street when they're serving the real Wall Street crowd. You also want to ensure that all staff wear slip-resistant shoes.

Black pants and a white shirt is a clean, practical look for FOH staff, and there are a lot of options today for more fitted, attractive styles. You can find lots of pictures of classic and trendy styles online and in your local restaurant supply store.

Hair

Kitchen workers must cover their heads and restrain their hair. Men with beards must wear beard guards. Always keep a box of disposable beard guards by the back door, so the bearded can put one on as soon as they enter. With many trendy young people sporting big, full, mountain man beards these days, you'll need a supply of beard guards.

> **POTENTIAL PITFALL**
>
> Some health codes stipulate that employees who touch cash should not touch food. Just think how many people may have touched the money, and how many of them may not have washed their hands. Gloves that touch money and then touch food are no better than bare hands.

Jody's kitchen workers were complaining about having to wear hats in the kitchen. Everyone was wearing caps, and caps can hold in the heat and make the head hot. So Jody told them they could wear any kind of hat they wanted, as long as it covered their heads and was a hat.

The next day, the restaurant's kitchen was filled with all types of hats: cowboy hats, surgeon's caps, baseball caps, berets, and woven panama hats. Everyone was smiling.

You could do the same thing with bandanas. Tell your BOH staff they can add any kind of bandana to their outfit. Let them express themselves in small ways; it makes your restaurant a more enjoyable place for people to work.

Hand-Washing 101

Coming to work properly groomed means that your staff arrives with clean hands. They should scrub under their nails with a nailbrush before they arrive at the restaurant. After they change into their uniforms, the first step in their routine is to wash their hands.

Demonstrate the proper hand-washing technique to all employees. Show them how to use soap and hot water, and dry their hands and properly dispose of paper towels. Also, jewelry such as rings, bracelets, and necklaces shouldn't be worn when preparing food.

Everyone's familiar with the signs that say, "Employees Must Wash Hands Before Returning to Work." Proper hand-washing will prevent the spread of E. coli, a bacterium that lives in the guts of humans and causes cramps, diarrhea, fever, and vomiting. Most people recover, but it can send children, the elderly, and people with weak immune systems to the hospital. You don't want your restaurant known for that!

Door handles can be filthy, germ-laden places. They should be at the top of your restaurant's cleaning checklist, especially in bathrooms. Over the course of a night, customers who don't wash their hands after using the toilet can spread germs to the door handles. When a separate staff washroom isn't possible, germs could be passed from customer to employees via the door handles. We suggest using a paper towel to grab the door handle to prevent the spread of germs.

SMART MOVE

If you participate in a special event offsite, such as a charity event where you're offering taste samples of your restaurant's food, the health department will have another set of requirements and they'll inspect all the vendors before the event begins. Often they require a hand-washing station. You can rig one up with a 5-gallon thermos with a spigot, or rent one.

Employee Health

Sick employees should not work around food. They should be sent home or at least given work that doesn't put them in contact with prepared foods. But really, they should not be in your restaurant at all. You don't want them to infect the rest of your team or the guests.

Cross Contamination

Raw meats and food can spread bacteria and viruses if they're not properly stored and handled. Chopping boards must be designated for raw meats only, and cooked meats must not be returned to a container that has held raw meats. Raw or finished products, such as salads or side dishes, also must not come in contact with raw meats or seafood or the boards they've been placed on.

One of the most pervasive infractions cited by the health department inspector is storing raw foods above cooked foods on the walk-in shelves. Raw blood and meat juices can drip or leak onto whatever is stored below. This is easily remedied with some simple systems changes. If you have two walk-in refrigerators, keep your proteins and vegetables in separate walk-ins. Keep seafood in sturdy plastic tubs with lids to prevent any unintended dripping of liquids. If you have only one walk-in fridge, keep meats on the lowest shelf.

Putting things where they belong is something you've got to drum into your staff. And in the heat of the moment on a sudden unexpectedly busy night, things in the walk-in can get jumbled. That's why chefs should do a nightly inventory of the proteins and a basic restoration of order.

Prepped meats and fish that will be used for the evening are kept in reach-in refrigerated drawers at each cooking station. Every shift starts with clean and patted-dry meat in fresh containers.

To prevent cross contamination:

- Don't let raw chicken or any surface it touches come in contact with ready to eat (RTE) products.

- Designate chopping boards according to use by color and have your prep cook prepare cuts of meat in advance of service, using safe practices.

- After raw chicken has been butchered or prepared on its designated chopping board, the board must be washed with soap and hot water, rinsed, and then sanitized using a chlorine solution, approved by the FDA and EPA.

- Bacteria are killed by cooking. Use a thermometer to determine whether meats have reached proper temperatures.

Preventing Foodborne Illness

Your chefs, cooks, kitchen staff, and managers must be trained in the dangers of foodborne illness and how to prevent it. The bacteria that cause food poisoning include the following:

- Salmonella: The most common form of food poisoning in the United States, it's caused most frequently by raw and undercooked chicken and eggs. This bacteria is killed by cooking and through pasteurization.

- E. coli: A harmful strain of this bacteria, which lives in the intestines of humans and animals, can cause severe bloody diarrhea. The most common cause is raw or undercooked meat, such as hamburgers.

- Norovirus: Made famous by outbreaks on cruise ships, this form of gastroenteritis can be passed directly from an infected food preparer to food or to another person.

- Listeria: A bacteria that can grow in cold temperatures, and can infect delicatessen meats, hot dogs, soft cheeses, pates, and raw sprouts. Recalls of listeria-infected products hit the news every year or so. Food poisoning from listeria causes fevers and stiff necks.

- Campylobacter: One of the most common causes of food poisoning is caused by contact with or eating raw or undercooked poultry. Cases tend to be isolated rather than widespread.

Chicken is a particular concern in the restaurant; it can carry salmonella, which is bacteria found in the guts of animals, especially poultry and reptiles. In the United States, poultry is the number one food associated with deaths caused by foodborne illness. When you think about how universally popular chicken has become and how often it appears on restaurant menus, you get an idea of how important it is to take precautions not to infect your customers with it. Salmonella can contaminate meat, milk, and eggs, or end up in the parsley because your prep chef didn't wash his hands after he cut up the raw chicken.

Salmonellosis causes upset stomach, vomiting, diarrhea, and fever lasting four to seven days. It's more dangerous for older and younger people and those with impaired immune systems. The bacteria is killed by cooking. The USDA recommends that chicken reach an internal temperature of 165°F to kill any harmful bacteria. Salmonella is usually found on the exterior of meat, but the cavity of a chicken can harbor the bacteria, too.

E. coli is a concern for restaurants serving burgers rare or medium rare. In 2014, an E. coli breakout that hospitalized 12 people was traced to a beef packaging plant that provided ground meat to, among other pubs and steakhouse, a place specializing in burgers cooked to 145°F degrees. The Centers for Disease Control recommends cooking burgers to an internal temperature of 160°F degrees.

E. coli can also contaminate vegetables, soft cheeses, apple cider, and unpasteurized milk. Washing fruits and vegetables thoroughly before using can help prevent E. coli. Cooking, however, is the only sure way to kill the bacteria.

Recommended Temperatures for Meat

Product	USDA Recommended Internal Temp	Lower Temp with Precautions
Steaks, roasts, and chops	145°F	130°F for medium rare as long as all of the exterior is seared
Ground meat	160°F	Some foodies believe 145°F is the perfect temperature for a burger. WARNING: E. coli is not killed at that temperature.
Chicken (roast)	165°F	Play it safe and cook it to 165°F
Chicken (breast filet)	160°F	160°F

Health departments require that restaurants post warnings about the dangers of eating raw or undercooked meats, seafood, and eggs. But the truth is there are plenty of customers who'll eat raw oysters, fish, and beef dangers be darned, because they like the way they taste. Plenty of people order their meat rare, and many chefs do, too.

Many restaurateurs and chefs pride themselves on sourcing excellent ingredients, and there's a certain disdain for the customer who wants his burger or steak *cremated* or *killed*.

> 📖 **DEFINITION**
>
> **Cremated** and **killed** is kitchen slang for well-done meats. The terms indicate a chef's feelings about what the customer is asking for.

Vermin

The presence of vermin is another frequently cited health code violation. Vermin-proof your restaurant by using wire mesh to fill any holes where mice or rats can enter. Store food in food-safe plastic containers with lids. Have an exterminator visit regularly to inspect and treat as needed. You can also set out glue traps or poison. The main point is to be proactive. If you see any signs of vermin, droppings, or bug casings, get on it right away. Don't put it off, because it's a problem that can multiply overnight. If you see meal moths fluttering through your kitchen, find the source and get rid of it. Remove the food source and their entry points.

Safety Precautions

When you get your business license, you'll receive a poster of the employee bill of rights. Employees have the right to a safe work environment. But restaurant kitchens can rank high for injuries, especially for adolescent workers, according to the National Institute for Occupational Safety and Health (NIOSH). To prevent occupational injuries, special rules may apply for people under the age of 18 as to what types of work they're allowed to do and what equipment they are and aren't allowed to operate.

Know your local labor laws. Your state Occupational Health and Safety Administration (OSHA) can provide more materials on how to maintain a safe restaurant. They often offer guidelines in Spanish, too.

OSHA provides information on how to prevent injuries from:

Water and steam burns

Hot oil burns

Flames

Knives

Equipment and machinery

Cold and freezer storage units

Lifting and carrying

Slips and falls

Ladders

Chemicals

For instance, walk-in refrigerators and freezers must have interior latch releases and lighting. Anyone who is working in a cold environment should dress warmly with the appropriate footwear and protective gear to execute their jobs.

Teach your staff how to lift heavy boxes of food using their legs so they don't strain their backs. Teach them effective techniques for lifting an object together.

Use high-friction mats in wet areas, and have all staff wear non-slip shoes.

SMART MOVE

In the kitchen, cooks use the shorthand "behind you" to let others know they're there or moving past. It prevents collisions, spills, and burns. Train your cooks to say it loudly. It's like honking the car horn as a warning. For example, when someone has a pot of water in their hands, train them to say, "hot behind you" so staff is aware of the potential danger lurking near. Restaurateurs who aren't familiar with the kitchen should get in the habit of saying it, too.

Knives should be kept well sharpened, because dull knives are dangerous. A good test of a chef is how well he sharpens a knife. But staff must practice safe knife skills, and always be aware. Knives should never be buried under meat or produce; that's an injury waiting to happen. When walking with a knife, your staff should keep the blade facing downward and toward themselves rather than pointing upward and facing others.

Preventing Burns

Cooks quickly learn to stand back and let the initial burst of heat dissipate before reaching into an oven. That initial blast can make you feel like you've had a face peel.

When using wine or alcohol to deglaze a pan, always pour it from a measuring cup rather than directly from the bottle. The flames on a kitchen stove can ignite a bottle, turning it into a fireball.

Use teams of two to lift heavy pots filled with liquids. In addition, always empty the frying oil after it has cooled.

Worker Violence

Worker violence is another common source of injuries in restaurants. You should always employ a management style that fosters teamwork and a sense of family; but remember this is a high-pressure and volatile business. And even families get into fights sometimes, and things can spiral out of control.

Violence must be stopped immediately. The parties must be separated and at least one of them sent home to cool off. Jody doesn't allow staff to be fired in the heat of the moment. He tells them they'll talk about it the next day. If someone needs to be fired, that's when Jody or a manager will tell them. (We'll talk more about managing your staff in the next chapter.)

Heat Exhaustion

How hot does it get in the kitchen? So hot even big strong dudes stagger away from a blazing hot grill, lean on the back door and walk out into the night never to be seen again.

Keep your kitchen staff well hydrated; make sure everyone begins their shift with a big bottle of water. When you get slammed, do your best to keep your team cool. Your grill guy works in the hottest spot in the kitchen. If it's getting too hot, have your sous chef take his place at the grill and let him cool down for a couple of minutes with a cold towel. There's no point in anyone on your staff working themselves into a state of heat exhaustion.

In addition, keep an emergency first aid cabinet well stocked with antiseptics and bandages to dress cuts, scrapes, and burns so they can continue to work. Any serious cuts and burns must be treated by a doctor.

> **POTENTIAL PITFALL**
>
> Cleaning and sanitizing solutions come in concentrated form and need to be diluted. These chemicals can splash in workers' eyes or burn their skin. Have safety goggles and heavy gloves available that are appropriate for any chemicals the staff uses, and make sure they wear them. Keep an emergency eyewash in your first aid kit just in case.

Keeping It Clean

Your local health codes may stipulate how often surfaces that come in contact with food and equipment should be cleaned. They may specify the types of cleaners, sanitizers, and degreasers that can be used.

All your cooks should be trained to keep their work areas clean. Wiping down their stations should be instinctive. Don't allow cooks to wipe debris from their workstation onto the floor; enough stuff will fall or drip onto the floor while they're working. At the end of the dinner shift, the kitchen floor is a mess. In fact, on busy nights someone might need to sweep the floor during a lull in the action.

At the end of every night, after all the cooks have cleaned up their stations and wrapped leftover mise en place in plastic, labeled it, and stored it in the walk-in, they can help clean the stoves, grill, and fryer. Two people should remove the heavy mats so the floors can be swept. The floors then are washed and hosed down, and the floor drains cleaned.

Have a cleaning regimen in place and use your checklists to monitor the work. (You can find the checklists in Appendix D.) When you come in the next morning, the kitchen is ready for the day.

Bar Safety

Your staff needs to learn to be safe behind the bar as well. The ice machine is where problems often happen. Train all staff to use the metal ice scoop when filling a glass or bucket. Using glass or plastic is not allowed—they can chip into the ice and end up in a customer's drink. Using a glass instead of a scoop also makes it all too easy for a hand to come into contact with the ice. The staff also needs to be trained to return the scoop to its proper place.

Train staff to use separate towels for wiping down the bar and wiping glasses, and store the towels in separate places. Your health department might specify what types of cleaners and sanitizers must be used. In addition, they will probably have rules for how often garnish-cutting surfaces must be cleaned and sanitized, and how garnishes must be stored.

The most unsanitary thing your bartender can do is lick a finger before picking up a napkin. There are a lot of tricks for fanning out beverage napkins, which makes it easier for staff and customers to pick up one at a time.

Open Kitchens

Good habits and good behavior are all the more important if your restaurant has an open kitchen. The open kitchen has become a stage for showing off to the public how wonderful and sanitary restaurant kitchens are. But sometimes chefs forget they're on a stage. All it takes is for a customer to glance at a pair of cooking tongs tucked under an armpit, a sweaty brow looming above a boiling pot, or a chef inappropriately adjusting his attire to dispel all the magic of your restaurant. Train your staff to be aware of their surroundings and their work habits, and you won't have these issues.

The Least You Need to Know

- Kitchen staff and restaurant managers need to be trained in safe kitchen practices that can prevent the spread of foodborne illnesses.
- Use the resources provided by regulatory agencies such as the CDC, USDA, and OSHA for multilingual guidelines for preventing illness and injury in restaurants.
- Be proactive in addressing safety and health issues to avoid the bad publicity of health code violations.
- Establish a nightly cleaning routine for your restaurant.
- An open kitchen requires exemplary behavior from your staff.

CHAPTER 21

Managing and Training Your Employees

Training should be an ongoing process in restaurant work. It's an essential element of effective management. In this chapter, we'll talk about how to train and manage your restaurant staff.

When you open a new restaurant, start by hiring managers and chefs. We'll discuss the importance of training them first, to get them thoroughly prepared for executing your concept and using your systems, before you allow them to train the staff who will work beneath them. We'll show you training exercises and management techniques that create a team spirit and reduce staff turnover.

In This Chapter

* Why training is the foundation of effective management
* Training exercises for your staff
* How to motivate your staff by making work fun
* Ways to reduce employee turnover

Training Staff

Jody has taken many classes in hotel and restaurant schools and he's learned something important. Like many restaurant people, he learns better on his feet, watching and doing, rather than sitting in a chair listening to someone talk. As a manager, he discovered that if you sit a bunch of restaurant people in a room and lecture them, they'll all shake their heads yes, and then when you unleash them on your restaurant, you'll be shaking your head no.

So to engage your staff, use a combination of classroom and hands-on training. In the final weeks before you open your restaurant, focus on basic training. Remember, you've built this training into your budget. At this point, your staff is still working at their current jobs. Let them come by for training during the afternoon hours when the restaurant is quiet, from 3:00 to 4:00 P.M., and pay them for that time.

Certification

Jody calls training "certification." Front of the house (FOH) staff must get certified in the basics of their jobs to earn permission to be on the *floor.*

 **DEFINITION**

> The **floor** refers to the restaurant's public spaces: the dining room, bar, and outdoor seating.

Set up stations in the restaurant, each devoted to an aspect of the job—knowing the table and position numbers, the steps of service, basic health codes, and how to use the POS system.

The trainees are given a lesson at each station, and afterward they're tested. If they pass the test, they're certified. If they don't pass the test, they have to retake the lesson before trying certification again. Every member of the front of the house staff should be able to tell you the location of Position 4 at Table 3. FOH staff must have a general overview of the restaurant, its concept, and the food. The focus at this point is the basics. We'll build upon this knowledge in the days to come.

Trailing

Most new restaurant staff is trained by *trailing,* though Jody doesn't find this an effective way to train. Training for new staff should take place from 3 to 4 in the afternoon and it should be with the owner or manager directly. Trailing or shadowing should be done only as part of training in order to get the rhythm, the flow of movement.

 **DEFINITION**

Trailing is a restaurant term for a potential employee following an experienced staff member around the restaurant and being trained by watching him or her do job. It's also called "shadowing."

One of the first assignments Jody gives new staff, in the training period before the restaurant has opened, and there's still a little debris, dust, and clutter from the renovation, is to have them set up the dining room. That's all he says; he purposely leaves the assignment ambiguous, and then watches the group exercise unfold. Who is going to take the time to find a ladder and dust the ceiling fan? Who is cleaning windows? Who is setting the table with dirty forks? Who is in the corner texting? An assignment like this lets Jody know what he's got going for him, the staff members with initiative and an eye for detail, the natural leaders, and worker-bee team members—and what he's up against. Then the staff does a mock service using the steps discussed in Chapter 19.

During the mock service you should have the staff wait on each other. That's when you'll catch things like a waiter opening a wine bottle by putting it between his legs. Teach them the way wine is served in your restaurant. Then have them wait on you, and do it over and over until it's like tying a shoe. You want it to be like dancing—when you know the steps so well you don't have to look at your feet. Service should look effortless.

Once your staff knows all the components, the restaurant will start to find its rhythm. The staff will start to come to together as a team, and that's important. Jody has put together all-stars and watched mock service become a disaster. They hadn't learned each other's moves. Opening a new restaurant can be chaotic and nerve-wracking. Think about it: you've got 24 new people in a new facility with a new menu, and you're about to put on a performance.

SMART MOVE

People want to belong to the best team. Equality in performance levels is an important aspect of building a winning team.

Wine Training

During the initial training, some restaurateurs will bring in an expert to talk to staff about wine, craft beer, or distilled spirits. Jody doesn't do that at this critical time. People can only accumulate so much information, especially when it's something new to them. Instead of jamming in more information that they're likely not going to remember, focus on what's important: the steps of service, knowing the tables and position numbers, and knowing the restaurant specializes in indigenous Southwestern cuisine.

As for knowing whether the cherry flavors and tannins of the pinot noir play well with the seared veal chop … that's not important now. If you want your servers to upsell the pinot noir by mentioning its cherry notes, tell them that in the staff's daily pre-service meeting.

When your staff is ready and comfortable with the basics, add some refinement to the training. Bringing in the wine expert can be a perk, but don't throw everything at them at once. Create a training regimen that encourages everyone to bond and feel part of the restaurant. The group exercises do that.

> **POTENTIAL PITFALL**
>
> Well-trained restaurant staff who work as a team will self-govern. If a new staff member is hired and isn't pulling his or her weight, watch out! The team might set on that person like a pack of wolves.

Dining Room Demeanor

Your manager, hostess, waitress, and bartenders are your sales team, and you must teach them never to let the customer see them sweat or show tension or anger. The guests are here to relax and enjoy. Anger and appetite don't mix.

Always smile. Always be in control. If something goes wrong, if a guest is unhappy, the staff lets the manager know. If a guest tells a manager about a problem, he'll say, "Let me find out about that for you." Don't get rattled. If you get rattled, people will be tense and start to watch you instead of enjoying the hospitality. Complaints are an opportunity to earn great word of mouth for how you resolved a problem, and how gracious and hospitable you and your staff were.

Jody tells his staff to think about an airplane pilot. If you saw him come running out of the cockpit looking perplexed and worried, you would immediately lose confidence. Your restaurant guests should never lose confidence.

> **SMART MOVE**
>
> During training sessions, teach your staff how to deal with difficult guests. Give them a script and role play until their responses are polite, positive, and solution-oriented.

Many of Jody's restaurants have had a loose and sexy feel. But to create that illusion, the back of the house ran like the Marines. However, the customers never had a hint of the demanding regimen. Remember, customers will pick up on any tension staff members bring into the dining room.

Dress Rehearsal: The Friends & Family Meal

In advance of the opening date, a restaurant hosts a *friends & family* dinner or series of dinners to practice a real-time meal service and fine-tune the flow.

> **DEFINITION**
>
> **Friends & family** is the name for a dress rehearsal meal before the restaurant officially opens. The guest list is made up of ... you've got it, friends and family.

The dinner is a complete run-through of dinner service. Think of it as a dress rehearsal before a friendly audience. A lot of people think the friends & family meal is about testing the food, so a lot of your guests will give you their opinions. But friends & family meals are more about the service than the food. You've blueprinted your menu way earlier in the process.

Some famous restaurateurs denounce friends & family night as a waste of money, feeding people for free. Eschewing a friends & family dinner might work for some, but if you're a first-time restaurant owner, we highly recommend having a friends & family dinner, and building that cost into your capital budget. The friends & family dinners can also serve as great opening word-of-mouth marketing, a way to get a buzz going. Focus on the hospitality aspects of the meal. Use this experience to make an excellent impression.

If you've planned your restaurant carefully, only tweaks will be needed after the friends & family meal. And people will spread the word about how great your place is. However, if the night goes dreadfully wrong, at least with friends and family you can say, "Okay, folks, we're going to start this evening all over. Everyone please have another glass of wine, and we're sending out more appetizers."

Compare this to the account we read on a blog. The guy opening a restaurant decided not to have a friends & family dinner for his new restaurant. He hired his staff 24 hours before the restaurant officially opened to the public. He gave them 10 minutes of training on the POS and table positions. Halfway through the opening dinner service the health department came in and shut down the kitchen for an hour as guests squeezed into tables. It was chaos. That's the impression his restaurant made on opening day. What do you think the paying guests talked about the next day? That's tough to recover from.

Motivating Your Employees

Cash is the main motivator in the restaurant business. Restaurant people work hard, get sweaty, and leave with a fist full of dollars. So make sure you *tip-out* the staff in cash every night.

> **DEFINITION**
>
> To **tip-out** means to reconcile credit card receipts against customer tips, and pay/ distribute that money to the servers and front of the house staff in cash. Because so few customers pay in cash these days, restaurateurs must bring in cash to the restaurant to tip-out.

Don't make your staff wait until the end of the week. Give them the cash each night. They want to go out and have fun with their friends. Cash on the barrel and at the end of the night is the way to control this crowd.

When Jody worked in corporate restaurants, he chafed under all the rules and regulations. In running his own restaurants (where he employs many of the systems learned in corporate restaurants), he learned from managing restaurant folk that they don't respond well to environments that are overly corporate. Restaurant work is hard and gritty. Owners and managers have to find ways to make the staff enjoy that work.

Scheduling can be used to keep your staff happy. Don't let your manager fiddle with the schedule every week. Lock in a schedule to let each staff member have specific days off every week, so they can make plans with their friends. A constantly changing schedule tortures the staff.

Jody doesn't like merit and demerit systems. Managers sending people home to punish them if they come in late is self-defeating. Send someone home, and then you don't have enough coverage. What do you win? That's why Jody tries to find ways to give dirty work to people who screw up and give privileges to those who shine.

One thing Jody did at his restaurant Bleu was to keep a fishbowl filled with scraps of paper that had all the worst jobs in the restaurant printed on them. And whoever screwed up the most—like if someone dropped a tray of glasses—they'd have to pull a piece of paper out of the fishbowl. Everyone would gather around to see what crummy job he or she pulled—like clearing out the employee's lockers. It was a fun way to reinforce good behavior.

Jody's team also rewarded the employee of the week, the person the whole staff decided had outperformed everyone else. That person got to sit in the dining room while everyone else was setting up, and could order anything from the menu. They got to sit there like a lord while the others worked and served him or her. The staff loved this. It was fun, and it had the effect of peers acknowledging peers.

Ultimately, showing that you care for your staff will reinforce good behavior. Be respectful; don't reprimand bad behavior in front of other staff members. Remember that staff often already know they did something wrong. Give them an out if it's a minor offense.

When a staff member does something really wrong, like questioning a customer about a tip or repeatedly not doing what he or she should have done, we suspend them for one week. They might say, "Oh, cool—I'm going skiing." And then they realize they've just lost a week of income.

When they come back, they will have learned the value of working at your restaurant. And you've shown you've got bullets in your gun. If you just wave it around, giving demerits, you're impotent.

Drug Testing

Drug testing of restaurant employees may be required in corporate restaurants. They may require a pre-hire urine test and random testing throughout the year. In that environment, employees who have an accident are immediately tested for drug use. Corporations often require drug testing to protect themselves from lawsuits.

Jody doesn't do drug testing, and neither do a lot of independent restaurant owner veterans. A chef told us a story about what happened at the yacht club where he was working. He was putting out an updated (less fried) New England Seafood menu, when the board of directors voted in a new rule: all club employees had to have drug tests. "I lost my best guys," he said. Truth be told, drug testing can deplete the talent pool. (Good thing they didn't require drug testing of potential club members!)

Terminating Employees

At Jody's restaurants, only the manager can fire people. Firing is a big deal, and you have to follow a certain procedure. You can't allow your chef or any other staff member to terminate someone. There's too much potential liability.

If an action is egregious, Jody's policy is that the employee must be sent home immediately. They're told they will have to meet with the owner before being permitted to return.. They leave thinking they still have a job. You've put them in a calm place. You don't want people stomping out shouting, fighting, or breaking things.

Your restaurant's employee operations manual will outline the behavior and actions that are unacceptable in your restaurant, and the consequences of those actions. Such offenses could include:

- Serving alcohol to minors

- Stealing

- Showing a lack of respect to customers and/or fellow employees

- Making derogatory remarks about the restaurant to customers

- Coming to work intoxicated

You should keep your employee manual short and sweet so people will actually read it. Use bullets and lots of white space to make it easy to read.

> **SMART MOVE**
>
> Customize your employee operations manual. Use it to underscore your core value of providing excellent hospitality. Let your staff know your restaurant's mission is to be profitable *and* a positive atmosphere where everyone—customers, co-workers, and management—is treated and spoken to with courtesy.

Dealing with Turnover

Jody has had managers who've worked with him a long time go off to start their own restaurants. They might team up with a chef or bartender who's been working for him, too. All that time Jody nurtured their careers … and now it's as if they're graduating or leaving home. At that point, the owner's job is to help them leave honorably and on good terms.

Sometimes people forget that the way you leave a job says more about you than the way you start it. So a restaurateur must work through the reality of turnover. Turnover is high with servers and bartenders. Kitchen staff and management can be long-term if your restaurant is well run and inspiring. Don't get upset when long-time staff moves on. Over the years, Jody has noticed something. They often come back—after they get a good taste of the complexities of running their own restaurant.

Creating a Family

Creating a restaurant family of staff is a glorious pinnacle when it can be achieved. Yet it can't be forced, and some restaurants never get there no matter how successful they are. The most effective way to nurture this closeness is by orchestrating the staff in a way that forces them to rely upon one another. Be fair and try to do what's best for the entire family. But also be considerate of the staff's personal lives, like letting a staff member out early to take care of personal or family matters.

Everyone needs each other to perform, because the team constantly depends on one another. The host greets the customers, then passes them to the bartender, who then passes them back to the host, who delivers them to the server, who needs the busser to assist. The chef relies upon his crew and the runners and servers. Finally, it's back to the host for the customers' exit. There are lots of opportunities to drop the ball, but when everyone is focused, the effort can be seamless. Their collective success is based upon "one for all and all for one."

Jody has also found that socializing strengthens the staff family bond. He throws great picnics at his house, where the staff join together to grill, relax, and play (adult slip 'n' slides). It develops their cohesiveness as a group. Travel is another inspiration. Jody has taken key staff on trips to experience cultures that inspired his restaurants—China, Tuscany, Paris, and Morocco. They've been great investments in motivating and bonding the restaurant family.

A new restaurateur won't have the time or budget for foreign trips, but depending on your restaurant concept, you can devise other motivational outings. Visit a local farm that provides your produce, eat dinner at another hot restaurant, or take a trip that will educate and inspire your staff.

The Least You Need to Know

- Train your staff in the basics and make sure they know the system cold before you unleash them on your customers.
- Combat staff turnover by making your restaurant a great place to work.
- Never fire staff in the heat of the moment. Minimize potential trouble by having the staff member leave immediately, and tell them they must meet with the owner the next day to be permitted to return to their job.
- Teach your staff to keep a calm demeanor and be solution-oriented when dealing with customer complaints.

CHAPTER 222

Growing Your Business

Now that your restaurant is open and running successfully, we're going to talk about growing your business. If you've followed the suggestions throughout this book, you've had a strong opening. Now you want to keep your first customers coming back, and bring in their friends and friends of friends.

In this chapter, we'll talk about how you can use word-of-mouth marketing, event marketing, and social media to keep your restaurant in the public eye. We'll also talk about how to handle your success, and the best ways to manage those long waiting lines. Getting more people into your restaurant on busy evenings is the goal, and hospitality is the key.

In This Chapter

- Traditional restaurant marketing practices
- Why word of mouth is the best kind of marketing
- How event marketing can work for you
- Using social media to promote your concept
- Handling success and managing wait lines

Growing Your Business

Take off like a rocket and keep climbing. For the first 60 days, focus on making friends rather than money. You can always fix a food cost overage or adjust your labor schedule later, but you can't change consumer opinion easily when their first opinion of your restaurant isn't a great one.

When your restaurant opens and becomes the place everyone wants to go, it's even more important to be good to your waiting guests and those who can't get a seat. Success is no excuse for arrogance. Your focus at this point should be on hospitality.

Marketing Milestones

There are a series of marketing milestones by which you can gauge your success. The major milestones are three months, six months, and nine months.

Three months' success is almost assured by virtue of curiosity in the marketplace. That's great, right? Well, yes, but don't mistake this wave of business as any measure of long-term success. Think of it as an introduction, an opportunity percolating, a getting-to-know-each-other experience for your guests.

The six months milestone will tell you if the folks who came earlier came back and brought along their friends. Everyone loves to turn their friends on to new discoveries, so seeing guests show off their newest restaurant find is a good sign. When those friends come back with their friends, you're off to a great start.

The nine months milestone is when the first economic reality takes hold. A new business can make it through its first three quarters coasting on initial credit terms, constantly rationalizing and making excuses, and hoping things will work out the way you want them to. The nine-month window is usually the face-to-face meeting with economic reality. It's the time when you learn whether or not your restaurant is really successful.

Traditional Marketing

Jody has never known traditional marketing to work—hiring someone to send out press releases or eblasts about his restaurants. Marketing isn't what most people think it is. It isn't a promotional postcard. Marketing is everything about your restaurant that people are going to talk about, the décor, the hospitality, and the food.

But if your restaurant isn't pulling in guests and you're feeling desperate to get more people in the door, should you throw dollars into traditional marketing?

Say your aspiration is to do $40,000 a week in sales, but you're landing at $30,000. Don't count on traditional marketing to increase sales that much.

You can't push people into coming to your restaurant. With hard work, maybe you can get your sales up to $32,000. It's better to recalibrate your model to $32,000 a week in sales with a decent profit margin factor than to keep pushing for and failing to reach $40,000.

> **SMART MOVE**
>
> To get buzz circulating about your restaurant, try introducing a unique and theatrical element to it. At Jody's Mexican restaurant, waiters welcomed guests with complimentary grapefruit granitas in bowls of steaming dry ice. It was a theatrical presentation that got people talking. The guests loved it.

Word of mouth is the greatest form of marketing for your restaurant. People *love* to talk about restaurants. They want to know about the newest places. They love reliving the pleasure by telling other people about it. Can you believe it was once considered bad manners to talk about food? Now it's central to cultural discourse. Exceeding customer expectations is the foundation of word-of-mouth marketing.

You may not have the time to devote to blogging or Facebook, and you shouldn't have to. If your restaurant is exciting and the food is presented beautifully, your guests will take photos and post them on Facebook, Twitter, and Instagram. Guests putting photos of dishes from your restaurant on social media will elicit immediate questions from their friends and followers: "Where are you?!" "That looks great!" "Yum!"

Websites

Very few restaurants create good websites. The best websites Jody has had for his restaurants had great music. People would say they put on headphones and listened to it all day in their office.

Your restaurant's website should be like a little commercial. Think less information and more attitude. One of the best websites we've seen was for the restaurant Casa Tua in South Beach, Miami. There are evocative photos of a beautiful young Latin family and their kids that make you want to step through the screen and take a seat in the candlelit garden. The website's bossa nova music offsets the mood to relax and enjoy.

Websites that work well utilize association. So many websites are literal with many clicks and categories. A restaurant's website shouldn't unveil all the restaurant's nuances. It should pique people's curiosity and encourage them to visit.

Your website should evoke the same mood as your restaurant. The website is a teaser to intrigue, provoke, and seduce customers.

> **POTENTIAL PITFALL**
>
> Website designers are often more concerned about the look of a website than how it will be used. It's up to you to make sure the text contains the keywords that will make your restaurant come up in online searches for your genre and location.

People who look up your restaurant's website are looking for a few basics:

- What your restaurant looks like
- What kind of food you serve
- What your price range is
- What people are saying about you
- What days and hours you're open
- Your address
- Additional services (catering, takeout, etc.)
- Upcoming events (wine or beer tastings, live music, etc.)

You should post your prices on your website. It's difficult to understand when restaurants don't do this. It can't be because they're concerned about raising prices, as they don't change their prices that often. *Market price* can be used if the main protein's price varies significantly.

> **DEFINITION**
>
> **Market price** is the daily menu price of an item, typically fish or lobster, that changes because the purchase price fluctuates daily in a material manner.

The new restaurant owner is better off creating a simple website and Facebook page that can be managed consistently. If you feel comfortable with what your restaurant is, then your customers will feel comfortable. It's the inconsistent message that scares people away.

Facebook

Many restaurants use Facebook rather than websites to keep their customers up-to-date. It's a vital tool these days to help you stay in touch with your family of customers. A photo of the chef's chocolate soufflé, with crème Anglaise pouring into it, will get your customers thinking about coming in for a taste.

If you don't want to manage your Facebook page, find someone on your staff who is excited about updating the restaurant's page often. Many restaurants start a page with verve and vitality, and then it goes stale as managers underestimate the amount of work it takes to keep it fresh. If you don't want to deal with that work, you should calculate whether it's worth hiring a social media person to regularly update your Facebook page. If you hire someone, make sure they understand your restaurant's needs and they are grounded in your restaurant's concept. If they do what you want them to do, it's worth paying for.

Blogger/Press Dinners

Often when a restaurant isn't doing well, the owner hires a restaurant marketer to invite local press and bloggers to a complimentary tasting dinner, which often results in a rush of fawning blog posts. Many restaurateurs have told us it increases business for about two weeks.

The thing is, if your restaurant doesn't live up to bloggers' praise, the first-time guests who follow their "likes" and "loves" won't return; nor will their friends. If you asked someone how a restaurant was and the reply was, "Ummmm, it was okay," would you rush to spend your money there?

Charity Events

Restaurants are often asked to participate in charity or business events put on by the Chamber of Commerce, Downtown Merchant Association, or media entities. At these events, guests pay an admission fee and restaurants set up stations where they offer tastes of their food. These events can help spread the word about your restaurant and they can create goodwill. However, they're also a lot of work and expensive.

When you're new on the scene, it's all about market penetration. But you need to be careful to align yourself with like-minded events. You're still establishing an identity. If you have an elegant French café, it doesn't make sense to participate in a blue-collar rock festival. If you have an organic vegan kitchen, it doesn't make sense to participate in a Blues and BBQ event. Align your restaurant with the appropriate events to reap the most correct kind of exposure.

It's good to help causes that mean a lot to you, but until your business is stable, don't leverage your promotional budget to a charity that doesn't fit with your business. If there are causes that are important to you that don't fit with your restaurant's concept, donate personally rather than through your business.

Warning: you can get a lot of requests to participate in events and to donate food. How do you say no? Tell them you love the idea and would love to participate, but you're new and you already went beyond your budget for events this year. Then add, "Please don't forget me next year." And say "Hey, have you tried the cornbread we make here? I haven't seen you in for dinner yet." Flip the tables, and sell the seller.

Wear Success Graciously

Learn to take your success in stride. Even when all the seats in your restaurant are filled, remind your staff not to gloat about it to the customers waiting or seated. Six months from now it could be a different story. Never act self-satisfied about not having a seat available for a potential guest.

If there's absolutely no way your hostess can get potential guests a seat tonight, train her to empathize: "I'm so sorry, but I could book you a great table in the corner—it's very cozy—for tomorrow. I'll be here; my name is Mary, and I'll take care of you." Now, instead of the potential guest feeling completely dejected, his spirits have been buoyed by the pleasant encounter with your hostess.

POTENTIAL PITFALL

Even if your restaurant has a strong point of view—loud music and low lighting—you never want your staff to brush off complaints with a flippant "Sorry, that's how the owner wants it." Train your staff to empathize with your guests (even if they don't get what your restaurant is all about).

Reservations

The number of tables you book by reservation has an effect on the dining room's energy. Boxing out the entire dining room with reservations creates a variety of problems. It annoys people to be told there are no tables when they see empty tables in the room. Empty tables are a cash-register drain as well as an energy drain. Taking too many reservations makes it more difficult to seat the walk-ins.

How long should you hold a reserved table for a late party? Once again, it's not what you do but how you do it. If you give away a reserved table and the party arrives afterwards, it must be handled carefully and tactfully, not as a punitive measure.

Managing Waiting Guests

People want to go to the hot new place, and they're willing to wait. Waiting, as much as it creates anxiety, can confer status. Customers feel this really must be The Place if all these people want to get in. Yet a restaurant owner always needs to manage lines and waiting times.

When giving estimates on waiting times, always speak in a general sense—around 15 to 20 minutes ... should be less than half an hour. Don't quote exact times for a table since it's impossible to have that exact a schedule. Don't apologize about wait times, either.

Offering the guest the option of beginning their meal with shared appetizers at the bar is also a way to diffuse their wait anxiety. When a guest is asked to wait in the bar, casually synch your watch with theirs. What you're really doing is confirming what time it is. Make a note on the seating chart that helps you remember a guest. Make sure your descriptor is something they can see such as "green sweater" rather than "red face," in case they demand to see where they are in line. You can also get their cellphone number to text them when their table is ready. That's much nicer than handing them a glowing, buzzing orb beeper.

Escort the guest to the bar area, after alerting the bartender that you're bringing this party to the bar. When you bring the guests to the bar, tell the bartender, "This is the Johnson party, and they're going to enjoy the bar for about 15 to 20 minutes until their table is set." This engages them, and they don't feel like cattle being told to wait in the field.

When the guest table is almost ready, checkin with those guests to say, "We're preparing your table, and I'll come get you in a few minutes, if you would like to close out your bar tab."

If you've guessed the waiting time incorrectly and the wait turns out to be much longer than quoted, the first thing to do is to approach the guests waiting in the bar with an appetizer-style shared plate. Say, "I figured you were getting hungry, and I thought this might take the edge off, as the diners are taking a little longer than we anticipated." Don't buy them another drink. They're hungry, and another drink might pour fuel on the fire.

The important thing is to communicate. Don't hide from a waiting table. When a member of a four-top leaves his group to see about their table, he needs to return to his group with a win. Make that happen. Apologizing is worn thin when guests are a little buzzed and hungry, and things can turn ugly. It's best to be honest and direct.

You need to be mindful of how you're putting tables together for your strategy. Only one host can run the show. Otherwise, it would be like picking up where someone else started in a chess game. The hand-off technique doesn't work.

If you have a four-top waiting and there are no two-tops waiting, and you have a *deuce* open next to a deuce that's on dessert, you need to be careful not to seat a walk-in two-top at that open table. Wait until the deuce has finished dessert and paid their bill, and then push the two tables together to make room for the four-top. That's why only one person can run the show.

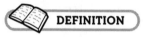 **DEFINITION**

A **deuce** is a two-top table. Restaurants use shorthand terms such as eight-top, four-top, and deuce to refer to how many people can be seated at a table.

Pre-Service Meeting

Before service, the staff gathers for a 5- to 10-minute meeting. These meetings are designed to align the group as a team just like a sports team huddles right before the game.

This is the time to pump up the staff to meet the evening and week's goals; discuss selling specials, wine, and desserts; and talk up new holiday promotions. The chef can offer the servers tastes of the specials. A server's firsthand knowledge of the food makes a favorable impression on the guests. You don't want your servers telling the guests about their "favorite dishes." That information isn't helpful. Staff instead should know how to describe the dishes. During the pre-service meeting, give your staff the key words to describe the night's specials. Train them to respond to a question to which they don't know the answer. "I don't know" is useless; "Let me find out" is the right response.

After service, some restaurateurs and managers hold a five-minute post-mortem meeting. Jody never found them effective. It's tedious listening to a critique of the day's performance while you're still in a sweaty uniform, tired, and achy. Plus, it doesn't boost morale to lay criticism on a tired staff. As an owner and manager, your job is to figure out the solutions to what went wrong and present that information to your staff when they're fresh and energetic.

Online Coupons

Companies like Groupon and Amazon sell consumers online coupons for a discounted meal at restaurants. For example, the customer will pay $30 for a $50 coupon good for dinner. Groupon can bring new customers, but often they bring in bargain hunters, who will use another coupon next week for another restaurant.

> **POTENTIAL PITFALL**
>
> Make sure your staff treats customers who are using discounted coupons with the same hospitality with which they treat all customers. If your goal is to expose more people to your restaurant by using coupons from organizations such as Groupon, make sure these new customers have a great experience they'll want to tell their friends about.

Online coupons can bring in incremental income, but they're dangerous for first-year operators. You have too many unknown elements to consider before you can effectively incorporate this form of marketing into a budget.

Stay True

Jody knew a man who started a restaurant that was struggling. The restaurant was across the street from where Jody lived, so he went there often. Every two weeks the owner was rearranging things. He'd put a new rug in the dining room. He'd buy a lot of palm trees and accent pieces. One evening, the owner had brought in three big Chinese screens. It was difficult for customers to commit to a restaurant the owner was always changing.

We're not in favor of putting out a "work-in-progress" message. We believe in laying it out there, and proudly saying, "This is it. I love it. I hope you do, too." When you show tentativeness, people are afraid to like it. People are afraid of liking something that's not complete. So our final words to you, the future restaurant owner, are to have the courage and conviction to pick a strong point of view. People will respect that. Waffling doesn't make anyone feel good. Say you've taken over a space that used to be a traditional, classic high-end French restaurant, the kind of place that does the table-side duck à l'orange. You create a contemporary French bistro, serving a rustic roasted chicken in a vintage copper pan. It's an excellent dish, but the old customers say they don't like it.

This is the moment of truth—the moment not to retreat. You should empathize with the old customers about how great that old dish was. Show them how wonderful the new dish is, the quality it shares with the classic dish, and how it has been updated. It's like when you go to a concert and the band is excited to play their new album, but they'll throw in a beloved hit between the new songs. A restaurant has to do the same thing. Keep enough of the familiar flavor, but strongly execute the new stuff. Before long, the new dishes will become old favorites.

The desire to entertain, nurture, satisfy, and indulge others is a special calling. When a small team of renegades (otherwise known as restaurant people) band together to create and execute a unique restaurant plan that pleases and takes good care of customers, the reward transcends money. When you perform well enough to make a profit, then you can call it a business. Running a successful restaurant business—well, there's just nothing else like it. That's why we chose this path and never looked back, and we hope you will, too—with the help of the tools you've obtained from this book.

The Least You Need to Know

- Keep focusing on hospitality, even after you've become successful, especially when you're trying to seat waiting customers on a busy night.
- Train your staff to empathize with your customers when something goes wrong or they're complaining, and to provide a solution to the problem.
- Promote your restaurant in the community by participating in charity tasting events that align with your concept and are attended by potential customers.
- Stay true to your restaurant's concept, and don't change just because one or two customers don't like it. Your conviction and belief in your restaurant will have a strong influence on the majority of your customers.

Glossary

Americans with Disabilities Act (ADA)   National legislation that requires upgrades to buildings to allow access for people with disabilities. Check your local zoning and health departments for their guidelines.

articles of organization   The legal document that establishes your limited liability company (LLC) for doing business in your state.

back of the house (BOH)   This area contains the kitchen, delivery area, storage rooms, staff changing rooms, and office.

"behind you"   In restaurant kitchens, cooks use this shorthand to let others know they're behind or moving past a staff member. It prevents collisions, spills, and burns.

bitters   Concentrated botanical extracts made from herbs, flowers, roots, or seeds, which are a trendy ingredient in cocktails.

boeuf bourguignon   A beef stew made with red wine from the Burgundy region of France.

bring your own [booze or bottle] (BYOB or BYO)   Restaurants without liquor licenses that allow customers to bring their own alcohol, and will often charge a corkage fee to cover glass breakage and maintenance.

campylobacter   Bacteria that is a common cause of food poisoning caused by contact with raw poultry or by eating undercooked poultry.

capture   A marketing term that describes a restaurant that attracts customers who happen to be walking or driving by.

certificate of occupancy (C/O or COO)   The official paperwork from the town's building department that says a restaurant meets all building, fire, and health codes and can open for business.

charger   A large decorative plate used as part of a formal service that is placed under the plate upon which customers dine.

chef de cuisine   A French term for the chef responsible for the daily running of the kitchen. In contemporary American restaurants, the chef de cuisine is often known as the "executive chef." When a restaurant group owns several restaurants, the executive chef oversees the menu concept for the group, and the chef de cuisine would be in charge of the daily workings of one of the restaurant kitchens, and might have the title of "head chef."

code compliant   A restaurant currently meets the local zoning, building, fire, and health codes.

commodity-based liquor license   In some states, liquor licenses are a tangible asset that is regulated by quota. The state runs lotteries to sell them, but it's difficult to obtain these licenses. Licenses can be bought on the open market from restaurant owners.

cremate   Kitchen slang for an order of well-done meat.

cross contamination   Occurs when foods such as raw meat and seafood spread bacteria and viruses because they're not properly stored separately or are chopped using knives or boards not designated for them.

crowdfunding   An online form of fundraising, such as Kickstarter.

crudo   An Italian raw fish that is traditionally served like tartare and is chopped and seasoned. Today's contemporary Italian restaurants often serve it thinly sliced, topped with sea salt, herbs, spices, and olive oil.

destination   A marketing term to describe the type of restaurant people deliberately leave their homes to visit.

dry county or town   A municipality that doesn't allow alcohol to be sold in stores or restaurants. Restaurants in dry towns usually allow guests to bring their own bottle (BYOB).

E. coli   A harmful strain of bacteria that lives in the intestines of humans and animals and can cause severe bloody diarrhea. The most common cause is eating raw or undercooked meat, such as hamburgers.

enterprise zone   Municipal areas targeted for economic growth in a city. Tax breaks are offered to new local businesses willing to locate there.

expeditor   The executive chef who acts as the connection between the front of the house (FOH) and back of the house (BOH) during service. The expeditor calls out orders, tells chefs to fire dishes, and inspects finished plates before sending them to the dining room.

fee-based liquor license   An annual fee that some states charge for a liquor license. This is a more affordable proposition than the commodity-based liquor license.

fire   A kitchen term used by an expeditor that orders the line cooks to begin cooking a certain dish.

French brigade system   A hierarchical structure in which the chef de cuisine and sous chef oversee the work of other chefs located at 10 different stations.

front of the house (FOH)   The public areas of a restaurant, which includes the dining room and bar.

grandfathered   In terms of buildings, this means conditions that existed before the current zoning codes are allowed to continue even though they violate current codes.

in the weeds   Restaurant slang for falling behind during service.

kill it   Kitchen slang for an order of well-done meat.

limited liability company (LLC)   The most commonly used business entity that restaurant owners form because it protects them against personal liability, and provides tax benefits.

liquor license classifications   States have a system of different classes of establishments, such as live entertainment, cabaret, tavern, or café, which have various building requirements and restrictions. Check your local zoning laws.

listeria   Bacteria that can grow in cold temperatures and infect delicatessen meats, hot dogs, soft cheeses, pates, and raw sprouts.

mise en place   A combination of all the raw and cooked ingredients cleaned, chopped, and portioned, in containers and ready for use at the appropriate chef stations. Sometimes referred to simply as "mise."

mock service   A training technique in which FOH staff practice waiting on one another and the manager and owner.

norovirus   A form of gastroenteritis made famous by outbreaks on cruise ships; it can be passed directly from an infected food preparer to food or to another person.

operating agreement   A legal document that establishes the way your limited liability company (LLC) will operate, defining the roles and responsibilities of members and how the profits and losses are shared.

par stock   The minimum amount of inventory a restaurant should have on hand before ordering more.

point of sale system (POS)   A computer system that tracks every transaction from order to check and manages cash control systems. Credit card purchases are deposited daily through the POS system. This system can also be used as a staff time clock.

popularity, preparation, and profitability (PPP) test   The test restaurants run on all foods and drinks to rate their cost-effectiveness and determine if they should be included on the menu.

post-off   A price reduction that state liquor authorities run on wholesale prices of alcohol.

private equity funding   The act of raising money from individuals and investors. Because banks are reluctant to lend to restaurateurs, they usually raise funds this way.

reach-ins   Small refrigerators and freezers that kitchen staff can reach into for items.

restaurateur   The French word for restaurant owner, from *restaurer,* meaning "to restore." Restaurants, places where food and drink are served, were first referenced in print in Paris in the 1700s.

salmonella   The most common form of food poisoning in the United States, caused most frequently by contact with or eating raw or undercooked chicken and eggs. This bacteria is killed by cooking and pasteurizing.

shrinkage   The amount of inventory lost through spoilage, errors, sloppiness, and spilling.

sous chef   A French term used in American kitchens for the chef who is second-in-command, under the direction of the chef de cuisine and/or executive chef.

sous-vide   A cooking technique in which food is cooked super slow and low, creating exceptionally tender proteins.

The Man   Restaurant slang for a health inspector or fire department inspector.

tip-out   To reconcile credit card receipts against customer tips, and distribute that money to the servers and front of the house staff in cash.

variances   Official exemptions that vary from zoning regulations. The approval process for variances can be long, expensive, and painful.

walk-in   Large refrigerators and freezers where staff stores large quantities of food products.

walk-ins   Customers who arrive at a restaurant without reservations.

well liquor   Generic or lower-end brands of distilled spirits, also called "rail."

wrap-around costs   The costs of items a restaurant gives away, such as chips and salsa, salt, pepper, ketchup, lemon wedges, hot sauce, or cookies at the end of the meal.

yield test   The difference between how much a food item weighed when it came in the door and its edible net weight after it has been processed.

Resources

For further information on starting and running a restaurant, check out these online and text resources.

Websites

Bureau of Labor Statistics: bls.gov/ooh/food-preparation-and-serving/

Food and Drug Administration:www.fda.gov/default.htm

foodsafety.gov/index.html

Online Reading

Brown, Laura Green, Shivangi Khargonekar, Lisa Bushnell, and the Environmental Health Specialists Network Working Group. *Frequency of Inadequate Chicken Cross-Contamination Prevention and cooking practices, Journal of Food Protection* 76, no. 12 (2013), 2141–2145, doi:10.4315/0362-028X. JFP-13-129.

The Environmental Health Specialists Network. *Explaining the Risk of Foodborne Illness Associated with Restaurants.* Accessed at www.dir.ca.gov/dosh/dosh_publications/Rsg.pdf

Jurafsky, Dan, Victor Chahuneau, Bryan R. Routledge, and Noah A Smith. First Monday. Narrative on framing consumer sentiment in online restaurant reviews. Accessed at firstmonday. org/ojs/index.php/fm/article/view/4944/3863.

Text

Jurafsky, Dan. *The Language of Food: A Linguist Reads the Menu.* New York: W.W. Norton & Company, 2014

Preopening Checklists: The Critical Path

Use the following checklists to ensure that you're on the right path for opening your business. Check off each item as you go.

Phase 1

Not Started	% Complete	Done	Target Opening Date:___ Six Months Out	Responsible Party
			Concept definition	
			Develop concepts	
			Define target guest experiences	
			Review concepts and create concept descriptions	
			Approve concepts	
			Interface with kitchen designer	
			Interface with kitchen supplier to determine equipment needs and layout	
			Interface with bar supplier to determine equipment needs and layout	
			Review timeline	

Phase 2

Not Started	% Complete	Done	Target Opening Date: ___ Five Months Out	Responsible Party
			Facility design	
			Obtain kitchen design and mechanical drawings	
			Logistics: flow of products, supplies, trash	
			Design/construction plans are finalized	
			Approve outlet storage plan	
			Define audio needs by outlet	
			Review FF&E	

Phase 3

Not Started	% Complete	Done	Target Opening Date:____ Four Months Out	Responsible Party
			POS requirements	
			Get drawings for kitchen/bar equipment	
			Provide job descriptions for all positions	

Not Started	% Complete	Done	Target Opening Date:____ Three Months Out	Responsible Party
			Work with chef on working menu	
			Review OS&E	
			Budgets	
			Operating budget	
			Finalize budget	
			Review outline grand opening	
			Review training program	
			Review uniforms	
			Review menus	
			Start designing of tabletops, day part of set-up	
			Define key managers search, produce ads for employment, offer letter for general manager	

continues

Phase 3 (continued)

Not Started	% Complete	Done	Target Opening Date:___ Two Months Out	Responsible Party
			Produce working menus for all meal periods and outlets, including events, catering, takeout, wine list, and special house cocktails	
			Start to identify purveyors (food and beverage, small wares, etc.), and finalize meat purveyor	
			Source tabletops (tablecloth/placements)	
			Finalize beverage program (beer and cocktail list)	
			Decide on hours of operation	
			Finalize training program (dates, times, and content)	
			Finalize decision on tabletops and all major components	
			Review contracts: coffee and ice tea machines, linen, PR, oil recycle, fire suppression, refrigeration, pest, HVAC, soda/CO_2, overnight cleaners, valet parking, waste removal, utilities (electric, gas, water), rental of ice machine, dish machine, and/or espresso machine	

Not Started	% Complete	Done	Target Opening Date:___ One Month Out	Responsible Party
			Assemble all recipes	
			Sequence of service developed	
			Run ads: interview and hire key players	
			Begin to assemble FOH training packets	
			Create bar small ware needs, source them	
			Continue to identify purveyors	
			Food tastings: set your goals, along with the time and date	
			Coffee/tea programs: create programs for regular coffee breakfast and French press for dinner	
			Create initial order to begin recipe testing	
			Make final decisions on tabletop and service wares. Have purchase orders out	
			Finalize the sequences of service	
			Receive kitchen equipment, orders of food and supplies	
			Begin recipe testing and costing of dishes	
			Create inventory sheets for food and liquor	
			Continue to hire staff, running ads if necessary	
			Receive construction and timing update	

continues

Phase 3   (continued)

Not Started	% Complete	Done	Target Opening Date:___ One Month Out	Responsible Party
			Begin weekly meetings with top staff	
			Sample music for custom CD burning	
			Create outline for grand opening party	
			Continue with recipe testing, costing, taking pictures, and creating menu descriptions for food, beverages, etc.	
			Set up first food tasting	
			Implement training schedules for FOH	
			Weekly meeting with top staff	
			Finalize all menus, liquor, beer, and wine lists	
			Create theoretical costing for all consumables	
			Hold tasting for friends, family, and investors; hold dusty shoe	
			Have all FOH training materials finalized and printed, including scheduling spreadsheets, staff training, and operations manual; record operations manual and restaurant standards on CD	
			Perform your final edit menus and lists	

Not Started	% Complete	Done	Target Opening Date:___ Three Weeks Out	Responsible Party
			Start BOH training	
			Finalize and print up BOH training materials, including a standardized recipe book with photos, menu descriptions, menu yield tests, menu mise en place, food purchasing bid analysis form, food and liquor perpetual inventory forms, food and liquor ordering forms, and FOH and BOH scheduling spreadsheets	
			Provide final menu and liquor lists for POS provider	
			Create, print, and send out grand opening party invitations	

Not Started	% Complete	Done	Target Opening Date:___ Two Weeks Out	Responsible Party
			Begin training program for FOH	
			Begin training of FOH, including taking reservations, using the POS, and purchasing	
			Identify "fires" and assign responsibility to follow up	
			Hold a cook-through for staff with key players	
			Begin daily recap with GM and top staff	
			Start uniform distribution	

continues

Phase 3   (continued)

Not Started	% Complete	Done	Target Opening Date:___ Two Weeks Out	Responsible Party
			Put all service wares in place	
			Set lighting and music level presets for different day/ evening parts	
			Create daily task list	
			Determine outlet opening sequence	

Not Started	% Complete	Done	Target Opening Date:___ One Week Out	Responsible Party
			Continue training all staff	
			Schedule mock services	
			Start taking reservations	
			Place initial orders and prep for opening	
			Begin holding a daily recap and reportswith GM and top staff	
			Perform daily task list	

Not Started	% Complete	Done	Target Opening Date:___ Opening Week	Responsible Party
			Hold grand opening and opening	
			Hold daily recap and reports with GM and top staff	
			Adjust training materials, if necessary	
			Train and retrain staff, as needed	

Not Started	% Complete	Done	Target Opening Date:___ Opening Week	Responsible Party
			Evaluate daily performance with key players	
			Tweak any computer glitches	

Not Started	% Complete	Done	Target Opening Date:___ One Week In	Responsible Party
			Continue training	
			Hold daily performance evaluation with key players	
			Hold daily recap and reports with owner and key players	
			Hold all staff meetings	

Not Started	% Complete	Done	Target Opening Date:___ Two Weeks In	Responsible Party
			Have all permanent restaurant staff members take one day off	
			Hold daily performance evaluation with key players	
			Have restaurant players "do" analysis	
			Continue training	
			Tweak "hardware"	
			Hold weekly recap with owner and key players	
			Hold individual FOH and BOH meetings addressing issues from last week's meeting	

continues

Phase 3 (continued)

Not Started	% Complete	Done	Target Opening Date:___ Three Weeks In	Responsible Party
			Continue training	
			Hold weekly recap with owner and key staff	
			Hold key player evaluations	
			Key player evaluations discussed with key players	

D

Operational Checklists and Forms

In this appendix, you'll find all the checklists and forms you'll need to begin, run, and manage your successful restaurant. Feel free to copy them and make them your own.

host/hostess Responsibilities

Department: FOH

Reports to: Manager on duty

Job Summary: The host or hostess's job is to supervise and coordinate the activities of the dining room in a restaurant while being one of the first points of contact for the guest. The host/hostess provides professional, friendly, and responsive service to extend an exceptional dining experience to each guest. Every host/hostess's primary objective is to create such an excellent dining experience that a guest will want to return again and again.

Qualifications

- 1 year of experience in host/hostess position and/or industry/operation
- High school or higher education
- Must have excellent customer service skills
- Must be organized and personable
- Must be able to communicate effectively with associates, management, clients, and vendors
- Able to work flexible schedule in order to accommodate busy periods
- Familiarity with reservation systems a plus

Essential Job Functions

Maintain professional communication etiquette while on the phone, and when speaking with customers and staff.

Maintain a professional appearance per company protocol.

Ensure all menus are clean and presentable, free of spots or stains, and complete.

Ensure all menus and specials are current and reviewed for incorrect information.

Ensure entry way, doors, windows, and floors are clean, free of debris, and inviting.

Check reservations for large parties and inform the proper staff, kitchen, servers, and management.

Answer any reservation messages and confirm the business for the current shift.

Confirm reservations for upcoming business in a polite professional manner.

Ask the kitchen if there are menu changes or problems that will affect business for your shift.

Customize the seating chart and organize the reservations.

Help arrange tables to accommodate the shift's reservations needs.

Welcome guests, escort them to their table, and present menus to them.

Ensure servers know when guests are seated.

Keep track of server customer count and do the best to evenly seat servers.

Control the flow of business to ensure an efficient spacing of service, FOH, and BOH.

When needed, prepare the coat room for use by organizing the hangers and cleaning the space.

Be a point of contact for the lost and found efforts.

Know and follow all restaurant emergency and safety procedures.

Attend and participate in all scheduled meetings and training sessions.

Standards

- Protect the assets of the property.

- Maintain professional appearance and behavior when in contact with guests and associates.

- Follow policies and procedures found in training manuals and employee operations handbook.

- Always remember we are in a partnership with our guests, fellow employees, and owners to provide quality service and profitability.

- Regular attendance in conformance with the company standards, which may be established by the restaurant from time to time, is essential to the successful performance of this position.

EMPLOYEE'S STATEMENT:

I have read this job description and fully understand that failure to comply with any of the stated responsibilities is grounds for disciplinary action.

This job description is an outline of job requirements and may not include all job functions that may be required. This job description is subject to change without notice.

_____   _____

Employee Signature   Date

_____   _____

Supervisor Signature   Date

Bartender Responsibilities

Department: FOH

Reports to: Manager on duty

Job Summary: Restaurant bartenders are responsible for a positive guest interaction while accurately mixing and serving beverages to guests and servers in a friendly and efficient manner. At all times, bartenders are expected to be attentive to our guests' needs and make them feel welcome, comfortable, important, and relaxed.

Qualifications

- 2 to 5 years of experience as a bartender
- High school or higher education
- Excellent oral communication skills
- Positive interpersonal skills
- Knowledge of wines, beers, and spirits
- Ability to communicate effectively with associates, management, clients, and vendors if necessary
- Able to work flexible schedule in order to accommodate busy periods

Essential Job Functions

Take beverage orders from customers and servers.

Prepare and serve alcoholic and nonalcoholic drinks consistent with the company's drink recipes.

Enter drink orders accurately and immediately after receipt into the POS system.

Check identification of customers to verify age requirements for purchase of alcoholic beverages.

Be responsible for an assigned house bank and for following all company cash-handling procedures.

Accept guest payment, process credit card charges, and politely return the proper change.

Learn the names and personally recognize the regular customers.

Demonstrate a thorough knowledge of company food and beverage items, menu items, and promotions.

Ensure that the assigned bar area is fully equipped with the tools and products needed for mixing beverages and serving guests.

Maintain bottles and glasses in an attractive and functional manner to support efficient drink preparation and promotion of beverages.

Prepare garnishes for drinks and replenish snacks and appetizers for customers when necessary.

Maintain cleanliness in all areas of the bar, including counters, sinks, utensils, shelves, and storage areas.

Receive and serve food orders to guests seated at the bar and to any restaurant customer when necessary.

Report all equipment problems and bar maintenance issues to the restaurant manager.

Assist the restocking and replenishment of bar inventory and supplies.

Frequently lift/carry up to 25 pounds, occasionally lift/carry up to 50 pounds.

Perform all reasonable requests by the management team.

Follow proper time-keeping policies and procedures.

Know and follow all the restaurant's emergency and safety procedures.

Attend and participate in all scheduled meetings and training sessions.

Standards

- Protect the assets of the property.

- Maintain professional appearance and behavior when in contact with guests and associates.

- Follow policies and procedures found in training manuals and associate handbook.

- Always remember we are in a partnership with our guests, fellow associates, and owners to provide quality service and profitability.

- Regular attendance in conformance with the company standards, which may be established by the restaurant from time to time, is essential to the successful performance of this position.

EMPLOYEE'S STATEMENT:

I have read this job description and fully understand that failure to comply with any of the stated responsibilities is grounds for disciplinary action.

This job description is an outline of job requirements and may not include all job functions that may be required. This job description is subject to change without notice.

_____   _____

Employee Signature   Date

_____   _____

Supervisor Signature   Date

Server

Department: FOH

Reports to: Manager on duty

Job Summary: Provide professional, friendly, and responsive service to extend an exceptional dining experience to each guest. Every server's primary objective is to create such an excellent dining experience that a guest will want to return again and again.

Qualifications

- 2 to 5 years of server restaurant-related experience

- High school or higher education

- Ability to communicate effectively with associates, management, clients, and vendors

- Must possess excellent math skills, handle money, and have experience with credit card processing

- Experience with a POS system

- Able to work flexible schedule in order to accommodate business levels

- Able to work in a standing position for extended periods of time

- Ability to safely lift and easily maneuver trays of food and dishes weighing up to 30 pounds

- Punctuality and regular and reliable attendance

- Honesty and integrity are highly valued

Essential Job Functions

Have overall food knowledge with expert knowledge of the restaurant's menus.

Have ability to welcome guests and make them feel comfortable.

Inform guests of specials and menu changes.

Make suggestions you feel your guests would enjoy, and avoid offering personal preferences or opinion.

Have ability to upsell food and beverage menu items using suggestive selling techniques.

Answer questions regarding regions where food products come from and how food is prepared.

Answer questions about the wine list with attention given to wine regions, vintages, aromas, and flavors.

Describe in detail tastes and textures.

Answer questions about the food, beverages, and other restaurant functions and services.

Show expert knowledge of table numbers and guest seat numbers.

Take and organize food and beverage orders from guests, and efficiently enter orders in the POS system.

Deliver food and beverage orders from the kitchen and bar to guests in a timely manner.

Maintain clean service areas.

Monitor and observe guests' dining experience, ensuring that they are satisfied with their items.

Prepare and present the final bill to the guest, memorize types of payment the restaurant accepts, and make change when necessary.

Be ready, willing, and able to help other servers when the situation arises.

Be ready, willing, and able to assist server assistant with cleaning and resetting tables.

Thank guests for their visit and encourage a return trip.

Complete side work at the start and end of each shift as per schedule.

Be willing to fill in shifts as needed to ensure a smooth and efficient operation of the restaurant.

Accurately record reservations.

Help keep restrooms clean and stocked with necessary supplies.

Travel, as necessary, to different properties/venues for work.

Perform all reasonable requests by the management team.

Follow proper time-keeping policies and procedures.

Know and follow all the restaurant's emergency and safety procedures.

Attend and participate in all scheduled meetings and training sessions.

Standards

- Protect the assets of the property.

- Maintain professional appearance and behavior when in contact with guests and associates.

- Follow policies and procedures found in training manuals and employee handbook.

- Always remember we are in a partnership with our guests, fellow associates, and owners to provide quality service and profitability.

- Regular attendance in conformance with the company standards, which may be established by the restaurant from time to time, is essential to the successful performance of this position.

EMPLOYEE'S STATEMENT:

I have read this job description and fully understand that failure to comply with any of the stated responsibilities is grounds for disciplinary action.

This job description is an outline of job requirements and may not include all job functions that may be required. This job description is subject to change without notice.

_____   _____

Employee Signature   Date

_____   _____

Supervisor Signature   Date

Busser/Server Assistant

Department: FOH

Reports to: Manager on duty

Job Summary: A busser or server assistant's role is a supportive one. You will assist with the activities of both front and back end operations and help expedite work. While this is a support role, by no means is it minor in essence as the operations of a restaurant cannot be carried out properly without assistantship.

Qualifications

- 1 to 2 years of experience in the food service industry
- High school or higher education
- State Food Handlers Certification a plus
- Friendly, efficient customer skills and customer knowledge are necessary
- Able to communicate effectively with associates, management, and customers
- Able to work flexible schedule in order to accommodate busy periods

Essential Job Functions

Organize and set tables efficiently without disturbing guests.

Serve water and refill glasses as needed.

Overall food knowledge with expert knowledge of this restaurant's menus.

Expert knowledge of table and seat numbers.

Ability to professionally aid guests to locations within the restaurant.

Clean dining area and serving stations without disturbing guests.

Continuous cleaning of the dining area and serving stations during service.

Assist janitorial staff with trash removal.

Assist in cleaning up spills.

Greet guests with or in the absence of the hostess.

Make suggestions about menu selections when asked.

Ensure timely delivery of food orders.

Address customers' queries and concerns efficiently.

Travel, as necessary, to different properties/venues for work.

Perform all reasonable requests by the management team.

Follow proper time-keeping policies and procedures.

Know and follow all the restaurant's emergency and safety procedures.

Attend and participate in all scheduled meetings and training sessions.

Standards

- Protect the assets of the property.

- Maintain professional appearance and behavior when in contact with guests and associates.

- Follow policies and procedures found in training manuals and employee handbook.

- Always remember we are in a partnership with our guests, fellow associates, and owners to provide quality service and profitability.

- Regular attendance in conformance with the company standards, which may be established by the restaurant from time to time, is essential to the successful performance of this position.

EMPLOYEE'S STATEMENT:

I have read this job description and fully understand that failure to comply with any of the stated responsibilities is grounds for disciplinary action.

This job description is an outline of job requirements and may not include all job functions that may be required. This job description is subject to change without notice.

_____   _____

Employee Signature   Date

_____   _____

Supervisor Signature   Date

Opening Daily Checklist

This is a daily opening checklist that shows how a restaurateur adapts the list with specific tasks related to setting the atmosphere.

Opening restaurant:

- ❏ Bar bank reconciliations counted
- ❏ Opening side work posted
- ❏ Check ice

Check set up:

- ❏ Check side station and hutches
- ❏ Check for bowl of oranges on service bar
- ❏ Check lemonade
- ❏ Check tables
- ❏ Check candles
- ❏ Check water, salsa, coffee, iced tea, and chips

Station chart: (Create on Sunday night)

- ❏ Check reservations
- ❏ Check bathrooms:
    - ❏ Clean
    - ❏ Stocked
    - ❏ Writing on wall

Outside lights on:

- ❏ Two cords from patio near bathrooms
- ❏ One cord where fountain usually is
- ❏ One cord by antique podium

Turn on music:

- ❏ Check to ensure all volumes are on the first notch.
- ❏ Turn on all amps.
- ❏ Turn on sound mixer.
- ❏ Make sure sound mixer lever on far right is turned all the way down and volume knob is at first notch.
- ❏ Plug iPod into charger and into stereo. Choose restaurant playlist.
- ❏ Press play.

Outside by front doors:

- ❏ Check for sweeping
- ❏ Straighten mats
- ❏ Undo curtains

Walk outside and check cleanliness while light

Walk outside at dark to check light bulbs

Start session on POS

Check position of tables

Adjust lights:

- ❏ Turn on lights in mezzazine (two film lamps, not floor lamp)
- ❏ Check bar light levels and main light dimmer behind POS
- ❏ Turn on bathroom lights
- ❏ Adjust dimmers by main kitchen door and on back bar wall of service bar

Post side-work worksheet

Restaurant Manager's Opening Checklist

❏ Check building exterior as you approach. Be on the lookout for broken windows, loitering strangers, or other signs of burglary, as well as any litter or debris.

❏ Unlock doors, enter building, disarm alarm system, and turn on lights as needed.

❏ Check overall appearance of kitchen and dining room. Be sure all closing tasks were completed to standard.

❏ Check the manager's log for events, incidents, and information from previous night.

❏ Check to be sure all employees punched out appropriately from the previous night, and check labor hours.

❏ Be sure there are enough employees scheduled for the day's shifts.

❏ Check email and voice messages.

❏ Be sure all equipment, especially refrigerators and freezers, are properly functioning.

❏ Be sure food orders are accurate, and double-check inventory levels to be sure the restaurant is prepared for the daily operations.

❏ Prepare for employees to arrive. Unlock employee entrance. Oversee employees as they punch in, and be sure they're dressed appropriately for the shift.

❏ Assign opening kitchen workers their opening duties and side-work duties for the shift.

❏ Count the safe and assign cash drawers where needed. Check deposit slips and be sure all cash is in order from previous day's sales.

❏ Review reservations book with host/hostess, making appropriate plans and changes for large parties or events.

❏ Be sure all opening duties have been completed, and turn on all lights and sound system for music.

❏ Give an instructional, energizing pep talk to all opening staff members. Unlock entrance for service at scheduled time.

Restaurant Manager's Closing Checklist

❑ Cut labor as business slows, leaving enough staff for performing closing tasks.

❑ Check with kitchen manager to be sure all food orders have been completed.

❑ Check that all employees' side-work tasks are satisfactorily complete.

❑ Collect all server checkout sheets, cash drawers, and tip reports.

❑ Count the safe.

❑ See that the server stations, bar, and other areas are restocked where needed.

❑ Close the kitchen and bar at scheduled closing times.

❑ Lock the front door after all guests have departed.

❑ Check restrooms for lingering guests, cleanliness, and trash.

❑ Turn off sound system and any lights not being used.

❑ Be sure bartender cleans and stocks bar for next shift.

❑ Be sure bussers complete their closing cleaning tasks.

❑ Be sure all kitchen staff have completed their closing tasks. Make sure kitchen manager is satisfied.

❑ Balance checkout sheets, send credit card report, and record daily sales information.

❑ Fill out manager's log for the next day's manager to read.

❑ Make sure safe is locked.

❑ Lock liquor storage room, walk-in coolers, and storage rooms.

❑ Lock manager's office and all doors leading outside.

❑ Turn off all lights.

❑ Set alarm, exit building (in pairs or a group), and lock front door.

Shift Closing Sidework

- ❏ Clean and reset tables.
- ❏ Clean chair seats, backs, and legs.
- ❏ Wipe windowsills, shelves, and server stations.
- ❏ Clean table bases.
- ❏ Empty and clean iced tea and soda station.
- ❏ Restock straws, beverage napkins, and sip sticks.
- ❏ Empty and clean coffee station. Place items in back fridge.
- ❏ Stock plates, silverware, to-go boxes, bottled water, etc.
- ❏ Clean and fill all condiment containers.
- ❏ Clean and fill all salt and pepper shakers.
- ❏ Inspect and clean floor.
- ❏ Complete additional assigned closing sidework duties as scheduled.

Cleaning Checklists

Use these weekly, monthly, and yearly cleaning checklists to keep your restaurant in tip-top shape.

Weekly Cleaning Schedule

❑ Dining room tables and chairs: Wipe down where necessary. Check undersides.

❑ Pictures and mirrors: Remove dust, dirt, and smudges.

❑ Walls and ceiling: Remove obvious dirt, wiping them down where necessary.

❑ Shelves, ledges: Brush down and wipe over ledges.

❑ Ventilation: Clean filters. Wipe down canopy.

❑ Refrigerators: Clean down racks. Wipe all surfaces. Defrost if necessary.

❑ Refuse: Disinfect bins.

❑ Cupboards: Remove contents and wipe surfaces.

❑ Dry goods store: Tidy up. Check for vermin.

❑ Changing room: Clean the walls and mop the floor.

❑ Lights: Brush fittings. Clean tubes and bulbs.

❑ Empty reach-in coolers: Wash and sanitize coolers.

❑ Sinks and faucets: Delime them.

❑ Clean coffee machine: Deep clean, soaking machine parts when necessary.

❑ Clean ovens: Deep clean all removable parts.

❑ Floor drains: Use drain cleaners on drains.

Monthly Restaurant Kitchen Cleaning List

❑ Wash behind the hot line (oven, stove, and fryers) to cut down on grease buildup, which is a major fire hazard.

❑ Clean freezers.

❑ Empty and sanitize the ice machine.

❑ Calibrate ovens.

❑ Calibrate thermometers.

❑ Sharpen the meat and cheese slicer.

❑ Deep-clean walls and ceilings.

❑ Wipe down the dry storage area.

❑ Change any pest traps.

❑ Restock your first-aid kit.

❑ Update your material safety data sheets. (They outline how to use cleaning chemicals safely in your restaurant.)

Yearly Restaurant Kitchen Cleaning/Safety List

❑ Check fire suppression system.

❑ Check fire extinguishers. (This may need to be done twice a year, depending on where you live.)

❑ Clean hoods twice a year. Hire a professional company—it's very messy and time-consuming.

❑ Clean pilot lights on gas kitchen equipment. (Be sure to follow the manufacturer's instruction.)

Bar Purchase Log

BAR PURCHASE LOG								
DATE	/ /	/ /	/ /	/ /	/ /	/ /	/ /	WEEKLY TOTAL
	MON	TUES	WED	THU	FRI	SAT	SUN	
BEER/LIQUOR								
								$
								$
								$
								$
								$
								$
								$
								$
								$
								$
								$
								$
DAILY TOTAL	$	$	$	$	$	$	$	
WINE						Total Beer/Liquor:		$
								$
								$
								$
								$
								$
								$
								$
DAILY TOTAL	$	$	$	$	$	$	$	
						Total Wine:		$

Kitchen Purchase Log

KITCHEN PURCHASE LOG							
DATE	/ /	/ /	/ /	/ /	/ /	/ /	/ /	WEEKLY TOTAL
SUPPLIER	MON	TUES	WED	THU	FRI	SAT	SUN	
								$
								$
								$
								$
								$
								$
								$
DAILY TOTAL	$	$	$	$	$	$	$	
						Gross Food Total:	$

Food Cost Schedule

PLATE COSTING INDEX

click below links to view

Inventory
Recipe Index
Plate Template
Recipe Template

SORT BY PLATE NAME

SORT BY PLU #

Perpetual Cost Summary

Type	Cost %	Sales	Cost
App	0.0%	$0.00	$0.00
Entrée	0.0%	$0.00	$0.00
Dessert	0.0%	$0.00	$0.00
Side	0.0%	$0.00	$0.00
Total	**0.0%**	**$0.00**	**$0.00**

Type	Items Sold	Total Sales	Total Cost
		$0.00	$0.00
		$0.00	$0.00
		$0.00	$0.00
		$0.00	$0.00
		$0.00	$0.00
		$0.00	$0.00
		$0.00	$0.00
		$0.00	$0.00
		$0.00	$0.00

Click to view plate cost

PLU #	Plate Name	Type	Menu Price	Plate Cost	Food Cost %
Plate 01	enter plate name here			$0.00	0.0%
Plate 02	enter plate name here			$0.00	0.0%
Plate 03	enter plate name here			$0.00	0.0%
Plate 04	enter plate name here			$0.00	0.0%
Plate 05	enter plate name here			$0.00	0.0%
Plate 06	enter plate name here			$0.00	0.0%
Plate 07	enter plate name here			$0.00	0.0%
Plate 08	enter plate name here			$0.00	0.0%
Plate 09	enter plate name here			$0.00	0.0%
Plate 10	enter plate name here			$0.00	0.0%
Plate 11	enter plate name here			$0.00	0.0%
Plate 12	enter plate name here			$0.00	0.0%
Plate 13	enter plate name here			$0.00	0.0%

Labor Cost Schedule

Total Location Cost $

Approx. Weekly Sales

Week Ending

Employee	Hours Scheduled							Total Hours	Rate	Gross Pay
	Mon	Tues	Weds	Thurs	Fri	Sat	Sun			
Servers									$	$
Bussers/Runners										

(continues)

(continued)

Total Location Cost	$

Approx. Weekly Sales	

Week Ending	

Bartenders

Employee	Hours Scheduled							Total Hours	Rate	Gross Pay
	Mon	Tues	Weds	Thurs	Fri	Sat	Sun			
									$	$
								0.00	Total Wages	$
									AGM	$
									GM	$
									Est. Base Tax	$
									Est. Tip Tax	$
									Total FOH	

FOH Daily Report

FOH Daily Report					
Date	**Restaurant Name**				
Sales					
Dinner	$	Average Guest Spend	Dinner		Comps
Bar	$		Bar		Amount	Explanation
Lunch	$		Lunch			
Event	$					
Total Sales	$					
86 list					
VIPs					
Weather					

Recap

(continues)

(continued)

Guest Challenges

Staff Issues

Other Issues

Index

Q

R

S